Differentiated Staffing

In the
Prentice-Hall Series
In Curriculum and Teaching

Ronald T. Hyman,
Consulting Editor

Differentiated Staffing

RICHARD A. DEMPSEY
The University of Connecticut

RODNEY P. SMITH, JR.
Fellow, Yale University Center
for the Study of Education

PRENTICE-HALL, INC., *Englewood Cliffs, New Jersey*

Library of Congress Cataloging in Publication Data

DEMPSEY, RICHARD, 1932-
   Differentiated Staffing

   Bibliography: p.
   1. Differentiated teaching staffs.   I. Smith,
Rodney Pennell, 1930-   joint author.   II. Title
LB1029.D55D4   371.1'4   72-1815
ISBN   0-13-211854-8

*this book is affectionately dedicated
to two most special individuals—
our wives, Marion Dempsey and Elaine Smith*

10 9 8 7 6 5 4 3 2 1

Printed in the United States of America

PRENTICE-HALL INTERNATIONAL, INC., *London*
PRENTICE-HALL OF AUSTRALIA, PTY. LTD., *Sydney*
PRENTICE-HALL OF CANADA, LTD., *Toronto*
PRENTICE-HALL OF INDIA PRIVATE LIMITED, *New Delhi*
PRENTICE-HALL OF JAPAN, INC., *Tokyo*

Table of Contents

Foreword

This book may be considered a primer for those interested in pursuing the topic of staff differentiation as an educational innovation. Six years ago when I became the director of the Temple City Differentiated Staffing Project, there were neither books nor literature, and no precedent. It was exciting and scary. Today, much of what was learned in Temple City and Florida appears in this publication. Undoubtedly this book will save the educational planner considerable time and reduce his troubles.

Books on topics like staff differentiation have had to be written on the basis of field experience. There has been and continues to be a paucity of adequate theories. This is one innovation which has been built on small pieces of experience put together slowly and painfully. For that reason, practicing administrators will find this book useful and those at the university level may be motivated by it to begin the conceptual and theoretical research necessary to support significant change and innovation like staff differentiation.

As one reads this book, it is important to remember that an idea like staff differentiation is less a thing than a process. Basically, it is a process of matching people skills to pupil needs. As such it has been substantially refined since its early days in Temple City and Kansas City to such present models as the Mesa, Arizona "fluid hierarchy" coupled with internal performance contracting as the major vehicle of remuneration.

We need books on staff differentiation, lots of them. No idea can become institutionalized without a rather large body of information, diversity of opinion, and testable concepts behind it. From this base, substantive research may ferret out the more generalizable concepts. This book is welcomed, not only because the authors are dedicated and sincere professionals, but because the time is long overdue for us to ask the kinds of questions about staffing the authors have raised, and for those other questions which their book will provoke from its readers. We have not yet considered all the possible questions about and implications of staff differentiation in public schools. When we first began in Temple City there were those that said it could not be done. It provides me with some measure of satisfaction that the publication of this book and others about staff differentiation refutes those charges. It is a lesson we will have to keep relearning as we probe for more effective schools.

FENWICK W. ENGLISH, Ph.D.
Director, Mesa Public Schools
Differentiated Staffing Consortium
and Former Director, Temple City
Differentiated Staffing Project,
Temple City, California

Preface

Perhaps the most controversial issue that educators, boards of education, and laymen alike will have to face in the 1970s is that of differentiated staffing. What it is, how it can best be implemented, who will be involved in its planning, and what will be its impact on people, will be the subject of considerable debate during the next decade. Not since the one-room schoolhouse gave way to graded education has any educational innovation had such a potentially dramatic impact on the organizational patterns of our schools. For differentiated staffing proposes an entirely new way of organizing for education. It suggests new solutions to the problems related to the improvement of learning. It holds out to the classroom teacher, for the first time, the opportunity of a career in the classroom, a career which provides the teacher with the status, prestige, and monetary reward that are nonexistent in today's lock-step educational organization patterns. This book should not be viewed as a theoretical treatise on personnel organization and utilization. It is, instead, a practical do-it-yourself book for educators on the "firing line." It provides, as well, a volume for college and university professors of education in this entirely new area of differentiated staffing.

R.A.D.
R.P.S.

Acknowledgments

We wish to acknowledge those who helped to make this project a reality. Without their help and support this book would never have been written.

To Dr. Samuel Brownell of Yale University and The University of Connecticut, The Honorable Floyd T. Christian, Florida Commissioner of Education, Mr. Shelley S. Boone and Dr. Joseph W. Crenshaw of the Florida State Department of Education, and Arthur C. Croft of A. C. Croft, Inc., thanks.

In addition, this book owes much to other names prominent in research and application literature on Differentiated Staffing. Five in particular have had a major impact on its brief history. These creative pioneers, in alphabetical order, Dr. Dwight Allen of the University of Massachusetts, Dr. Donald Davies of the United States Office of Education, Dr. Roy Edelfelt, National Commission on Teacher Education and

Professional Standards, Dr. Fenwick English, Center for Educational Advancement, and Dr. Marshall Frinks of the United States Office of Education.

Special thanks go, also, to Dr. Keith W. Atkinson, Professor of Education, The University of Connecticut, Dr. Charles A. Blackman, Professor of Education, Michigan State University, Dr. Anthony F. Gregorc, Assistant Professor of Education, The University of Illinois, Dr. William T. Gruhn, Professor of Education, The University of Connecticut, and Dr. Ronald T. Hyman, Associate Professor of Education, Rutgers—The State University of New Jersey. Their support and encouragement has not been forgotten.

We are indebted, for their assistance, to the ever ambitious graduate students who provided the bibliographical research on this project—Sr. Therese Bernard, Sr. Jacquelin Crepeau, and Robert Kelly.

For the extended help and information offered through telephone, written correspondence, or through their press releases and differentiated staffing project information and descriptions, much thanks is due the indefatigable field workers, writers of projects, and project directors affiliated with the differentiated staffing school centers throughout the United States.

1. An Overview
of Differentiated Staffing

Gertrude Stein could have written A Teacher is a Teacher is a Teacher[1] as a companion piece to her classic "A Rose is a Rose is a Rose." Methods of staffing and staff utilization in most public schools suggest that there is a quality—called "teacherness," perhaps—which, when a person becomes a teacher, overrides all his individuating qualities. It appears that each state, through existing laws, boards of education, voters, and administrators, believes that when a person acquires "teacherness" he becomes like all others who have that quality. He can, with equal competence, do the job of any of his co-teachers; he can be assigned any task, fitted into any role without seriously altering the workings of the school. A second grade teacher, in this view, has second grade "teacher-

[1]Attributed to Dr. Dwight Allen, University of Massachusetts, Amherst, Massachusetts.

ness" and is like all other second grade teachers. Though certainly one of the tasks assigned teachers is to enable their students to become unique persons, and another to respect uniqueness and individuality, yet, in spite of this, practices of staffing in public schools perpetuate the myth of "teacherness." A Teacher *is* a Teacher *is* a Teacher—and so it has gone.

This myth has serious ramifications. Its perpetuation is making increasing numbers of teachers dissatisfied with the disparity between self-images as salaried professionals and responsible individual decision makers, and the mythic images of their employers and administrators. There are viable and deep-seated reasons for their dissatisfaction.

Teachers are concerned with the highly tentative nature of their recognition as professionals. Although lip service is paid to the concept of teaching as a profession, teachers are not accorded three of the benefits concomitant with professionalism: adequate compensation, promotion or similar forms of recognition, and decisional powers.

To talk about teachers' salaries is to probe already raw wounds, but the wounds deserve probing. By professional standards, teacher salaries rank from relatively to embarrassingly low. In a sharp criticism of the reward system for teachers Jacques Barzun wrote:

> Although it is true that a good deal of money is spent in and around education in this country, the prevailing style among those engaged in learning and teaching is shabby genteel. Money and good will have not been wanting, but the distribution has been haphazard, often wasteful, and almost always thoughtless. Wherein does it go wrong?[2]

A system of merit pay has been offered as an alternative to the often inadequate, across-the-board, years-of-service salary method, but visions of huge impersonal mechanisms for determining merit have prevented the widespread institution of merit pay scales. Meanwhile, teachers have grown increasingly unwilling to accept low pay status, which they feel reflects on their professional standing.

Teacher dissatisfaction over insufficient pay could be alleviated somewhat by possibilities for professional advancement. However, there is no system of promotion in the public schools designed to keep outstanding professionals in the classroom, as there is at the college or university. There a teacher may be rewarded by change in rank or pay without leaving the job for which he is being rewarded. In public schools, since there is no prestigious career ladder for teachers, the only rungs to climb are those out of the classroom, away from direct contact with students. For a teacher, upward mobility means to leave teach-

---

[2] Jacques Barzun, *Teacher in America* (Boston: Little, Brown & Co., 1945), p. 247.

ing and become a department head, guidance counselor, assistant principal, principal, district supervisor, or administrator. Too often it is the excellent teacher, the one most needed in the classroom, who seeks and obtains this advancement.

Even given their dissatisfaction with salaries and with the locked-in unprofessionalism that bars promotion within the job, many teachers would stay in the classroom if they had some sense of personal stake in the shape that education takes. But those who are ultimately entrusted with the education of children are denied effective roles in determining what that education should be.

After an intensive study of several educational systems, Seymour B. Sarason wrote in a chapter entitled "Teaching Is a Lonely Profession":

> Although a teacher is in a room throughout the entire day with 20 or more children, teaching is basically a lonely profession. A teacher presents material to children, and she may correct their work. On occasion, she may share a child's ambitions, his fantasies, or his worries, but it is rare that a teacher has the opportunity to discuss her problems or her successes in teaching with anyone else. There is certainly no formal structure for the discussion of the day-to-day concerns of the classroom. By and large, faculty meetings are devoted to issues of policy and to matters of general concern to the school. Depending on the school and the principal, faculty meetings may offer greater or lesser opportunities for open interchange of ideas. In one school general faculty meetings were not held. In another the meetings consisted almost entirely of the principal reading dicta and memoranda coming from supervisory personnel, from the PTA or from the superintendent and the board of education.[3]

Fenwick English suggests that teachers must be more involved in decision making through the establishment of new organizational structures. He maintains that:

> ...we say teaching is the most important activity in the educational enterprise, but all the rewards, financial and otherwise, encourage movement away from the classroom. The administrator is the one who has the status, power and prestige in education. Administration is the mark of advancement, the badge of success.[4]

Further expression of the teachers' sense of powerless futility is given in M. John Rand's statement quoted by Crenshaw and Smith:

[3]Seymour B. Sarason, et al., *Psychology in Community Settings* (New York: John Wiley & Sons, 1966), p. 64.
[4]Fenwick English, *Differentiated Staffing: Giving Teaching a Chance to Improve Learning*, Tallahassee, Florida: State Department of Education, September 1968, pp. 1-2.

Endless committees and councils have done little to change this sense of futility—too often decisions continue to be handed down from higher authority... in order for teaching to become fully professionalized, the decision making role of the teacher must be greatly expanded and most of the (education system) organizational plan changed. Also, it must be possible for teachers to earn more money and still work closely with children.[5]

These questions of professional standing have created a teacher identity crisis. Lacking public esteem through higher salaries, professional challenge through the possibility of upward advancement and, most important, the psychological satisfaction that comes in part with shaping the policies that affect their own and their pupils destinies, teachers are asking themselves "Who am I? . . . , Are teachers really important?" And without a tangible answer they leave the classroom or the profession. The result has been—over the years—such an appalling exodus of educators from the classroom that public education can only be weakened.

In summary, the teacher exodus can be seen to be caused by the following:

1. We have been unable to consistently retain good teachers for prolonged periods although we were initially able to attract them to the profession. Milton Kaplan clearly stated the problem when he said, "One of the most tragic ironies in education today is that the school administration, which is charged with responsibility of obtaining better teachers and improving teaching methods, is often responsible for doing just the opposite. With one hand it recruits frantically for teaching talent, and with the other it plucks that talent out of the classroom and allows the inexperienced and the inferior to do the actual teaching."[6]

2. We have relegated the classroom teacher to a position of isolation in the classroom and in so doing we have failed to tap his potential for leadership, thus depriving the profession of his needed skills.

3. We have developed a scheme of payment that shackles the teacher to lock-step salary schedules that pay only on the basis of years of experience and professional academic preparation. We have failed to recognize that one's age and number of courses taken are not the sole criteria for rewarding the outstanding teacher. Although knowing better, we have continued to profess, at least by our actions, that the older one

[5]Joseph W. Crenshaw and Rodney P. Smith, Jr., *Differentiated Staffing, Technology in Education* (Tallahassee, Florida: State Department of Education, 1968), pp. 1–2.

[6]Milton Kaplan, "Teachers Belong in the Classroom," *Education Forum*, November, 1968.

gets and the more courses he takes results in a better teacher, at least as evidenced by our rewarding system.

4. Power and prestige cannot always be found in the classroom. Too often the classroom teacher feels no more status in the profession or in the community than does the assembly line worker putting the red nut on the green bolt. Although the teacher may gain inner satisfaction in knowing that he has reached certain youth, his accomplishments are not recognized nor is his voice heard in the community.[7]

5. We have not placed teachers in responsible positions while bringing about educational change, yet we give lip service to the fact that in the last analysis teachers are the ones who ultimately effect significant educational change.[8]

6. There is a widening gap between teachers and administrators since the introduction of collective negotiations. A better relationship should be cultivated, ". . . and the function of the administrator is to promote the teacher, to create the conditions by which the teacher may respond creatively to the challenge of producing improved education and procure for the teacher the necessary materials and support to innovate."[9]

The obvious answer to the question "Are teachers important?" is "Yes!" Vital. On a mundanely practical level *someone* must staff the classrooms. That's where the masses of children are. Going beyond the immediate custodial importance of teachers, social changes are making the "yes" apparent. Some teachers are beginning to respond to that intangible but supportive affirmative.

Rapid technological changes, the rapidly narrowing gap between research and implementation and the recognition that education must keep pace with and be consciously involved in society have created an educational environment which few could envision a generation, even a decade ago. To more and more educators and concerned people it becomes apparent, that, in spite of itself, education is being changed. The awareness that education must meet the needs, however defined, of individual students is altering all aspects of public schools. A new category of books criticizing and analyzing the educational establishment has appeared on bookshelves and best selling lists. The media and the legislatures have begun to look closely and critically at the educational process. Are teachers important? The attention given to teacher "accountability" to national assessment attests to fervid public knowledge that they are.

[7]William B. Hedges, "Differentiated Teaching Responsibilities in the Elementary School," *The National Elementary Principal*, September, 1967, pp. 49–54.

[8]Hedges, p. 51.

[9]Fenwick English, *Differentiated Staffing: Giving Teaching a Chance to Improve Learning*, Tallahassee, Florida: State Department of Education, September, 1968, p. 4.

And how are teachers responding to the awareness that they *are* important? Those who are not leaving are actively involved in claiming their importance and in challenging all aspects of the system that deny or withhold it. The stereotype of the marginally intelligent, marginally successful male and the stern, sexless spinster teacher are becoming obsolete. Awareness of their importance and potential power has led teachers to transform docile unions and associations into active agents for change. Strikes, grievances, mediation, and arbitration have become accepted rather than rare practices. This is a beginning—for reshaping the image of teachers, for reshaping public education.

Nevertheless, too often the drive for recognition and change looks like, or even becomes, teacher militancy—with all its overtones of irrational, ineffective power-hunger. In part this new picture is the result of the frenzy that arises from the frequent failure of administrators to recognize new teacher demands as demands for decision-making involvement, for individual growth rather than for "merely" status or prestige. This misinterpretation of teacher activism allows administrators to maintain the status quo under the aegis of rational conservation.

Teachers are demanding recognition of their importance. Many are leaving the classroom or education. Simultaneously, new perceptions of what public education is about are demanding attention. All of these problems are coming quickly and surely to crisis—solutions must be sought.

A key to their solution may well be the reviewing of the roles of those most responsible for education—the teachers—and recognition of their varied worth, individuality and potential. Differentiated staffing may well be the way to practice what this review and recognition brings to light. Differentiated staffing seeks to put to best advantage the unique abilities of teachers through the development of a teacher hierarchy with a salary equal to job responsibilities. It is an organizational attempt to improve education by improving the utilization of the educational staff.

A complete definition of differentiated staffing would indicate that it is:

> . . . a plan for recruitment, preparation, induction, and continuing education of staff personnel for the schools that would bring a much broader range of man-power to education than is now available.[10]

> . . . a concept of organization that seeks to make better use of educational personnel. Teachers and other educators assume different responsibilities based on carefully prepared definitions of the teaching function.[11]

[10]National Commission on Teacher Education and Professional Standards, "A Position Statement on the Concept of Differentiated Staffing," *NEA*, 1969, p. 2.

[11]Donald Barbee, "Differentiated Staffing: Expectations and Pitfalls," *NCTEPS*, 1969, p. 1.

. . . the teaching staff is organized so that there are different levels of talent and responsibility.[12]

. . . a concept of organization that seeks to make better use of educational personnel. Teachers and other educators assume different responsibilities based on carefully prepared definitions of the many teaching functions. The differentiated assignment of educational personnel goes beyond traditional staff allocations based on common subject matter distinctions and grade level arrangements and seeks new ways of analyzing essential teaching tasks and creative means of implementing new educational roles.[13]

The goals of differentiated staffing are clear: the improvement of teaching (instruction), individualization of instruction, better utilization of the unique abilities of individuals (teachers and pupils), the provision for an upward-mobile career in the classroom for teachers, a mode of operation which begins with the strengths of a teacher, the placement of a person at the level at which he functions best, an increase in specialization, the involvement of teachers in decision making, and a provision to allow teachers to police and regulate their profession.

Differentiated staffing, as a policy for change in a school district, has implications for schools in general and for the professional image of teachers which must also affect the quality of education in public schools. Because it will channel teachers into positions for which they are best suited and will involve teams of educators who can better work with individual pupils, differentiated staffing may well enable breakthroughs in the implementation of new learning models. With differentiated staffing, teachers could advance in prestige and salary, and possibly rise in the decision-making hierarchy to become principals and central office staff. The teacher could insure his own positive image by achieving his fullest potential in one or an upward series of jobs.

There are implications in differentiated staffing for the training and certification of teachers and for breaking down the barriers that have prevented teachers and administrators from working together effectively. More often analyzed and criticized for their obvious ineptness in the past, today teacher preparation schools are reflecting spirited demands by instituting programs aimed at resolving age-old problems. Teacher preparation in the next two or three decades will, however, undergo its severest test—here the ultimate effectiveness of differentiated staffing will be resolved. The roles that teachers will be expected to fulfill call for something other than a traditional approach. Specialization calls for a differ-

[12]Rodney P. Smith, Jr., "New Patterns of Differentiated Staffing," *Educational Summary*, Croft Educational Services, May, 1969, p. 1.
[13]James L. Olivero, "The Meaning and Application of Differentiated Staffing," *Phi Delta Kappan*, LIT, September, 1970, pp. 36–40.

ent form of training from that presently given to generalists. Teachers will be expected to be far more effective in working with youth, far more expert in the academic disciplines, and far more proficient in the application of learning theory. They will need to learn to work effectively with other adults and to work through dominant and submissive roles as situations dictate.

The change in teacher function will ultimately have an effect on teacher certification. Educator teams will work with students, and teacher certificates, as they now exist, will not be applicable to some staff member functions. Certification provisions will have to be made for the use of assistant teachers and non-professional personnel in a youth-centered learning program. Differentiated staffing plans that have been developed and implemented have called for the use of community resources—non-educators—not only as guest lecturers or for assembly programs, but to be actively involved in the school as regular contributors.

If one were to consider administration as a force which administers support to the sophisticated system, then there is every expectation that some progress in the present teacher-administrator impasse might occur, as it has in a number of isolated cases under exceptional administrators. Under these, the teaching profession is truly elevated, morale is raised, and a new image of the teacher emerges. Innovation becomes primary and the learning-instruction core of American education begins to receive its due.

Differentiated staffing may solve many of the difficulties that have caused and grown out of the teacher identity crisis. The professional standing of teaching will be enhanced by the implementation of differentiated staffing. Teaching has not been a self-regulatory group as other professions have been. Certification standards are established by state or local agencies and teacher effectiveness is judged by mostly nonteaching administrators. Under differentiated staffing, teachers will be partners with or, in some instances, even replace administrators. They will be evaluated by their peers as well as those above and below them. Selection for promotion will be made by a panel of teachers who would have to work with the candidate. "Evaluation is a professional responsibility and should be practiced by the professional teacher. Competence is measured in terms of the degree to which the staff receives the services it has determined it needs."[14]

Through this new order some teachers will be paid salaries commensurate with those now paid administrators, and the decision-making arena will be opened to them. This will lead them to greater prestige and

[14]Rodney P. Smith, Jr., "A Teacher is a Teacher is a Teacher," *Florida Schools,* October, 1968, p. 5.

success. They may very easily earn salaries two or three times above their present maximum potential and command the status and authority equivalent to the administrator's. Such a restructuring will insure that the better minds of our age will be attracted to the classrooms, and will, of their own accord and desire, remain there.

The concept of differentiated staffing recognizes the individual differences of teachers by providing such an opportunity for them to become specialists. It recognizes the lost individual in an age of group identity. Each person has a special, vital position on the team—each is indispensable. This is important because the differentiated staffing pattern requires educational administrators to look upon teachers as individuals—each with his unique strengths, weaknesses, and contributions—in a manner in which teachers have been encouraged to observe and work with youth. Furthermore, the public can be shown that through the differentiation of tasks it is getting full value for its tax dollar. This is especially important in this period of competition for available tax revenues, for it is becoming more difficult to justify the money spent on an educational system whose relevance to society is already being questioned. Changes to meet these needs are necessary if public confidence and support are to be maintained.

Those who advocate differentiated staffing today, both theorists and practitioners, view it as a flexible instructional organization which may allow many improvements in American education. Primarily, it is a rearrangement of teaching roles to enhance student learning, which will allow the school to more nearly meet the contemporary ideal of individualized instruction—each individual child is of inestimable worth, and the development of his unique potential is a foremost endeavor. To the extent that differentiated staffing will help to meet the broad goals set by society epitomized by the phrase "individualized instruction," to this extent differentiated staffing is seen as inevitable in some form. It is for this that we need to know more about differentiated staffing. It is an idea which has come of age, and is being talked about and implemented in many places. It is important to know how to understand and use it, lest it, through our misunderstanding, manipulate us and our schools. Good ideas, in education, are only good insofar as they act as a catalyst to student learning.

Staffing patterns in American schools manifest themselves in several variations in the closing decades of the twentieth century. Where once the school staffing pattern was epitomized by one teacher in a one-room school, today's staffing patterns demonstrate remarkable growth: the proliferation of new staff positions such as principals and departmental chairmen; assistant principals in charge of curriculum and other areas; guidance counselors; specialists in art, music, and physical education;

school librarians, supervisors, resource teachers; fiscal and managerial personnel of all types. This growth might have been brought about by flexible adaptation on the part of schools to growing student populations and greater societal demands. Today, in fact, as society becomes increasingly more complex, as knowledge burgeons, as more and more demands seem to be placed on the schools, the school system itself seems to demand an even greater flexibility of staffing patterns.

Any discussion of differentiated staffing forces us to look at many items in turn—we may assume staffing does not exist in a vacuum. Given this, what framework do we use? What are components? One look, perhaps simplistic, may be seen in Figure 1–1.

In Figure 1–1 we have listed eight variables, which, though general, will suffice for our purposes. The reader will note that the section "staff-

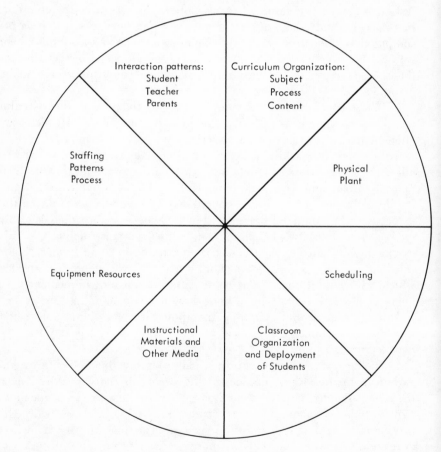

FIG. 1–1 PROCESS VARIABLES

ing patterns" could encompass the subcomponent: differentiated staffing; and that an overall staffing pattern, a particular pattern, ought to be designed to make other variables more effective. Thus a team teaching staffing pattern, for example, when superimposed on a school district or plan designed for independent self-contained classrooms, with time scheduling designed for this phenomenon, and with a system habituated to interaction patterns springing from this arrangement, could be assumed to establish a mismatch. Such an hypothesis concerning the weak influences of a dozen or so major innovations of the past several decades might be easily validated.

Not only the early core curriculum, but such recent innovations as non-graded schools, programmed instruction, computer assisted instruction, E.T.V., and interdisciplinary courses all contain or should contain within themselves the germs of a system. The core curriculum, for example, may not proceed on its own. Accommodations must be made; a system must be devised for its containment or implementation. For core curriculum entails different arrangements of other variables such as:

Staffing patterns
Equipment resources
Instructional materials
Classroom organization
Interaction patterns
Physical plant
Scheduling

In this regard, staffing patterns arranged for a time when teachers did little planning could not accommodate the increased need for teacher decision making implied in the curriculum. As well, to use a simplistic example, equipment (such as an opaque projector for class viewing of a magazine brought by a student) for using broader approaches to curriculum must be present. To continue: the difficulty of using old fragmented instructional material in core curriculum; the self-contained classroom in a static physical plant with bolted-down desks and little bulletin board space; the older teacher-centered lecture interaction patterns; the inelastic scheduling of time—all were designed for another system.

One can easily see that innovative variables are not apt to fit as well in a random system which is not designed to take advantage of the particular uniqueness of each. Systems must be uniquely designed to contain their variables. To the extent that these eight variables (or others) fit into a planned system the system will be balanced and more efficient, and will operate as it has been designed to.

A Look at Related Variables

Since we cannot ignore the interrelationships which present themselves, let us now look at how other variables in Figure 1–1 connect with and affect the larger system.

Classroom organization, scheduling, and staffing are vital to the process of differentiation. In classroom organization, for example, the solution must be actively sought to determine what learning can best be accomplished with various groups of students. This might lead to one, two, or three hundred or more students meeting for large group presentations, while small classes of nine to twelve meet for small group interaction, while still others are scheduled for individual consultation. Some teachers have talent and ability for large group instruction, others for small group, still others are better at one-to-one counseling and instruction.

The variables of facilities and self-instructional materials offer even greater flexibility; through large "quest-centers," independent study laboratories, programmed instruction centers, libraries, and even computer-assisted instruction centers, large numbers of students and their learning needs can be accommodated, thus freeing teacher time for more productive endeavors. Housing facilities for all these activities must be given prime consideration and, ideally, when long-range planning of these facilities is completed, great numbers of variations may be tried.

Certainly content is a variable. The teaching of certain subjects, such as English and the social studies needs minimal facilities (although this is rapidly changing), while other subjects, such as physics, chemistry, even multimedia driver education centers, require greater material support. Content does matter. If one takes time to notice it, content affects staffing—trained teacher-aides could possibly supervise the organized content in a programmed instruction laboratory. Only a highly capable specialist, though, could instruct a large group or work with "loaded" small group sessions. This, then, is a brief, perhaps cursory, examination of some variables and how they interrelate. Our assumption must be that the teacher is an important variable. How flexible instructional patterns and analysis of the relationships of other variables to the teacher may lead to an improved learning system and a more responsive school, will be discussed further in following chapters. For the present, let us return to our overview of differentiated staffing.

Further Views of Flexible Instructional Organization

We have said that differentiated staffing is a part of what we might call a flexible instructional organization. Figure 1–1 was meant to illustrate several possible variables in the educational system. Staffing was one of these variables. Given the belief that teachers are important, the authors presented a problem or two involving only this one variable, the teacher. Is the teacher effectively involved in decision making? And if the teacher is not involved, would something like the academic senate help his involvement? We shall look at the senate idea in a later chapter.

We then considered several additional variables, our assumption being that flexible instructional organization almost legislates flexibility in the several other variables. We shall return to this important point, flexibility, in later chapters. Perhaps it would be well to see flexibility included under the concept of differentiated staffing and ask the questions: What are some of the recent stirrings of differentiated staffing? What does a differentiated staffing model look like?

A Look at Some Models

In differentiated staffing models several levels of staff positions have emerged in the hierarchy pattern. Let us look at Figure 1–2. Note that there are six different positions indicated in it involved in classroom management. These positions are the paraprofessional (educational technicians, teacher aides, and teacher clerks), academic assistant, staff teacher, senior teacher, teaching curriculum associate, and teaching research associate. These are foreign terms in the traditional school setting, but when applied to a differentiated staffing model they become uniquely significant. To illustrate this it might be well to define the kinds of roles and functions that each would play.

EDUCATIONAL TECHNICIAN. Many teachers estimate that 25 percent of their time is spent on clerical tasks alone. This, coupled with other less productive tasks, indicates a waste of at least one third of a teacher's efforts and energy. The Educational Technician performs the routine tasks of the classroom, relieving the teacher of these lesser duties. His function varies, depending on the subject area or grade level in which he works. His job includes such routine tasks as ordering supplies, developing bulletin board displays, mixing paints, record keeping, duplicating materials, typing, playground supervision, setting up materials for labora-

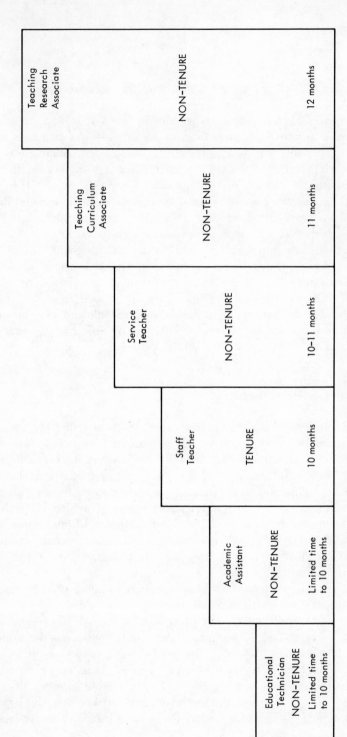

FIG. 1-2 SIMPLE DIFFERENTIATED STAFFING MODEL

tory experiments, or any number of other activities essential to the process of the classroom.

The Educational Technician need not be an adult. For many years high school students have been performing some of these chores on a less organized basis. A high school program designed to train Educational Technicians, laboratory assistants, and clerical help could be developed which could guarantee immediate employment to certain high school graduates. Before graduation the student could serve in an assistant or apprentice category, and on graduating become a full-time member of a differentiated staffing team.

ACADEMIC ASSISTANT. In most models the Academic Assistant is seen as a non-tenured person with at least two years at a recognized college. His work with students and teachers in the instructional program involves the use, the preparation, and the evaluation of materials. He could be responsible for maintaining clerical materials and supplies, grading papers, and giving specialized instruction in remedial enrichment areas, directed by a member of the professional staff, as well as supervise student study and be responsible for resource-centered activities. It is very realistic to think that an Assistant could start as an Educational Technician and, taking courses at night and during summers, complete the requirements and become a career Academic Assistant.

STAFF TEACHER. The Staff Teacher is the core of the educational program and his strength lies in his ability to communicate with students, work with parents, and effectively implement the goals of the educational program. He must be an accredited teacher and have at least one academic degree. He would be given the usual ten month teaching contract with a salary based upon a regular salary schedule. The Staff Teacher spends 100 percent of his time in classroom teaching. He must be able to plan daily for groups, meet individual student needs, keep classroom control, maintain pupil rapport, select and organize materials, confer with pupils and parents, effectively utilize educational assistants, function as a member of a teaching team, and make use of his opportunities to grow professionally.

Teachers now do all of these plus quite a few things not listed above. The Staff Teacher, freed from curriculum development and nonteaching clerical tasks, can be expected to be a full-time teacher.

It is a goal of differentiated staffing to utilize the special qualifications of all teachers through more efficient management of talents, space, time, and materials. Team teaching becomes one excellent method of achieving organizational flexibility but this is not necessarily mandated in a differentiated staffing plan.

SENIOR TEACHER. The Senior Teacher's primary responsibility is the application of curricular innovations to the classroom. He modifies new ideas and works out the details for implementation. From his work emerge refined, sound, and practical curricula ideas ready for immediate implementation.

The Senior Teacher must have demonstrated excellence as a teacher, and must continue to teach, though on a limited basis. He must have manifested leadership capabilities and be considered a master practitioner, with a great deal of experience and training, who remains vital and imaginative. The Senior Teacher must know the most recent developments in teaching and his subject/skill area.

It is proposed that the Senior Teacher spend most of his time in doing what is most needed—teaching effectively. He might conceivably be on an eleven or twelve month contract and spend about 50 to 60 percent of his time in class. The remaining 20 percent of this time might be spent on staff development and inservice education programs, workshops, and seminars. He could give assignments to student teachers, develop pilot programs, perhaps even function as a teaching team leader, planning schedules and programs with his team. He could help the Staff Teacher meet student needs, develop creative techniques and materials, serve on an academic senate and be responsible for the educational assistants in his area. The Senior Teacher could coordinate the work of all teachers in his subject/skill area. Using this model, only Staff Teachers are tenured, and all staff members are either on tenure as staff teachers or working toward tenure. Their tenure as Staff Teachers is not affected by working in higher positions, but tenure might not be held in the higher position. Also, all personnel employed in positions above the staff teacher will receive compensation based first upon their positions on the regular salary schedule, and second upon factors of additional responsibility and time. This latter consideration creates the improved salary schedule for the higher non-tenured positions.

TEACHING CURRICULUM ASSOCIATE. The Teaching Curriculum Associate's primary responsibility lies in curriculum development. Using the most promising educational trends, he could develop new curricular material which might eventually become part of his district's or county's educational program. He should be able to conduct sound research, demonstrate an understanding of the learning process, and utilize instructional resources efficiently. The Teaching Curriculum Associate could contribute to the development of new methods and new programs of education. He must be able to organize materials in ways that will be meaningful and amenable to classroom use.

The Teaching Curriculum Associate, like the Senior Teacher, is first a teacher. He would spend some of his time teaching, since everyone in the instructional program above the Staff Teacher must first be a teacher, and the rest of his time as follows: The Teaching Curriculum

Associate develops new curricula, and works with Senior Teachers in pilot programs in actual classroom situations. He conducts inservice programs and attends workshops, conferences, and other meetings. By refining and revising curricula with the Senior and Staff Teachers he keeps programs up to date and teachable. He might as well work with the same teachers on school programming and scheduling.

The Teaching Curriculum Associate would have the credentials and academic background expected of the Senior Teacher, but would also have considerable experience in curriculum design. He must, of course, be considered an excellent classroom teacher by his peers and superiors.

THE TEACHING RESEARCH ASSOCIATE. The Teaching Research Associate would keep pace with the very latest developments in his educational field or fields. Expected to read and investigate widely, he would bring to the staff a constant flow of ideas culled from research centers, universities, forward-looking school districts, and innovative schools. He must be able to critically select those ideas and materials most valid and practical for the program of instruction under his survey.

Working on a twelve-month contract, the Teaching Research Associate would spend about 60 percent of his time in the classroom. His salary would be near the top of the expanded salary schedule. His activities would include the establishment and maintenance of a continual program of research and evaluation in curriculum development and new teaching methodologies. He should read reports of related research, conduct inservice classes and workshops, attend research conferences, and work with the Teaching Curriculum Associate in developing curricula which incorporate the latest research. He would coordinate the efforts of all teachers along with his other responsibilities.

The Teaching Research Associate must have all the qualifications described for the Teaching Curriculum Associate and more. Teachers with a doctorate or the equivalent might be the Teaching Research Associate. They should, as well, have experience in research design and applications, statistical measurement, and curriculum preparation.

The illustration in Figure 1–2 should not be construed to be the final answer to differentiated staffing models. It is only a prototype, and would have to undergo numerous, perhaps significant, changes in order to be adapted to given staff and school district needs.

Note that Figure 1–2 lists the length of the work year for the respective personnel categories. Usually those positions beyond the staff level are based upon a longer contractual year. The use of a professional staff during the summer for nonteaching activities is an idea foreign to many boards of education. It becomes the task of the superintendent to "sell" the board of education and the community on the value of summer employment. Some of the activities in which eleven and twelve month professional employees can be engaged are:

1. *Research and writing of specific curricula* for subject area or grade level.

2. *Teaching* that involves the presentation of innovative course materials, such as pilot programs or the use of new instructional materials.

3. *Modification of existent curricula* to the specific needs and facilities of the school in question.

4. *Attendance at classes, institutes, and workshops* in which the work relates directly to the growth of the individual professionally.

5. *Traveling* to gain experience or study of similar innovative programs that have a direct relation to the assignment and which contribute to the effectiveness of the individual and the team.

6. *Developing materials* intended for classroom use and preparing guides for the use of such instructional materials.

7. *Presenting staff development or inservice classes,* seminars, and workshops in the use of materials and methods developed as a result of differentiated staffing activities.

8. *Working in business or industry* to develop related skills, principles, and practices in computer development, business techniques, scientific methodology, or other fields.

9. *Selecting and training of educational assistants.*

10. *Studying independently* to produce a specific educational goal related to the individual's assignment.

11. *Organization planning* to fulfill the assigned duties of their specific assignments.

12. *Project writing* intended to obtain outside sources of information.

These are but a few of the professional types of experience that could enhance the effectiveness of a differentiated staffing plan and could justify the expenditure of an eleven or twelve month academic plan.

We have looked at a rather basic theoretical model. Now let us consider an operational model, the one probably best known to educators —the Temple City (California) model.

The Temple City Model

The Temple City plan grew from a Charles F. Kettering Foundation grant for an eighteen-month study. Dwight Allen, then of Stanford University, was instrumental in providing the impetus for the project.

In April, 1966, Allen presented a differentiated staffing plan to the California State Board of Education. His model can be seen in Figure 1–3.

This early plan was redrafted at Temple City and took on a substantially different look—a look that has become the prototype for many subsequent models. Figure 1–4 diagrams the Temple City plan that evolved from Allen's early work. Note that there are only four categories in this organization plan, two tenure—Associate Teacher and Staff Teacher—and two nontenure positions—Senior Teacher and Master Teacher. The paraprofessional personnel—clerks, educational technicians and academic assistants—are seen as providing the support services for the differentiated staff hierarchy. Let us now describe nontenure, tenure, and paraprofessional positions in this flexible organizational pattern hierarchy as advanced by Temple City.

STAFF TEACHER. The Staff Teacher is an experienced teacher, probably with tenure or close to receiving it. A highly experienced and seasoned teacher, he offers a wide range of instructional talent in his dis-

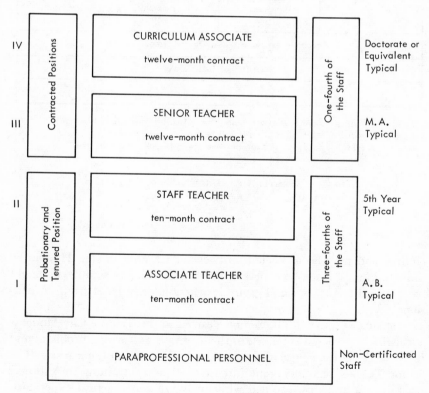

FIG. 1–3 EARLY DWIGHT ALLEN MODEL (around 1965)

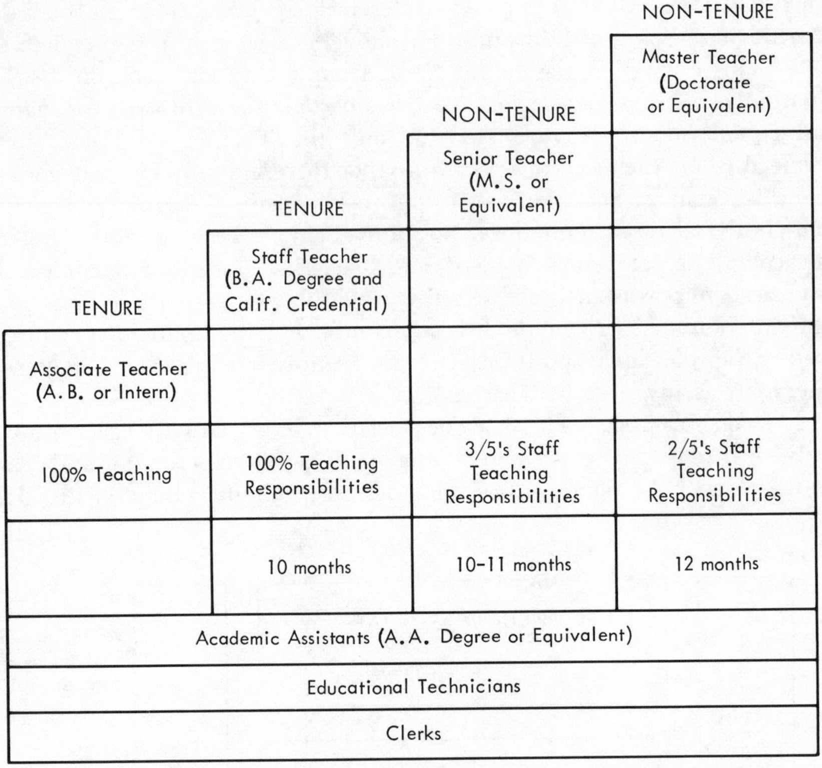

			NON-TENURE
			Master Teacher (Doctorate or Equivalent)
		NON-TENURE	
		Senior Teacher (M.S. or Equivalent)	
	TENURE		
	Staff Teacher (B.A. Degree and Calif. Credential)		
TENURE			
Associate Teacher (A.B. or Intern)			
100% Teaching	100% Teaching Responsibilities	3/5's Staff Teaching Responsibilities	2/5's Staff Teaching Responsibilities
	10 months	10-11 months	12 months
Academic Assistants (A.A. Degree or Equivalent)			
Educational Technicians			
Clerks			

* Teaching responsibilities are denoted on a flexible schedule rather than a traditional schedule. Thus it will be possible for a teacher to instruct as many, if not more, students per week even though the actual time interval may be reduced.

FIG. 1–4 TEMPLE CITY UNIFIED SCHOOL DISTRICT:
A MODEL OF DIFFERENTIATED STAFFING

cipline, and may be a specialist in several learning modes. He would, though, in most cases, be expert in at least one. As an example, he might have special talents in small group instruction, or in large group instruction.

SENIOR TEACHER. The Senior Teacher in the Temple City Model is a learning engineer, a specialist in the diagnosis of learning problems and in the relation of new teaching strategies to the needs of the learners. The Senior Teacher has undergone intensive, advanced training in a subject or skill area and this, coupled with many years of practical experience, offers other teachers a host of tested ideas for the improvement of learning.

MASTER TEACHER. The Master Teacher is first of all a very competent teacher, although perhaps not as good as the Senior Teacher. The Master Teacher is a scholar in his field, one who understands the technique and practice of the most promising research-tested ideas to improve learning. This requires a sound grounding in research and a knowledge of how people adopt innovations. The Master Teacher and the Senior Teacher form the "self-renewal" unit in the subject or skill area. They feed a steady flow of relevant new teaching practices, curriculum content, and ways and methods to enhance learning into the main stream of the school. In keeping the school up-to-date, they avoid much of the obsolete content and instruction so common in our schools today. This system, far from being an effort to stifle teacher creativity, is seen as a better, more formal system of fostering and more quickly nurturing teacher creativity than is being done today.

ASSOCIATE TEACHER. The Associate Teacher in the Temple City plan is a neophyte, the first year teacher. His actual teaching load is lighter and less demanding than that of the Staff Teacher. The beginning teacher, far less sophisticated in methodology and in pupil diagnosis than his more experienced counterparts, is not expected to be a fully functioning teacher during his first year. The first year might even be a year of internship. Easing the Associate Teacher into teaching could go a long way toward saving potentially good teachers from prematurely leaving the field due to disastrous first year experiences.

PARAPROFESSIONALS. A number of paraprofessional positions are envisioned in the plan. Today's teachers are called upon to perform a number of tasks too often markedly clerical or secretarial in nature. The performance of these functions is a waste of taxpayers' money and of professional time and talent, as well as being fatiguing and inefficient. Teachers should not fear employing paraprofessionals to remove these unnecessary classroom chores and administrivia. If there is no obvious difference in competence of performance as a result, the teacher ought to be replaced by a paraprofessional. The job of the teacher is to diagnose, prescribe, analyze, encourage, criticize. All of these tasks require the unique judgment of one human being working with another; this is the essence of the teacher's task.

Differentiated staffing challenges the career teacher to shed the cloak of subprofessionalism for full professional status with all its responsibilities and privileges. It challenges administrators to capture the desire of teachers for greater voice in the system of education and maximally deploy their talents. It challenges Boards of Education to let their professional staffs initiate substantially new programs with increased quality, instructional individualization, and relevance to contemporary problems. And it challenges teacher organizations to provide the impetus to help the profession break away from the image of Ichabod Crane and to take a new stance among the other professions.

2. Cost Analysis

There are two overriding factors in the management of any differentiated staffing project, one of which involves the district or school budget, the other the governance of the new differentiated staff, sometimes referred to as the academic senate, or faculty board.

After we have explored both *costs* and *governance* as these items have applied to actual differentiated staffing models, we will discuss overall planning strategy as this affects various school personnel and the community at large.

COSTS IN DIFFERENTIATED STAFFING

Districts which are considering differentiated staffing must necessarily think of the costs involved. To plan otherwise would be folly to a good administrator. How does one approach the cost analysis of a differentiated staff? It will be seen by a perusal of rough cost descriptions elsewhere in this book that the major costs occur in planning, research and development, and implementation of a model. A look at the fiscal outline of several differentiated staffing projects seems to say that after this initial cost for planning and development, costs are comparable with those of a school budget for a traditional staffing pattern.

Thus there are two costs to be considered: those of planning and implementation, and of maintenance. In his first thinking the administrator must consider both of these costs together. He must know what his present budget constraints are, particularly as these relate to salary. If he does not have a fairly close idea as to what he can afford in financing a differentiated staff, any money he should spend for planning could be spent futilely. He might come up with a model which he cannot begin to afford.

Some analytical purists suggest that by working within budgetary constraints we are not truly performing a proper task analysis. Such thinking is perhaps simplistic however, for no such thinking as regards learning theory and curriculum development is operant. There are budget constraints just as there are restraints in learning theory; for example, we do not expect a six year old, as an ordinary feat, to be able to master the calculus, nor do we expect a given curriculum guide to be completed in one day, nor a building to house two thousand students if it had been built to house seven hundred. There are constraints in the many factors of planning that the good administrator is forced to keep in mind, of which the budgetary constraint is only one.

How may an administrator conceive of possible models? If an administrator can not imaginatively project alternative models of staffing just for budget calculation reasons, then he must have access to this information. It is for this reason that several prognostications are included in this chapter.

Note the comparison in Figure 2–2 between traditional staffing and differentiated staffing in the Kansas City Model, the Mary Harmon Weeks Elementary School. The differentiated model is within reasonable cost distance of the traditional staffing pattern.

Notice as well the closeness of budget fit between the Martin Luther King Junior High School and a comparable traditionally staffed junior high school in Figure 2–1, and as well the budget outline of the Mary Harmon Weeks school—both schools in Kansas City, Missouri.

For yet another approach to cost analysis consider the planning proposal in the Nevada model, Figure 2–3.

COST COMPARISON OF DIFFERENTIATED STAFFING AND TRADITIONAL STAFFING

Let us observe the salary costs of an implemented model of differentiated staffing as contrasted with a traditional staff in schools of approximately the same size. Note the comparable costs in Figure 2–2. One

FIG. 2–1 PUBLIC SCHOOLS, KANSAS CITY, MISSOURI: COMPARATIVE ANALYSIS BE-
TWEEN MARTIN LUTHER KING JUNIOR HIGH SCHOOL AND A TRADITIONAL HIGH
SCHOOL OF COMPARABLE SIZE

Administration:	Differentiated Staff		Traditional	
Principal	$ 15,400		$ 15,400	
Vice principal	13,475		13,475	
Total		$ 28,875		$ 28,875
Instruction:				
2 Coordinating instr.	$ 24,310			
7 Senior instructors	64,400			
@ $9,200				
31 Instructors	267,840		(48)[1] $401,760	
(incl. librarian)				
8 Assoc. instructors	31,200			
2 Special education	16,740		16,740	
instructors				
Total		$404,490		$418,500
Certificated Serv.:				
3 Interns	$ 12,000.00			
8 Teachers' Aides	22,874.00			
2 Counselors	21,263.50		(2) $ 21,263.50	
1 Nurse	8,370.00		8,370.00	
1 Home-School Coordinator	8,370.00		(4/5) 6,696.00	
2 Accompanists	4,845.00		4,845.00	
Total		$ 77,722.50		$ 41,174.50
Noncertificated:				
1 Library Clerk	$ 3,530			
3 Secretaries	11,680		$ 11,680	
1 Registrar	5,088		5,088	
1 Textbook Clerk	3,650		3,650	
TOTAL		$ 23,948		$ 20,418
GRAND TOTAL		$535,015.50		$508,967.50
	DIFFERENCE	$ 26,068.00		

[1]Number of personnel in traditional model appears in parenthesis if different.
Where no personnel or the same number of personnel appear, no special notation
is made.

cannot help but mark the differences. Differentiated staffing costs approximately $15,000 more than traditional staffing. Why is this so? There
are no differences in principal and vice principal salaries in the two
models, and for the instructional category the differentiated staffing pattern costs approximately $14,000 less. In the two final categories of cer-
tificated services personnel and non-certificated personnel, however, we
find larger averages occurring in the differentiated staff than in the total
for traditional staffing. The differences are as follows:

Certificated Service Personnel	Differentiated Staffing		Traditional
3 Interns	$12,000.00		None
8 Teacher aides	22,814.00		None
2 Counselors	21,263.50	(2)	$21,263.50
1 Nurse	8,370.00	(1)	8,370.00
1 Home school coordinator	· 8,370.00	(4/5)	6,686.00
2 Accompanists	4,845.00	(2)	4,845.00
	$77,662.50		$41,164.50

Clearly, it is in Certificated Service Personnel that the $26,068.00 difference is found—the differentiated staffing costs exceed the traditional costs by almost $30,000. Thus the savings in instruction of approximately $14,000 by differentiated staffing is really no savings, since additional costs in certificated service personnel eat up this savings and in fact add addi-

FIG. 2–2 PUBLIC SCHOOLS, KANSAS CITY, MISSOURI: COMPARATIVE ANALYSIS BETWEEN MARY HARMON WEEKS ELEMENTARY SCHOOL AND A TRADITIONAL ELEMENTARY SCHOOL OF COMPARABLE SIZE

Administration	Weeks		Traditional	
Principal	$ 15,400		$ 14,350	
Adm. Coor.	12,155		9,340	
Total		$27,555		$ 23,690
Staff				
2 Coordinating Instr.	24,310			
7 Senior Instructors	64,449			
11 Instructors	92,070	(31)[2]	259,470	
4 Assoc. Instructors	15,600			
4 Interns	16,000			
8 Student Teachers				
1 Vocal Music Teacher	8,370	(1/5)	1,674	
1 P.E. Teacher	8,370	(2/5)	3,348	
1 Art Teacher	8,370	(1/6)	1,395	
1 Speech & Reading Teacher	8,370	(2/5)	3,348	
1 Librarian	8,370		8,370	
1 HSC-PSWC	8,370	(1/10)	837	
1 Prof. Nurse	8,370		5,022	
1 Music Instr.	2,092		5,092	
1 Ad. Sec.	4,000		4,000	
1 At. Clerk	3,467		1,949	
1 Library Clerk	3,353			
8 Teachers' Aides	22,876		1,080	
TOTAL		$306.807		$295.585
GRAND TOTAL		334,362		315,275
	DIFFERENCE	$ 15,087		

[2]See footnote 1, p. 24.

tional costs. What, then, costs extra in this Martin Luther King Junior High School model? It appears to be partial costs for interns and aides. And what caused this? Perhaps the demand of teachers for more aides or the establishment of an intern program, or task analysis, or mere extrapolation.

In any case, the illustration shows that differentiated staffing can sometimes cost more, even in excess of planning and implementation costs. If one were to assume a student population of 1500, the approximate cost per pupil for traditional staffing would be $344 as opposed to a cost per pupil in differentiated staffing of $356. Only further evaluation could answer if it is worth it.

Comparison of Another Kansas City Model

Look now at the comparison between the Mary Harmon Weeks Elementary School and a traditional school of comparable size in Figure 2–2. Here again the differentiated staff costs exceed the traditional staff expenditures, here by $15,000. Assuming here a student body of approximately 900, the differentiated staffing cost per pupil runs approximately $371, as against $350 for traditional staffing. Here again, in the differentiated staffing model, the extra costs seem due to interns. One might again ask if the additional cost is worth it? Only time and evaluation will tell.

Preview of Following Charts

By way of preview of the following charts (Figures 2–3, 2–5, 2–6, 2–7, and 2–8), let us hasten to add that differentiated staffing need not necessarily cost more.

In the Nevada model (Figure 2–3) for example, the instructional salary is not only not exceeded, but through careful task analysis and consequent staff design a $28,000 cash resource is established.

In the hypothetical model in Figure 2–5, differentiated staffing is also $280 less, and in the hypothetical model in Figure 2–6 the cost is over $1500 less for the differentiated staffing model. A similar saving is seen in the hypothetical model in Figure 2–7. In relation to the hypothetical model costs, one should give consideration to Figure 2–8 which gives the rationale for percentage allocation of differentiated staff personnel on a cost basis.

What the Nevada model and the hypothetical models seem to say is that with the same salary allocation a differentiated staffing plan can be implemented. This realized, the burden of proof no longer falls on differentiated staffing. If it can hold its own on a cost basis and an instructional-learner outcome basis, then the benefits otherwise accruing to differentiated staffing mentioned in Chapter One certainly begin to carry weight.

In plans for a differentiated staff at the William E. Ferron Elementary School in Las Vegas, two objectives were listed. One was to show that a workable model for differentiated staffing could be operated in an elementary school with the same personnel salary budget as that allotted to other elementary schools with the same enrollment. However planning costs and implementation costs would be additional expenses for the first year.

A second objective was to demonstrate that a differentiated staffing model would allow funds to be freed which would ordinarily be a part of the personnel salary budget. This freed money would be used to create a dollar pool, a separate budget category for contracting with individual teachers to do curriculum and program development work beyond the regular school day. Freed money would be used as well for training teachers to fill the new differentiated roles of instructional leaders, and to train paraprofessional instructional technicians, both of whom would use the developed curriculum program materials with students. The uniqueness of this plan is illustrated in Figure 2-3.

FIG. 2-3 DIFFERENTIATED STAFFING PROPOSAL: WILLIAM E. FERRON ELEMENTARY SCHOOL, LAS VEGAS, NEVADA

Total Salary budget	$244,400.00
Traditional staff 26 teachers at average salary $9,400.00	$244,400.00

Differentiated Staff
  9 Instructional leaders and
  6 Staff teachers	

15 Teachers @ $9,400.00	$141,000.00
26 Instructional technicians	$ 75,200.00
Cash resource for contracting and training	$ 28,200.00
TOTAL BUDGET	$244,400.00

Let us now look at a hypothetical model in cost analysis.

In the following differentiated staffing plan we consider the allocation of instructional units based on student/teacher ratios. On reviewing district figures we may further calculate the average individual salary for all instructional personnel. The hypothetical figure in our case is $8,626 per year. The ratios of students to teachers varies according to grade level which we calculate as follows:

Fig. 2–4

School	Students	Teachers
Elementary	24.7	1
Junior High	22.0	1
Senior High	21.1	1

Now, with these basic figures in mind, several theoretical models may be constructed. In this way we can show some typical schools under projected differentiated staffing plans.

It is evident in studying the following (Figures 2–5, 2–6, and 2–7) that we have, given the constraints of our allocation of salary funds, stayed well within these limits.

It is also a point of importance illustrated in Figure 2–8 that percentages may be devised in order to balance the staff.

Fig. 2–5   Model A—Elementary School

Student Population	750	
Allocation based on one instructional staff person for every 24.7 students		
$\dfrac{750}{24.7}$ =	30	
Allocation of salary funds		
30 × 8,626	$258,780	

No.	Job Title	Annual Rate	Cost
1	Principal	$18,000.	$ 18,000.
1	Teaching research specialist	17,500.	17,500.
1	Teaching curriculum specialist	15,000.	15,000.
3	Senior teacher	12,500.	37,500.
7	Staff teacher	10,000.	70,000.
8	Associate teacher	7,500.	60,000.
4	Assistant teacher	5,500.	22,000.
1	Educational technician	4,500.	4,500.
4	Teacher aide	3,500.	14,000.
30			$258,500.

COSTS IN PLANNING AND DEVELOPMENT

We are now ready to see what the costs of planning and development together with costs of implementation might be. Looking at some examples of planning grant requests we can get some idea of what others may have done. Note that one might call or write directly to any one of several differentiated staffing project proposals.

Notice that a number of important items are included in the following planning budgets: released time for teachers for planning, extended teacher contracts for planning, travel for visiting other differentiated staffing projects, inservice training costs, consultants for help in

Fig. 2–6 MODEL B—JUNIOR HIGH SCHOOL

Student Population   1,500
Allocation based on one instructional
staff member for every 22.0 students

$$\frac{1500}{22.} = \qquad 68$$

Allocation of salary funds
68 × 8,626 $586,568

No.	Job Title	Annual Rate	Cost
1	Principal	$18,000	$ 18,000
2	Teaching research specialist	17,500	35,000
2	Teaching curriculum specialist	15,000	30,000
8	Senior teacher	12,500	100,000
19	Staff teacher	10,000	190,000
16	Associate teacher	7,500	120,000
10	Assistant teacher	5,500	55,000
2	Educational technician	4,500	9,000
8	Teacher aide	3,500	28.000
67			$585,000

Fig. 2–7 MODEL C—SENIOR HIGH SCHOOL

Student population   3,000
Allocation based upon one instructional
staff member for every 21.0 students

$$\frac{3,000}{21.} = \qquad 143$$

Allocation of salary funds
143 × 8,626 $1,233,518

No.	Job Title	Annual Rate	Cost
1	Principal	$18,000	$ 18,000
3	Teaching research specialist	17,500	52,500
3	Teaching curriculum specialist	15,000	45,000
20	Senior teacher	12,500	250,000
43	Staff teacher	10,000	430,000
32	Associate teacher	7,500	240,000
25	Assistant teacher	5,500	137,500
3	Educational technician	4,500	13,500
13	Teacher aide	3,500	45,500
143			$1,232,000

the project, printing costs, project director's costs, secretarial help, and the like. All of these are fairly common to most planning grants, but each school or district also has its own unique needs.

FIG. 2–8 ALLOCATION OF DIFFERENTIATED STAFFING PERSONNEL

This adjusting of various levels of personnel to conform to a total school salary budget would have to be limited to prevent loading of any one teaching level. For example, a large number of high salaried Senior Teachers offset by a large number of low paid teacher Aides with no Staff, Associate, or Assistant Teachers would probably not provide the most desirable teaching/learning situation. Staffing percentages per position could be as follows:

	Percentage of Total Staff
Teaching research specialist	2–4%
Teaching curriculum specialist	2–4%
Senior teacher	10–15%
Staff teacher	20–30%
Associate teacher	20–30%
Assistant teacher	12–18%
Educational technician	2–4%
Teacher aide	5–15%

SAMPLE PLANNING BUDGET NUMBER 1

1. Specialized Training (Academic Year and Summer)		$19,500
a. Trainers	10,000	
b. Expenses	2,000	
c. Learning Coordinator's Sustenance	7,500	
	19,500	
2. "State of the Art" Survey		2,300
a. Data gathering and analysis	2,000	
b. Written copy preparation and reproduction	300	
	2,300	
3. Evaluation Planning		3,750
a. Consultation	3,000	
b. Expenses	750	
	3,750	
TOTAL COST		$25,550

Sample Planning Budget No. 1

Notice that in Sample Planning Budget Number 1 funds are included for a staff which will ostensibly conduct on-site training. This has proved to be important to every differentiated staffing project which the authors have surveyed. The rationale for inservice training is no doubt based on either the failure or weak start of other past innovations whose failure might largely be attributed to a lack of teacher readiness. For education is largely a technology dominated enterprise, since 85 percent to 90 percent of the educational budget goes for the technologists or the teachers. Facing this, innovators need go no further than involving teachers, but they must for minimal success go at least *that* far.

Note, too, in Sample Planning Budget Number 1 the attention given to the gathering of data, a "State of the Art" survey. For the fast moving, rapidly changing world has affected schools, and educators must be kept up to date. There is no time or need for wheels to be reinvented. While one looks for better wheels, a jet, rocket, or even an antigravity device might have been invented only a few hundred miles away. Thus, there will be a need for outside consultants. Today as in the times of the seventeenth century preacher and poet John Donne, "No man is an island."

Sample Planning Budget No. 2

In Sample Planning Budget Number 2, project planners have allowed for a director—an administrator who can see the project through. For what is everybody's job is nobody's job. There is, as well, allowance for released time for teachers, an extended contract for involved personnel, and clerical help needed to process the added business in travel, consultants, substitute days, extended contracts, equipment rental, supplies, materials, and the like. Note also the elaborate planning for all sorts of inservice training.

Sample Planning Budget No. 3

In Sample Planning Budget Number Three funds have been set aside for a project director (part time), secretarial and clerical help, part time instructors and substitute teachers to release regular staff for training, workshop and training expenses, honoraria for lecturers and consultants, employee benefits such as social security, travel and subsistence for home staff visitation and visiting consultants, supplies, and a Task Force Team five-day workshop.

Sample Planning Budget Number 2

1. Personnel Services
   a. Administrative $ 15,000
   b. Staff—High School and other
      selected district personnel
      (1) Released time 38 teachers 1/5
          time = 1368 substitute days
          @ $27.00/day   36,936
      (2) Extended contract for staff
          38 teachers 8 weeks @ 185/week   56,240
      (3) Extended contract for addi-
          tional staff 14 teachers 6
          weeks @ $185/week   15,540
      (4) Clerical   7,182
   c. Staff from participating agencies
      13 people 10 days at $100/day   13,000
   d. Consultants 80 days @ $150/day   12,000
   e. Advisory board 30 days at $150/day   4,500
   f. Travel
      3 man teams to make one or more visits
      to other agencies & institutions en-
      gaged in planning and implementing
      differentiated staff.
      Average cost jet coach, tax
      exempt   223.00
      Airport to hotel R.T.   10.00
      Per Diem $30/day trip   90.00
      Three people making 12 trips   11,628

2. Other Direct Costs
   a. Employee services & benefits (15 percent of salary)
      Items a and b under Personnel Services   19,635
   b. Communications   600
   c. Rental of data processing equipment for
      scheduling   5,000

3. Total Direct Costs   197,261

4. Total Federal Funds subject to direct costs   197,261

5. Indirect Costs—8%   15,781

6. Total Costs   213,042

7. Total Funds Requested   213,042

School District's financial contributions to the planning and implementation of the pilot project have been or will be as follows:

a. Have been:
  (1) Expenditure of fifty days planning at $50/day   2,500
  (2) Partial sponsorship of write-in conference on Developing Approaches to Differentiated Staffing   2,000

b. Will be:
  (1) Major involvement and commitment of district inservice education programs to include personnel (salaries of instructors, consultants and present teaching staff), supplies and materials   35,000
  (2) Major involvement and commitment of district adult education program to include personnel (salaries of instructors, consultants and students) supplies and materials   20,000
  (3) Two week interpersonal relations and theory of organizational structure laboratory for pilot school staff   15,000
  (4) Provision of all supplies, materials and reproduction costs directly attributable to and necessary for the implementation and conduct of the project   5,200

TOTAL COST $79,700

SAMPLE PLANNING BUDGET NUMBER 3

---

1. Direct Cost—Administrative and Instructional Staff Salaries
  a. Director—The Principal director of the project will be paid, from project funds, 1/3 of his yearly salary $ 3,755.00
  b. Secretarial and Clerical—The secretary to the project will be paid, from project funds, 1/3 of her yearly salary $ 1,260.00
  c. Part-Time Instructors—The Teacher-Administrators Task Force will be composed of six teachers and four administrators. There will be three five-day workshops held during the school year. Therefore, substitute teachers must be employed for the six teachers during the workshops. Substitute teachers will be paid $15.00 per day.
    6 teachers × 15 days × $15.00 per day $ 1,350.00

SAMPLE PLANNING BUDGET NUMBER 3 (Continued)

---

   d. Lecturers and/or Consultants—The project will
consist of four five-day workshops. It is
planned that four consultants, one per workshop
or any other combination of a total of twenty
consultant days, will work with the Task Force.
Consultants will be named at a later date.

4 consultants ✕ 5 days ✕ $150.00 per day, $ 3,000.00

                                      TOTAL $ 9,365.00

2. Other Direct Costs

   a. Employee Services and Benefits—9%
of lines a, b and c,—Part 1 $ 572.85

   b. Travel and Subsistence—

       a. $200.00 per consultant for four consultants   800.00

       b. $20.00 per diem for 20 consultants days   400.00

                                  TOTAL $ 1,772.85

   c. Office Supplies, Duplicating, Publicity and
Communications $ 842.00

   d. Instructional Supplies   250.00

                                  TOTAL $ 1,092.00

3. Stipend Support

   a. Participants—Ten members of Task Force Team
will be involved in a 5-day workshop during
the month of August. Members are to be paid
$15.00 per day for five days. 10 ✕ 5 ✕ $15.00 $ 750.00

                                  TOTAL $ 750.00

                                TOTAL COST $12,979.85

SUMMARY

    Cost analysis is of great importance to any management considera-
tion. In differentiated staffing, costs to be considered include those of
planning, implementation, and maintenance of the new faculty. The
major constraint is of course the overall salary budget. Given that most
boards of education and administrators expect some reasonable costs for
development of a differentiated staffing model, the problem then becomes one of a careful weighing of needs in advance, even before task
analysis is undertaken. In this regard, general guidelines can be set for
approval by the board, and these guidelines can be of inestimable value
in later planning. Thus cost analysis becomes at first merely a candle to
light the way. As will be seen, this estimate later gives way to the full
light of day in a thorough mission and task analysis.

3. Other Management Considerations

THE ACADEMIC SENATE, OR FACULTY BOARD

Any discussion of differentiated staffing must include some coverage of the idea of governance in the faculty composing this staff. In this arena of group management some new concepts of teacher involvement in decision making have arisen in innovative projects around the country. Such groups as the faculty senate, the academic council, the faculty board, and the building senate go far beyond the older, less structured (and somewhat inoperative) democratic faculty meetings where all too often the authoritarian presence of the central office, and the sometimes heavy hand of the school principal hold forth.

Let us look at the academic senate in the differentiated staffing project of the Temple City Unified School District. In the Temple City District, the differentiated staffing concept gives the teacher authority commensurate with his responsibilities. Policy making at each school is vested in an academic senate composed of senior teachers and staff teacher representatives. At the secondary level, members of the student government are represented as non-voting participants at appropriate meetings. Parents and other lay members are also a part of the non-voting participants.

The size of the senate depends upon the school, of course, but generally the number in the senate varies from five to eleven.

All senior teachers are not automatically part of the local academic senate. When the number of senior teachers at a school exceeds eleven, subject area representation is the criterion for selection. This body conducts school business pertaining to instruction, including decisions on class size, course offerings, course requirements, grading policies, and schedules; determines school discipline policies; functions as liaison with the district or county office and other schools; and coordinates evaluation of colleagues at the school level.

The Temple City plan uses not only the nucleus of an academic senate, but also implements, at a district or county level, academic and curriculum coordinating councils, and a managerial council.

The Traditional Model

Observe for a moment the so-called traditional model of school governance illustrated in Figure 3–1. In its nuclear form, it consists of a principal and *his* staff. This is the often criticized patriarchal pattern: What decisions or orders there are come down from the top. Teachers follow a predetermined scheme of things. There are, of course, many principals who do not follow this particular scheme; nevertheless, the design (stereotyped as it is) is modal and not exceptional even in the latter part of the twentieth century.

The Academic Senate and Differentiated Staffing

On the other hand, the differentiated staffing patterns allow for new schemes. There is a structured model which makes teacher involvement legitimate. In this model, illustrated in Figure 3–2, the academic senate functions as a strong staff to advise the principal. In some instances, the principal has only one vote on the academic senate. In other models the principal simply implements and manages the carefully thought out plans of the professional staff as voiced by the academic senate.

Are such models bound to be threatening to the principal? Should

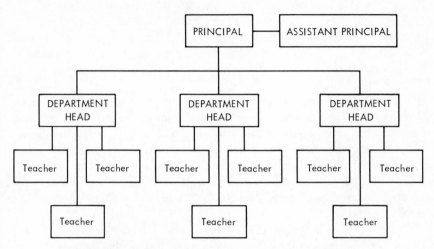

In the traditional model of government orders came from the top down. The model operation is designed for very little teacher decision making; teacher input varies with the leadership style of the principal. The organizational structure does not encourage teacher input at the top decision making level.

FIG. 3–1 SIMPLIFIED ILLUSTRATION OF A TRADITIONAL MODEL

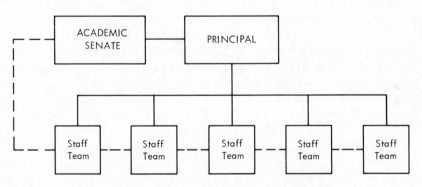

COMPOSED OF DIFFERENTIATED STAFF MEMBERS

In the simplified differentiated staffing model, the Academic Senate is the major source of decision making. The principal seeks advice and the organizational structure insures that advice will be sought. The role of the principal changes from that of line administrator to that of staff manager. He oversees the various group processes from discussion to decision to implementation. Here again, the principal's style of leadership greatly influences the total system; however, there are policy safeguards against arbitrary authoritarianism embodied in the model.

FIG. 3–2 SIMPLIFIED ILLUSTRATION OF A DIFFERENTIATED STAFFING MODEL

they be? Someone must always have a total view of the management paradigm, but to the extent that principals delegate responsibilities and authority to faculty bodies, faculties may in return be held accountable by higher management. In this, differentiated staffing puts the principal in the "cat-bird seat."

Another example in governance is found in the Sarasota, Florida Model where there is a faculty board, made up of the principal or principal-teacher, and consulting and directing teachers of a school. In addition a school staff may request one or more of the school faculty, other than those specified, appointed to the faculty board for a specific period of time, if a particular subject, discipline, or functional area was not represented by a directing or consulting teacher, if such representation seemed desirable.

The faculty board of the Sarasota model is the official body for school governance, and though it functions within the limitations of state law, school district policy, and district administrative regulations, it nevertheless exercises a wide latitude of freedom and influence into the everyday world of its school.

The faculty board oversees the operation of the school and makes decisions relating to the operation. Each member of the board has one vote; the principal does not have veto power. Further, where in traditional staffing the principal delegates authority to staff members, in the Sarasota model the faculty board normally does this.

How might school districts or total systems be organized to coordinate separate school programs better handled through central authority; busing for example, or central purchasing of standard supplies? For this, and to be able to make recommendations which affect a limited or large number of schools in the system, a central coordinating board is suggested in the Sarasota model. This board is composed of all principal-teachers—principals who also teach at least one class, consulting teachers—teachers who serve as helpers and leaders in the subject area but who also teach, and directing teachers—teachers who serve as inservice specialists at various levels of instruction in nongraded schools. In addition there are a prescribed number of elected delegates nominated by each school faculty board. This latter delegate assembly is proportional to its school's enrollment.

It should be noted that in the Sarasota model whether the system's staffing is predominantly traditional (for local schools have the option of maintaining traditional staffing patterns) or differentiated, the final administrative and ultimate legally constituted local authority remains with the board of education.

Two other models for decision-making bodies are found in the two differentiated staffing pilot schools in the Dade County (Miami area)

Florida school district. The faculty senate is found at Norwood Elementary School, and the building senate is the decision-making body of North Miami Beach Senior High School.

The Norwood faculty senate is the policy-making group for the total school operation. Members of this group are the principal, all team coordinators, and master teachers. Although required meetings are held at least every other month, the senate may request additional meetings. Each member has one vote, but the principal may only vote to break a tie. A majority of members present constitutes a quorum and may make binding decisions. Though the principal does have veto power, this veto can be overridden by a two-thirds majority in the senate. Student representation is encouraged but not mandated, and every fourth meeting is open for discussion between any single parent or parents group and the senate. Given these guidelines, the Norwood senate may establish its own roles.

Relationships within the school and the relationship of the effect of decision making on the district office are illustrated in Figure 3–3.

Teacher decision-making involvement in North Miami Beach Senior High School resides in the building senate, which is the policy making organization for the entire school. The high school is composed of subdivisions known as "little schools." Senate membership belongs to the principal, an elected member from each little school, two members of the student body selected at large, and a representative from the core unit. (See descriptive chart on p. 41.)

The kinds of decision-making processes carried on include the establishment of operational procedures, voting procedures, and needs, the creation of budget priorities, determining staff training needs, creating curriculum alternatives, and decisions on such issues as rules, regulations, salaries, tenure, and changes in school philosophy and objectives. A decision-making flow chart is presented in Figure 3–4.

Governance, then, ranks very high among considerations given to any study of differentiated staffing. The whole cloth, the total philosophy of a belief in group processes and group decision making is facilitated by a new organization, an organization meant to insure teacher involvement in decision making. In Chapter Six, the section on models, each pattern represented stresses the importance of faculty involvement in governance of the school.

Yet there is more than fancy democratic theorizing involved in governance, via the academic senate, in differentiated staffing. Differentiated staffing is not calculated to work where there is no structured machinery for teacher input. The decision must, in differentiated staffing, be as close to the implementation as possible. To make an analogy, the firing pin must be close to the powder. The general who gave the order to the lost

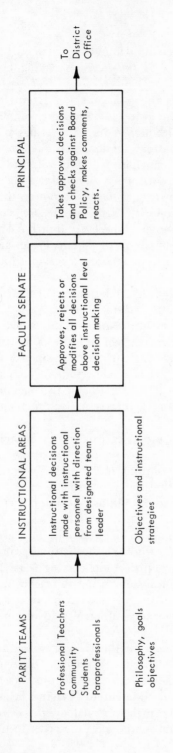

PARITY TEAMS

Professional Teachers
Community
Students
Paraprofessionals

Philosophy, goals
objectives

INSTRUCTIONAL AREAS

Instructional decisions
made with instructional
personnel with direction
from designated team
leader

Objectives and instructional
strategies

FACULTY SENATE

Approves, rejects or
modifies all decisions
above instructional level
decision making

PRINCIPAL

Takes approved decisions
and checks against Board
Policy, makes comments,
reacts.

To
District
Office

Decisions may be sent back along this line for modification.

Instructional leaders may send back to Parity Teams a decision for further clarification; Faculty Senate may
return a decision to the Instructional area; Principal may return a decision all the way across the decision
making "apparatus" for modification.

The Principal informs the district office of the decision if approval for decision is not needed from the district
office. If approval is needed from the district office, the principal informs, consults, and seeks decisions at
that level. The district office may take some decisions to the Board of Education at the District level.

Fig. 3-3 Norwood Elementary School: Decision Flow Chart

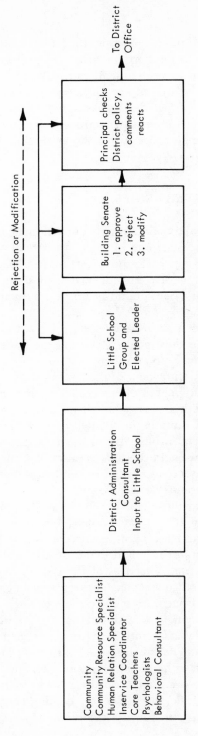

Community
Community Resource Specialist
Human Relation Specialist
Inservice Coordinator
Core Teachers
Psychologists
Behavioral Consultant

District Administration
Consultant
Input to Little School

Little School
Group and
Elected Leader

Building Senate
1. approve
2. reject
3. modify

Principal checks
District policy,
comments
reacts

To District
Office

Rejection or Modification

Approval may not be needed, in which case the Principal merely informs the
district office. If approval is needed the principal seeks this at the District
Office.

Fig. 3–4 North Miami Beach Senior High Decision-Making Flow Chart

brigade was three hundred miles away from the scene of battle. Thus, the illustrative point here is to develop and trust the professional teacher. No one principal, no one superintendent, can make multiple decisions for even a dozen teachers in a given five minute period. The only chance for proper action today is through delegated decision making. Further, dispersed leadership encourages internal commitment. It is only through internal commitment and high concern that any profession is apt to grow and give better service to society.

MANAGEMENT STRATEGIES

Starting, managing, and maintaining a differentiated staffing project is not difficult. Those who start one in their own school or district can take advantage of several years of study, starting in 1965, and observe some of the better known, earlier models, such as those in Temple City, Kansas City, Beaverton, and Sarasota all of which are discussed in Chapter Seven.

How did these projects start? What were the goals and objectives? How did the system attain those goals? What did the leaders do to start differentiated staffing in their school system?

Mr. John Rand, Superintendent of the Temple City Unified School District, is said to have originated differentiated staffing in a discussion on staff differentiation with Dr. Dwight Allen. Rand, a good administrator, liked the idea, but, cautious, he thought of what his school board, central office staff, teachers, principals, and general tax-paying public might think about it. How could the total educational staff and lay public be sounded out and involved so as not to feel left out, or left behind?

Most good administrators realize people must be involved if they are to develop internal commitment. No doubt in Temple City, as in other successful projects on differentiated staffing, how to get involvement, and to find or generate internal commitment, were motivating factors.

Every good administrator is bound to ask questions about the overall philosophy, the goals, and objectives of the system, if differentiated staffing fits in with short range and long range plans, and what parts of the school system will be affected? Most successful school districts involved in differentiated staffing went in fact through a step by step outline of *what to do* as long as two years before the system itself first started.

What are these steps? First one must ask how the people, students, teachers, all concerned, view the broad philosophy of education in their community? What are the overall goals of the system? What are specific (and sometimes not so specific) objectives for reaching those broad philosophic goals? What tasks need to be accomplished to attain those objectives and what kind of staff does it take to do them? Only after a superintendent and his entire community and school have asked these searchingly can they ask: "Is differentiated staffing for me? Will it work here?"

Let us look more closely into the management of a systems approach to differentiated staffing. In Weiler and Guerin[1] a systematic approach to planning for a differentiated staff is given, using an "imaginary" city, Elmwood.

Elmwood

The Elmwood Community had a history of school support, for though Elmwood did not have a large tax support base for its system, within its budget constraints its school board was particularly open to new and better ways of doing things. Board members were always looking for better services, for increasing the productivity of educational programs, to increase learning *without* increasing costs.

Thus, the superintendent and his assistant were permitted to contact consultants in some universities, to look into new ideas of organization of school personnel. They consequently discussed with the board what the fruits of a year's look at new organizational processes and patterns had been. The superintendent suggested that the board authorize a system-wide study of flexible scheduling and differentiated staffing. With further board support, the superintendent also proposed that a private foundation grant pay for the flexible scheduling-differentiated staffing study.

The second year soon saw the development of a formal, board authorized study. Consultants from colleges and universities nearby were called in to examine alternative choices for the time schedule, curricular program, and personnel organization or staffing patterns. Note that in all this study the overriding issue was students' learning, supported by the surrounding needs of the community.

Some of the suggestions and alternative staffing patterns and programs seemed almost revolutionary. Yet all these new ideas seemed headed toward a better educational system, a system that could improve learning by retaining and rewarding good classroom teachers. Modification of the teaching role would lead toward more involvement, more leadership responsibility; the new role would nevertheless emphasize the importance of classroom teaching.

Keeping pace with the conjectures was an ongoing analysis of costs

---

[1]See Weiler and Guerin, in *School Community Relations and Educational Change* (Washington, D.C.: U.S. Office of Education, n.d.), for an extremely interesting and well-written case study.

associated with the alternative proposals. Would the new and better ideas fit in the present budget of the school system?

Looking at his short and long range plans, the superintendent saw the changes and modifications needed. He considered his present staffing patterns, and turnover, and wondered how his present personnel would work in the new system. His whole future plans hinged on whether or not his teachers and principals accepted and would be committed to the new idea. How could he bring this about?

First, he could place all principals on full pay for the entire summer and let them begin working with the new idea. Planning for this was undertaken and board approval was obtained. With the summer, seminars, workshops, and study groups began, discussing topics like new roles for principals and teachers, group processes, personality theory, and human relations. For two weekends, the principals and administrative staff even became involved in T-group "sensitivity training." They not only came to understand, accept, and contribute to new ideas for change, which would lead toward differentiated staffing, but acquired interpersonal skills in communication and task accomplishment as well. They learned to understand and work with one another, and they developed skills to work with various groups which would involve people in decision making.

The third year was spent in system wide discussion of the process and plan for differentiated staffing and all associated factors. Teachers met in groups of five to nine or more, asked questions, and made suggestions for more specific plans. Even at the planning stage they were becoming involved in decision making.

There was, to be sure, resistance, much of which came from union members whose major objection was that the differentiated staffing plan would destroy the single salary, across the board, unity of teachers. They worried that some teachers' salaries would be considerably higher than others, how these teachers would be placed in these jobs, and what would be the evaluation process.

The administrative staff had, however, anticipated the argument surrounding the difference between merit pay and differentiated staffing, and had considered the necessary plans for evaluation, and were generally ready to mutually and sincerely explore these and other matters.

With such communication throughout the system, the superintendent could now appoint task forces, study teams, and a steering committee to come up with a workable plan for change. Here it was necessary to make clear committee assignments in curriculum, for example, in time scheduling, and in actual patterns. It was also important to have representation, even better, elected representation, from each school. The superintendent would himself *select* three appointees to the main steering committee, or advisory board.

A somewhat surprising turn of events came about when only a very few union teachers were elected to the committee. However, the superintendent utilized two of his three selections for key union members, for it was no time to cut off debate. A wise administrator listens to and learns from his critics; he can not afford to be surrounded by nor can he encourage "yes" men.

Toward the middle of their third academic year the new staffing committee began its major work. Chosen to work with the committee was the district's most able leader, a person skilled in human relations and group processes, a dynamic and well respected principal.

Several things happened in the committee. The need to change was discovered and subscribed to by most committee members. There were assets in the new patterns of instruction which were not present in the old order of one-teacher-one-classroom-thirty-pupils.

Union members, forming a cohesive block, still resisted the new ideas. However, the committee, not skirting this resistance, met it openly and asked that opposition views be put in writing, so that the items of opposition could be met through negotiation.

When the annotated list was finished, the committee addressed itself as a whole to the points of opposition. These fell around two groupings: the varying roles of new differentiated staffing members, and the selection-evaluation process. Conciliation was reached when both the union members and the rest of the committee agreed to clarify all points, and answer the challenges posed.

Two sub-committees were formed to study the two areas, and the two committees finished the year discussing these points. A final outcome of the role committee was a complete listing of the duties or tasks of a teacher, and which of these most directly improved the educational program, and led to better learning for children. The committee also looked for new duties which would improve the teacher role in student learning, and finally separated all of these aforementioned duties, responsibilities, and other items into separate tasks. These tasks were then allotted to various job categories. Both union members and non-union members came to an agreement.

While the roles committee was meeting, the committee on selection of teachers for new roles met, and came up with a plan which would involve the total faculty in the selection of teachers to be placed in the new hierarchical positions. The committee found that this same plan could also lead to peer evaluation on all staff levels as a fundamental basis for annual reports and promotions.

Both such committees then presented their findings to the overall committee. After minor revisions the overall committee prepared a final report, and it was taken back to the individual schools, and discussed at the school level. Personnel were asked to make suggestions for change, and by the end of the year all personnel in the system pretty much accepted the plan.

Opposition still existed, but it, reduced through group decision making and further negotiations, was just an irate few, who yet demanded of the superintendent on threat of resigning, that he stop all future differentiated staffing plans. The superintendent, confident in a great majority of his total personnel, stood his ground.

The following summer saw the completion of a final editing of the district plan. A full description of the new differentiated staff was compiled, and selection and evaluation criteria were polished and finalized. This, along with the superintendent's recommendation that it be approved, was presented to the board.

The following fall the total report, which now had the board, administration, and advisory committee approval, was presented to the total teaching staff for an almost total majority approval.

In the new year which was now begun, an implementation program would be devised. All would be involved, all would understand, and group decision making had been accomplished.

SUMMARY

We have seen in Chapter Three that there are several management considerations in investigating, planning for, and implementing differentiated staffing. One factor is of overriding importance: governance.

Governance, and the academic senate, are discussed in some detail in this chapter. What differentiated staffing proposes may represent a major shift in policy formulations and decision making at the school level. Here teacher involvement in the process of decision making provides a critical point. Several models are given to elaborate on this.

Finally, the chapter provides a case study utilizing a hypothetical city in order to pursue in a familiar way those managerial aspects of planning which are almost common knowledge to the educational administrator in considering differentiated staffing.

4. Understanding the Change Process: A Prerequisite to the Implementation of a Differentiated Staffing Model

The past two decades have seen considerable literature published related to the importance of the curriculum change which leads to curriculum improvement. Much of this has been written from the perspective of the administrator, the curriculum worker, or the teacher preparation institution, imploring each to provide a magical atmosphere in which all "good things" could occur. In this literature, the classroom teacher has been treated as a catalyst—someone to accelerate and make the reaction work. All too often, however, the ultimate reaction has not been what the administrator, supervisor, or curriculum worker expected. Often the reaction seems to have produced situations ranging from no reaction whatsoever to a violent reaction of catastrophic proportions. A major reason for the failure to produce the desired results, one rarely considered in the ensuing evaluation, is how the individual teacher perceives and reacts to the curriculum alteration or innovation.

It is evident whenever one talks with teachers about curriculum improvement and change that to them certain barriers or obstacles often exist which tend to impede the change process. While these barriers are all "real" to the individual, on close neutral evaluation they sometimes appear to be mere rationalizations. This, in part, may be due to the teacher's desire to maintain the status quo, or because a teacher lacks security in coping with new and different circumstances. It is highly unlikely that all the individual teacher's fears or felt barriers to a specific change could be allayed, but if those who are initially responsible for change understand what others perceive as obstacles to it, and if sincere effort is made to remove or reduce these obstacles, then a proposed curriculum change might be more successful. Regardless of what the teacher expresses as barriers to curriculum change, it becomes necessary for the curriculum worker to try to discern what constitutes, in the mind of those who ultimately effect change, obstacles to change, so that he may work toward a more immediate and lasting solution to the many existing curriculum problems.

But can the curriculum worker, realistically, do much to alleviate the obstacles which exist in the minds of teachers and which impede the change process? The answer, unqualified, is "yes." When educators sincerely become aware of and attempt to cope with the beliefs, concerns, and problems of those who implement a change or an innovative practice, then they will be on the road to resolving the many conflicts confronting education today.

Educators cannot continue to function as they have in the past. If innovations are to succeed, educators responsible for curriculum modification must drop the facade of knowing what is all important for all people. If educators are going to attempt to institute an innovative program such as a differentiated staffing pattern, they must understand the components of the change process, for it is unreasonable to assume that, without this, effective and lasting change can be brought about.

CHANGE

It would seem appropriate to first clear away some semantic obstacles. The word "change" often produces rather strong emotional reactions, primarily because, to many people, change is threatening. Not a neutral word, "change" often conjures up visions of a manipulator, a dissatisfied idealist, a troublemaker, a revolutionary, a malcontent. Nicer and safer words referring to the process of changing people are "education," "training," "orientation," "guidance," or "therapy." We are usually more ready, for example, to have others "educate" or "train" us than we are to have them "change" us. We feel less guilty in "training" others than in "changing" them. But why do we have conflicting emotional responses about words somewhat similar in definition? The safer words carry the implicit guarantee that only the changes acceptable within the framework of a commonly held value system will be produced. Cold, unmodified, "change" promises little respect for values; and might be perceived as altering those values. It might, then, foster straight thinking to use the word "change" and force ourselves to struggle directly with the implied problems of values that are involved. Words such as education, training, or guidance, because they are not quite so disturbing, may close our eyes to the fact that they also involve values.

We have not yet defined "change." The authors see change as the perceived phenomenon which occurs when the balance and stability of a situation is altered; when there is a substitution of one thing for another. This phenomenon may result from a complex of forces such as new ideas, a readjustment to a new set of perceptions, or realignment to a new environment, arising out of any dynamic situation which involves the interaction of an individual with his perceptions of the unknown. To further clarify, this concept of change must consider changes resulting from structure of framework, technological innovations and processes, as well as altered behavioral characteristics.

We have already said that change elicits frequent varied reactions within people, but perhaps the idea of the process of change has an even greater impact. It is pleasant to hold to familiar ideas, procedures, and materials—this engenders a sense of security; at the same time, it is not unpleasant to meet the new and unexpected—this adds variety to our lives. In any event, change, found present in every culture, proceeds at an accelerating pace in American society. The cultural conflicts in even seemingly ambivalent attitudes toward change cause frequent strains within a group of people trying to work together, and indeed within any one person in a group. Why some changes are smooth while others are resisted, why some people welcome change while others reject it, and why emotion is so often easily aroused in connection with change have been the subject of concern among educators for no little time. Much more needs to be learned about people and change. Let us look briefly, then, at two types, unplanned change and planned change.

TYPES OF CHANGE

Unplanned change occurs when the stability of a situation is altered in a manner best described from a maturation point of view as spontaneous or developmental. The unplanned change is not anticipated, nor are its results easily predictable. It may be pictured by some as an "act of the gods." Unplanned change represents the opposite of a planned attempt to initiate, to innovate, or to move toward carefully defined objectives.

Planned change is founded on a conscious premeditated decision to accomplish certain objectives. An example of this in a specific system is when one or more educators identify a specific school or school-community problem or need and then seek to mobilize all existing resources within their command to solve the problem or resolve the need. If planned change is the most effective way to deal with change, certain basic assumptions must be made.

1. Individual and group behavior can best be modified through a systematic approach. A well planned and well organized plan of operation which considers the needs of people and the principles of prevention of resistance to change has a greater chance of success than does one which is disorganized or unplanned.

2. A change in one part of a system will always influence other parts and, therefore, alter the total system. As one facet of a system changes, the system is perceived differently by those in it. They begin to behave differently. This different behavior sets up a chain reaction, for those observing it in turn begin to alter their behavior and the total system undergoes modification.

3. Any modification or changes which the initiator of the change deems desirable will usually progress on several levels of desirability by those most affected by it. The varying ways people perceive a change, from good to bad, beneficial to unprofitable, will determine the degree to which they enter into, unquestionably accept, or reject the change.

4. Within reasonable limits, the overt effect of change may be predicted. People in a position which requires them to implement new ideas or innovations can and do develop a sense predictability about the success or failure of a proposed change. Needed for this sense are large quantities of "common horse sense," and an ability to read the sociopolitical handwriting on the proverbial wall. Upon completion of this chapter, this should be clearer to the reader.

5. Within the framework of a rapidly changing society, the maintenance of the status quo may represent a form of planned change. In a planned change it is sometimes held strategically sound to hold one or more variables constant—to put things on the shelf or plan for plateaus—in an effort to obtain the highest degree of success in achieving the ultimate goal.

PHASES OF THE CHANGE PROCESS

Let us now direct our attention to the phases of the change process. Numerous studies of the dynamics of change have constantly pointed to several discernible phases, In his pioneering analysis of group and individual performances related to the process of change, Kurt Lewin suggested three phases:

> A change toward a higher level of group performance is frequently short-lived; after a "shot in the arm," group life soon returns to the previous level. This indicates that it does not suffice to define the objective of planned change in a group performance as the reaching of a different level. Permanency of a new level, or permanency of a desired period should be included in the objective. A successful change includes, therefore, three aspects: *unfreezing* (if necessary) from the present level, *moving* to the new level, and *freezing* group life on the new level. [1]

From Lewin's original work, Lippitt, Watson, and Westley[2] discovered in their comparative study of a population of consultants that there were seven phases which can be identified with some degree of consistency. That is, the relationships between the initiator of the change (often called the change-agent) and the client-system (the person or group that is being helped to change), appears to move through seven distinctive change phases.

Let us first consider this vignette to more clearly illustrate each of the seven phases listed below.

George Brown is a first-year principal. While working on an advanced degree at State University, he became interested in the concept of differentiated staffing. He read extensively about the subject and even wrote two research papers on the topic for his administration courses. He felt so comfortable with it that he decided to include his plans for its implementation in some remarks that he was preparing to deliver to the first parent-teacher meeting of the year. George had not found the time, however, to discuss the concept with the faculty. At last Wednesday evening's meeting, George explained his plans to the assembled parents and teachers and told them how he would like to see the program implemented by the following September. On Thursday afternoon the presi-

[1]Kurt Lewin, "Frontiers in Group Dynamics," *Human Relations.* Vol. 1 (New York: McGraw-Hill, 1947), p. 34.

[2]Ronald Lippitt, Jeanne Watson, and Bruce Westley, *The Dynamics of Planned Change* (New York: Harcourt, Brace, and Jovanovich, 1958), pp. 122–123.

dent of the local teachers' organization paid a visit to George and presented him with a grievance.

How does George extricate himself from this dilemma? George and
his superintendent will proceed through the following seven phases of
the change process as they attempt to resolve George's problem. The
reader will keep in mind that in this case the superintendent is the
change-agent and George is the client-system.

1. *Development of a need for change.* In order for the process of
planned change to begin, the individuals involved must become aware
of the existing situation or problem. This awareness must be translated
into a desire to change and finally, into a help-seeking action on the part
of the client-system (George).

In the vignette described above, George would probably consider
the alternatives for resolving his problem and decide to seek help from
the superintendent (the change-agent).

2. *Establishment of a consulting relationship.* The manner in which
a client communicates the need for help to the change-agent and how he
decides whether or not a particular change agent is the best for him to
have, is basic in the development of a helping relationship. This second
phase must involve a clarification of expectations that both the client
and the change-agent bring to the relationship.

The degree to which George and the superintendent are able to
establish a working relationship in an attempt to resolve the problem is
important. This relationship would involve the clarification of roles and
expectations of each other.

3. *Clarification of the client problem.* The movement into the third
phase of the change process is really a movement from the preliminary
"unfreezing" phase to a new level of functioning performance. After a
clarification of role expectation, the client-system and the change-agent
are ready to collaborate on the diagnostic activities that should bring
about an agreeable solution.

At this point George and the superintendent are now able to define
George's problem and they are ready to jointly begin to resolve it.

4. *Functioning of alternative solutions and goals.* After clarification and diagnosis of the client-system's problem, there follows a need
for setting specific goals and objectives (a strategy if you will) to attain a
desired change. It is necessary to examine alternative solutions to the at-
tainment of the desired goals. Related to the setting of specific goals is
the selection by the change-agent of appropriate points for the initiation
of change.

With the problem clarified, George and the superintendent now begin to develop a strategy to bring about an agreeable solution to George's
problem.

5. *Transformation of intentions into actual change efforts.* This transformation requires a commitment on the part of client-system and change-agent to actually begin attempting change. It is here expected that the mutual relationship gain the necessary support from whatever the source or sources needed to effect the change.

George and the superintendent are now at a point where they must take some definite action and they would probably establish communication with the president of the teachers' organization and present him with a plan that might result in a withdrawal of the grievance.

6. *Generalization and stabilization of the new level of functioning or group structure.* Any movement from one level of behavior to another requires a stabilization of driving and restraining forces in order to develop a new level of equilibrium. If the status quo is thought of as an equilibrium between the driving and restraining force in existence, change must be thought of as a realignment of these forces. The probability of the development of maintenance of the equilibrium may be increased by building some kind of reinforcement into the environment of the client.

An agreeable solution to the problem is reached and George is now ready to reassume his role as principal with some altered behavior.

7. *Achieving a terminal relationship with the consultant and a continuity of changeability.* This last phase requires that the client-system gradually assume responsibility for effecting lasting change. The means by which there is a harmonious and positive termination of the client-system change-agent relationship, and through which there is the least trauma, will depend upon how the pattern of dependency has been maintained and how easily it can be disengaged.

With the problem resolved, George is now able to terminate the relationship that had been developed to find a solution to his problem, and return to his school to reassume his responsibilities.

It should be understood that the authors do not imply that all planned change proceeds in such an orderly fashion through the seven distinct and separate phases described above. In most cases a specific phase is not discernible. Usually more than one phase can be seen operational at any given time.

CATEGORIES OF ADOPTERS IN THE CHANGE PROCESS.

Common sense tells us that in a group of people its individual members do not adopt or accept change at precisely the same time, but along a continuum. Because they do, it is possible (through careful scrutiny and observation) to categorize individual members of the group on the basis of their readiness to accept a given change. When this is done, the classification is commonly referred to as adopter categories. There have been numerous titles given to the categories of adopters (authors who use such titles are, to name but a few, Ross;[3] Chaparro;[4] Carter and Williams;[5] Darhof[6]), but most scholars in the field of change believe that there are five general adopter categories. To place an individual in an adopter category, one must realize that there is an adoption continuum, and that there are no pronounced breaks on the innovativeness continuum among each of the five categories. With this in mind, let us now consider the five important adopter categories of which school administrators should be aware in their effort to bring about significant change.

The Innovators

Innovators are people eager to try out new ideas, who are rash and daring in their ideas, and often in their mode of operation. Perhaps because of this, innovators tend to spin out of the immediate social circle and develop social relationships of a more cosmopolitan nature. Communication and friendship patterns among innovators tend to span great geographical distances, because innovators are often viewed with alarm in the local setting because of their rash ideas. Generally speaking, innovators are seldom in leadership positions, though they usually have financial resources which permit them to assimilate any losses that may result from unprofitable ventures; they can accept rebuke from others should an innovation fail, and they are able to understand abstractions and often technical knowledge to make concrete applications of their ideas.

Early Adopters

The early adopters are more acceptable in the immediate social system than are the innovators. They choose the best of the innovators'

---

[3]Donald H. Ross, *Administration for Adaptability: A Source Book Drawing Together the Results of More Than 150 Individual Studies Related to the Question of Why and How Schools Improve.* (New York: The Metropolitan School Study Council Teachers College, Columbia University, 1958), p. 31.

[4]Alvaro Chaparro, *Role Expectation and Adoption of New Form Practices* (Unpublished Doctoral Dissertation, University Park, Pennsylvania State University, 1955), p. 81.

[5]C. F. Carter and B. R. Williams, *Industry and Technical Progress: Factors Governing the Speed of Application of Science* (London: Oxford University Press, 1957), p. 110.

[6]Clarence Darhof, "Observations on Entrepreneurship in Agriculture," *Changes in the Entrepreneur*, in *Change and the Entrepreneur*, ed. Harvard Research Center on Entrepreneurship History (Cambridge, Mass.: Harvard University Press, 1949), pp. 20–24.

ideas and profitably employ them in their operations. This category of Adopter, probably more than any other, can exert the greatest degree of opinion leadership in his social community. Those who seek information regarding an innovative idea look to the early adopter for advice. Because the early adopter is not as "far out" as the innovator, but is yet ahead of the majority, he is respected by his peers as the embodiment of success and leadership. The early adopter is discreet in the use of new ideas. He knows that if he is to maintain his esteem among his colleagues, he must be mindful of the use to which he puts new ideas.

In his book, *Diffusion of Innovation*, Everett Rogers cites the following as being characteristic of those in the early adopter category:

> Early adopters tend to be younger in age than later adopters.
>
> Early adopters usually have more specialized operations than later adopters.
>
> Early adopters have a different type of mental ability than later adopters.
>
> Early adopters tend to be more cosmopolitan than later adopters.
>
> Early adopters have greater opinion leadership than later adopters.
>
> Early adopters tend to utilize a greater number of information sources than later adopters.
>
> Early adopters have more social participation than later adopters.
>
> Early adopters are influenced less by their peers than later adopters. [7]

The Early Majority

The early majority, far more deliberate in their thinking, tend to adopt new ideas and innovations just prior to the average member of the population. The early majority tend to participate and interact a great deal with their peers, but they rarely hold positions of leadership. They deliberate for a considerable time before they completely adopt a new idea, and because of this position between those who are early to adopt and those who are late to adopt an innovation, they serve as a unique link that tends to make innovations acceptable and legitimate.

The Late Majority

The late majority is generally skeptical of new ideas. They often adopt more out of social pressure or economic necessity than out of the willingness to change. They approach innovations cautiously, and tend

---

[7]Everett Rogers, *Diffusion of Innovation* (New York: The Free Press of Glencoe, 1962), pp. 311–14.

to exert limited opinion leadership. They are generally tuned to the early majority for direction and leadership. They might be considered obedient followers. The late adopters can be convinced of the worth of new ideas, but the weight of public opinion must favor the change, and pressure from peers is necessary to motivate adoption.

Laggards

The last category to appear on the adopter continuum is that of the laggards. It is not uncommon to find laggards adopting an innovation at a time when it has been superseded by another innovation. In any social system laggards are near-isolates and possess almost no opinion leadership. In fact, their opinions often have a reverse impact—people realize that their opinions are not in tune with the times. Laggards are traditionists by nature, suspicious of new ideas, and they consider innovations from the point of reference of the past. When most individuals in a social system are looking to the future, the laggard has his gaze fixed on a rear view mirror. Let us now look at the personal characteristics of adopters.

PERSONAL CHARACTERISTICS OF ADOPTERS

Research studies tend to indicate important differences among the five adopter categories with regard to values, attitudes, abilities, group memberships, and social status. This suggests that the most successful change agent will need one approach to reach the early adopters with an innovative idea and still a different approach to reach the late majority. To use the most effective technique to reach each sub-audience, a change agent must understand the personal characteristics of each adopter category. Below are some generalizations about adopters.

Attitudes and Values

1. Innovators have a more positive attitude toward science and technology then do those in other adopter categories. Laggards have less knowledge about research and are more suspicious of scientists. Innovators are more likely to have direct contact with the scientist and are more prone than the average person to adopt new practices on the basis of research findings.

Innovators tend to place a high value on the role of science, technology, and research and readily recognize the contribution that each particular field can make. In contrast, the laggards and the late majority place much less value on science, technology, and research and tend to put their trust in "the way we've always done it."

2. Laggards and late majority trust more in traditional beliefs than do innovators or early adopters. Examples are those educators who believe that all children who exhibit marginal academic performance will naturally benefit from a repeat of the year's work; or those who steadfastly believe that instructional media is a crutch rather than a tool.

3. In agriculture and business, it has been found that the first to adopt new practices tend to place less value on the security of being debt-free. They are willing to borrow money and take risks to realize a profit. Similarly, in education, early adopters tend to be more secure in their ability to very successfully perform assigned tasks. This security allows them to implement new ideas with a limited amount of concern for themselves. Laggards, on the contrary, are reluctant to borrow money (in agriculture and business) or try new ideas.

4. Innovators have more venturesome attitudes than do those last to adopt new ideas, techniques, and practices. Innovators reach decisions more quickly than others and often adopt new practices soon after they learn about them. In one agricultural study, the innovators adopted a new weed control spray the same year they learned about it, while some laggards took ten years to finally adopt it. Since uncertainties are involved in the initial use of a new idea, innovators take certain risks that their later-adopting neighbors are unwilling to take.

Older age tends to be associated with more conservative attitudes and an emphasis on security. Although research findings as to the relationship between age and time of adoption have not been entirely consistent, most studies have found laggards older than innovators. In one study laggards' ages averaged 55 years while innovators' and early adopters' ages averaged 38 years.

Abilities

1. Research findings generally indicate that those among the first to adopt new practices have more formal education. In one Midwestern study of farmers (note that rural sociologists have long been at the forefront of research in the field of change), innovators averaged slightly more than a high school education—about twenty percent were college graduates. By contrast, the laggards averaged slightly more than a grade school education. This can often be borne out when one reads polls about controversial issues on matters of national interest. Those who are in the highest educational categories tend to view issues in a more liberal and perhaps a more enlightened manner.

2. The first to adopt new practices tend to have special *mental* abilities. For an innovator, adoption requires a high level of intelligence and an ability to deal with abstractions. Research has shown that innovators read far more in their field than do laggards in the same field. The first to adopt an idea, practice, or technique must be able to secure much new found information from printed sources, while late majority and laggards depend heavily upon personal contact with neighbors or coworkers who have already adopted the innovation.

Group Memberships

Research indicates that those who are relatively early in adopting new practices are more active in formal professional organizations. Laggards belong to fewer such groups—this tends to mean fewer contacts with sources of new ideas. Note that innovators belong to more *kinds* of groups than do laggards.

Innovators and early adopters are more active in local, state, and national organizations; the late majority and laggards, when active at all, usually confine their activities to within the local community. Also, the informal friendship patterns of the laggard tend to be confined to his locality, while those of the innovator are more cosmopolitian. Innovators are less likely to exchange work and equipment with their coworkers or neighbors, less likely to visit with them, and more likely to disregard their coworkers' opinions of new practices. Innovators recognize that their coworkers do not have respect for their work-related practices. This does not disturb the typical innovator, who has a wider range of contacts.

Community norms on adoption affect the respect that innovators receive. In progressive communities or schools, innovators may be looked to by their neighbors for information and advice, while in backward communities or schools, their method of operation or practices are usually viewed with suspicion by those less likely to change.

Social Status

Sociological research generally finds that innovators have a higher social status than do laggards. The innovator ordinarily has greater community prestige, a higher income, and, generally, more wealth than others in his field. Even though innovators may have high social status, their practices may not be respected. Laggards usually have the lowest social status among their coworkers.

Change agents have frequently referred to the "trickle-down process" whereby the first adopters influence others, who, in turn influence still others to adopt. Research indicates that information (the diffusion of an innovation) generally spreads from higher to lower status individuals, and that most people tend to look up the status ladder to others who have a somewhat higher status than themselves and to those whose judgment they respect. Figure 4–1 below summarizes the characteristics and communication behavior patterns of the five adopter categories.

An understanding of the concept of the adopter categories can be most beneficial to the educational change-agent who is looking to implement an educational innovation such as differentiated staffing. If significant change is to be made, he should not surround himself with those he would classify as either innovators or laggards. He needs to look for balance in the types of people whom he selects to carry out a new program or idea, for if any important change is to be made, it will be helped by those or an opinion leader. He should also know that within limits, the roles people play on the adopter continuum will vary from one innovative idea to another. (More will be said about people on the adopter continuum in Chapter 6.) With this, the authors deem it appropriate to focus attention on the causes for resistance to change.

RESISTANCE TO CHANGE

In essence, it has been said that man's life is constantly changing. Most of these changes are slow and gradual; so slow in fact that the individual is often not aware of them. For the most part, changes exist in the subconscious or unconscious; some self-imposed, some voluntary. A greater portion of man's life is change in this voluntary manner, and, thus, he accepts change with little or no resistance. When changes are externally imposed, however, and the individual is forced to accept an unwanted change, then rejection of or at least resistance to change often occurs. This is most vividly seen when change is imposed as part of a supervisory function, whether in education, business, industry, or the military.

Perhaps a significant reason for this reluctance or resistance to external change stems from the individual's perception of himself—his self-image—in relation to change. Imposed change implies that the individual or his mode of operation is not as acceptable to others as he would like it to be. This may result in varying degrees of insecurity, anxiety, and tension. This coupled with the concept that most people like themselves the way they are, and usually find themselves and their behavior acceptable to others, may be a prime factor in the individual's reluctance to change. The most reputable research on this topic is found in industrial studies, which have found that there are three basic reasons

Fig. 4-1 Summary of Characteristics and Communication Behavior of Adopter Categories

Characteristic or Behavior	Innovators	Early adopters	Majority		Laggards
			Early	Late	
1. Time of adoption	First 2.5 per cent to adopt new ideas	Next 13.5 per cent to adopt	Next 34 per cent to adopt	Next 34 per cent to adopt	Last 16 per cent to adopt
2. Attitudes and values	Scientific and venturesome	Progressive	More conservative and traditional	Skeptical of new ideas	Highly traditional beliefs; fear of debt
3. Abilities	High level of education; ability to deal with abstractions	Above average education	Slightly above average education	Slightly below average education	Low level of education; have difficulty dealing with abstractions and relationships
4. Group memberships	Leaders in local, state, and national organizations; travel widely	Leaders in organizations within the community	Many informal contacts within the community	Little travel out of community; little activity in formal organizations	Few memberships in formal organizations other than church; semi-isolates
5. Social status	Highest social status, but their practices may not be accepted	High social status; looked to by neighbors as a leader	About average social status	About average social status	Lowest social status
6. Sources of information	Scientists; other innovators; research; books and magazines	Highest contact with local change agents; magazines	Few magazines; friends and coworkers	Friends and coworkers	Mainly friends and coworkers

why people resist proposed changes: economic, personal, and social in nature. All of these may be interrelated at any one given point. All of these have a logical carryover into the field of education.

Economic Reasons

People frequently fear that proposed changes may result in unemployment, in the loss of a tenured position, in a substantial reduction in their total working hours, in an ultimate demotion, in a reduction of their basic pay if failure occurs, in loss of merit or bonus pay, and hence in loss of self-esteem and status among their peers. The economic reason is of particular importance in any discussion of differentiated staffing, since differentiated staffing might be perceived by the individual as an innovation which could cause unemployment or employment at a lesser salary.

Personal Reasons

People resist because they resent the implication that their present method of operation, work routine, or role is inadequate. They resist because they may believe that the change may bring about a higher degree of specialization resulting in greater boredom and monotony, as in a substantially decreased feeling of accomplishment. They may resist because they fear that the change will require skills and training which they do not possess or are unable to acquire, or because they fear that they may be transferred to another department or building where they will have to reestablish themselves in their work roles. In education, with special regard to differentiated staffing, one might feel that loss of a degree of individual uniqueness in functioning as a team player rather than a star.

Social Reasons

The individual often looks to his occupation to satisfy certain social needs. Some people will resist change, then, because they fear that it may break long established social contacts and working relationships with people whom they know and like. Related to this are those who might resist change, such as differentiated staffing, because they strongly dislike making new social adjustments and fear that a new social situation may bring about reduced personal satisfactions. The change may cause resistance when it involves the lives of the individual's family as in the case of transfers to a new location. Or, it may meet with resistance because the person perceives a loss of prestige when required to make occupational role adjustments.

It might help to clarify these economic, personal, and social factors by relating to a problem faced by a group of educators and observed firsthand by one of the authors.

A New England community was experiencing overcrowded conditions in both its junior and senior high schools. A second junior high school was in its final stages of construction, and was being built not only to ease the overcrowded conditions in the other schools but, also, to allow for unique and innovative educational practices to take place. To make maximum use of its facilities, the board of education had, several years ago, appointed a citizen's group to undertake a study of projected enrollments and return with recommendations for the number of schools needed and the grade alignment necessary to resolve the problem. The citizen's committee recommended that one junior high school should be built and that the grade realignment be changed from a 6–2–4 plan to a 6–3–3 plan. When it was announced that the board of education had accepted these recommendations no major concern was expressed. The *fait accompli* was several years away. But as the new building neared completion anxieties began to be displayed.

The greatest concern expressed was from those teachers who had direct contact with the ninth grade students, because the ninth grade was to be moved to the junior high school level. These teachers realized that unless a vacancy occurred in the high school—one for which they were qualified—they would have to leave the school district or be transferred to the junior high school level. As concern mounted, it manifested itself in wild rumors, hastily called meetings "to do something," and a general atmosphere of discord. On this note, arrangements were made by the school district's chief administrators to interview each teacher in hopes of allaying their fears.

The administrative staff, working in one-to-one relationships with the teachers, began to discover some interesting comments based on some carefully worded questions. When the notes of the interviews were compared, they disclosed that nearly all fell into some combination of categories of reasons which were economic, personal, or social in nature. Some of the reasons stated are summarized below:

ECONOMIC REASONS.   Since there was only one teachers' salary scale in the school district the base salary would not have been affected by moving from one school or one level to another. However, economic reasons for not moving from the high school to the elementary school did appear, most obviously with those involved in coaching athletics. In athletics the freshman coaches of interscholastic teams in the high school received more money than did those who coached intramural athletics in the junior high school. Ninth grade coaches assumed that there would be no interscholastic athletics for the ninth grade when it moved to the junior high school and, hence, they would realize an economic loss if they, too, moved to the junior high school level. This factor was also important in several other cases where a teacher was receiving extra pay for extra duty and counted on it for "making ends meet."

PERSONAL REASONS. There were numerous personal reasons expressed by teachers who expected to be transferred to the junior high school level. Among these reasons was the concern that the individual teacher might not be able to perform to the expectations that "they" might expect. ("They" were a nondescript group who appeared in many sizes, shapes, colors, and numbers but who were never really defined.) But the expectations of the "worst" surrounded even those judged "best" as they viewed a new educational plant designed for new techniques of teaching and learning, for although some teachers had "proved" themselves at the high school where many had taught a decade or more, they feared that they were going to have to "prove" themselves all over again in a grade seven, eight, and nine assignment. And the belief that the traditional academic disciplines that had served some so well for so long might disappear and that interdisciplinary teams would take their place (thus necessitating a major realignment of oneself in a new environment with, perhaps, new and different responsibilities) created a major and traumatic concern within many.

SOCIAL REASONS. It became most obvious to those who were interviewing the teachers who were most likely to move that a major cause of their resistance was social. For the ninth grade science teacher who shared his lab with a colleague for over twenty years and who, also, played poker and golf religiously with the same group of cronies for nearly as long, a move to another location—even though within the same school system— was a major traumatic experience. The thought of beginning anew with a different group of people was nearly too foreign for him to comprehend. And yet, the knowledge that if he did not take this opportunity he might have to uproot his family in order to work in a high school in another town was even more difficult for him to comprehend.

We are certain that what this school district's chief administrators learned from this experience will have a major impact on their decisions in the future. For when all of the data was analyzed they took immediate steps to embark on an information program designed to anticipate questions, head off rumors, and formally help those who had to make the change to see how they might make it in the easiest manner possible.

It was fortunate for this school district that it had chief administrators who were concerned for others. For all too often resistance to change makes people appear stubborn, perverse, or contrary, at least to those who favor a specific change.

But people do not naturally resist change. They only resist change when: (1) they believe their basic securities are threatened; (2) they do not understand the change; (3) they resent being forced to change.

It is very easy for the change-agent who sees the value of a proposed change and feels adequate in taking the initial steps toward accepting the change to assume that others perceive the situation the same as he. Consequently, any reluctance in the latter looks to him like stubbornness or senseless opposition. In reality, one or more of the above factors or, perhaps, even other more covert conditions may be operating to hinder the change process.

But people are able to change without any seemingly significant resistance. Change occurs when it is recognized that certain factors such as the individual's behavior are preceded by his thoughts, his past experiences, his beliefs, his perceptions, and his attitudes, all tempered by years of habit patterns; when it is recognized that all lasting change must be personalized in relation to these factors.

OVERCOMING RESISTANCE TO CHANGE

Thus far, the authors have focused their discussion on why people tend to resist change. If it is possible to isolate those factors which cause resistance to change, then it should be possible to suggest the means for overcoming or preventing that resistance. (It should be noted here, however, that for individuals to overcome all resistance to change is probably never possible, but to reconcile and reduce the resistance factors within oneself to the lowest terms will make the change easier on all concerned.) Aware of certain factors, one may be able to cope more intelligently with the problems of change resistance. The change-agent in the leadership role can, then, be more sensitive to people's needs and can vary his working relationships to meet these needs. With this in mind, the following principles have been developed for consideration.

1. *People change when they see a need to change.* People can be expected to change only when they see a need for it. When they are discontent with their present situations, an altered or a changing concept of their self-images or the belief that the change will positively benefit them are the most common reasons for them to see a need for change.

2. *People change when they know how to change.* In order to effect change an individual must modify his beliefs, attitudes, and values. He must, then, see himself in a different role and make some value judgments about himself in that role. When he can do this and have some

degree of certainty about the outcome, and when he believes that he knows how to accomplish the change and how this change will affect him in the eyes of others, there is every reason to believe that the change may be so accomplished as to produce the least resistance.

3. *People change when they are actively involved in the change process.* Change in people's attitudes, beliefs, or behavior does not come about if they remain passive—they must take an active part in the change process if lasting change is to take place. The individual must see himself as an integral part of the entire change pattern. His perceptions of what is happening to himself and how he will be affected will do much to influence his attitude and degree of resistance to change.

4. *People change when they are secure in changing.* People know how things are in the present and how they were in the past, but they are often unduly fearful of the new because they are unsure of themselves and their abilities to adjust to something different. The degree to which the individual's fear can be allayed will usually determine his willingness to accept and cooperate with the proposed change.

5. *People do not necessarily change on the basis of new knowledge alone.* Newly acquired knowledge does very little by itself to bring about change, especially where longstanding habits and beliefs are involved. Furthermore, new knowledge may threaten the individual—he may fail to understand its implications or may be unable to perceive how to use it to make his job more productive.

6. *People change when they are encouraged and supported in changing.* Change is usually perceived as involving a certain degree of risk. An individual is more likely to initiate and carry through change if he believes that those whom he respects are supporting him, since the knowledge that others are engaging in similar activities and efforts often provides considerable support to the individual and his change. But to live in an atmosphere of self-doubt, expectation of the worst, and unsupported risk will not enable an individual to undertake the change in the most positive manner.

7. *People change some attitudes slowly.* Abrupt changes in attitudes occasionally occur from some dramatic experience, but change is generally gradual. Change in a person's conceptions are often painful for him to achieve, for his current perceptions are deeply rooted in earlier experiences, unquestioned assumptions, and unanalyzed beliefs.

When people sincerely work toward these basic beliefs, real and lasting change behavior can be accomplished. For people often fear, reject, or resist the unknown or untried, reject the new, and hold to the secure that has served them so well. But once their fears are alleviated, and once they see that they will not lose, they usually accept change as a challenge and cooperate with it.

THE GROUP AS A MEDIUM FOR CHANGE

Up to this point, the emphasis has been on the sociopsychological components which the change-agent must consider when working with individuals in the group. The authors have stressed the need for the change-agent to understand the individual's concerns, his beliefs, and his needs. These are all vital factors in the change process, and the authors cannot stress their importance enough. But as the educational change-agent works toward a differentiated staffing model or, for that matter any other innovative program, he does not work entirely with individuals; but also with groups.

The behavior, the attitudes, the beliefs, and the values of the individual are all firmly grounded in the groups to which he belongs. His fundamental beliefs and prejudices are determined to a very high degree by his group memberships. These beliefs and prejudices are the components both of groups and of the relationships among and between individuals in the groups. The extent to which individuals change or resist change will, therefore, be modified by the characteristics of the group. Attempts to effect significant change among large numbers of people must be concerned with the dynamics of groups.

The educational change-agent, when studying how groups might enter into a change process, may find it valuable to consider groups in three ways. First, he should view the group as a source of influence over the individuals in it, since efforts to help the group alter its attitudes can be supported or blocked by pressures exerted upon individual members of the group by the group itself. To make the most constructive use of these pressures the group must first be thought of as a *medium of change*, after which, second, it can become the *target of change*. To alter the attitudes and behavior of its individuals, it may be necessary to help the group to alter its standards, style of leadership, emotional environment, and stratification into cliques and hierarchies. Although the objective may be to help individuals to alter their attitudes, the target of the change becomes the group. Third, some changes in attitudes and behavior can be brought about by organized efforts of groups as agents of change. A committee to combat intolerance, a teachers' association to increase the pay of teachers—such groups have varying degrees of effectiveness, depending upon the way in which they are organized, the satisfaction they provide to members, the degree to which their objectives are understood by members, and a host of other group components. Only the first two aspects of the problem will be considered: the group as a medium of change and the group as a target of change.

1. *When viewing the group as a change medium, the client-system and the change-agent must have a strong sense of belonging to the same group.* The chances of change in people are greatly increased when a strong "we-feeling" exists, whether it is a large committee working to improve a school district's reading program, or simply one teacher and one student working toward a common goal. The chance for reeducation and a change in value patterns appear to be greatly increased whenever a we-feeling develops within a group.

2. *The group will have a greater influence on its members if the group is attractive to the individual members of the group.* If the individual members like each other and are comfortable in the environment of the group, a cohesiveness develops that satisfies many needs of the members. A group that satisfies these needs is, to its members, an attractive group. The more cohesive groups are, the more ready the individual members are to attempt change. Early studies by Festinger[8] indicate that in cohesive groups there is greater readiness of members to influence and be influenced by others, and a stronger attitude toward conformity when conformity is a relevant matter for the group.

3. *The greater the status of a group member, as perceived by other members, the greater is the scope of influence he can exert.* The degree to which an individual group member is able to conceptualize a common problem, synthesize group thinking, or state with clarity the nature of a problem, most often influences the status of that member in the eyes of the group. Connected to this is the common observation that the group's official and actual leader are not necessarily the same individual.

4. *Efforts to change individuals within a group which, if successful would have the result of making them deviate from the norms of the group, will encounter strong resistance.* In recent years considerable evidence has been accumulated which tends to indicate that there are tremendous pressures which groups can exert upon individual members of the group to conform to the group's norms. The price paid by the deviant, or at least for unacceptable behavior is rejection by or even expulsion from the group. If an individual wishes to become a member of a group and be accepted by it, he must adopt and maintain a certain acceptable mode of behavior—he usually cannot withstand this type of pressure. For this reason, efforts to change people's attitudes and behavior by removing them from the original group and providing them with special training have so often been disappointing. This most important fact accounts for the recent finding that people who are removed from a group and thus trained often display heightened tension, more

[8]L. Festinger, et al. *Theory and Experiment in Social Communication:* Collected Papers (Ann Arbor, Mich.: Institute for Social Research, 1950).

overt aggressive behavior toward the group, and/or a tendency to form cells or cliques with others who have shared their experiences, in an effort to subvert the group's activities.

5. *In attempts to alter attitudes, values, or behavior, the more relevant they are to the basis of attraction to the group, the greater will be the influence that the group can exert upon them.* This principle provides us with a possible explanation of some extremely puzzling phenomena. How does it happen that a group, for example a teachers' educational association, appears to be able to exert strong discipline over its members in some matters (such as presenting an attitude of militant unity when negotiating with the school district's central office administration and board of education) while at the same time it appears unable to exert the same influence in other matters (such as social activities or political action)? If we examined the fundamental reasons why individuals are attracted to a particular group, we would discover in all likelihood that a fundamental reason for the association relates more to some than to all of the group's activities. Teachers gravitate to professional and quasi-professional organizations to get what they could not get individually. They are much less likely to join one of these organizations because of its bowling league, Saturday night theatre parties, or some employment improvement in their professional status that membership might bring.

Note that these five basic concepts concerning the group as an instrument or condition of change have their readiest application to groups which have been created to influence and produce changes in people. It might serve this purpose well here to focus on the group as a target of change.

6. *When changes occur in one part of a group they usually produce stress in the related segments which can only be reduced or altered through the elimination of the planned change or by effecting a readjustment in the related parts.* It is not uncommon to try to improve the functioning of a group by providing educational programs for certain individuals or sub-groups within the organization. An inservice or staff development educational program for principals, first grade teachers, or selected representatives from specific grades or schools is the established format in educational circles. If the educational program's content is to be relevant and bring about certain changes, it is essential to recognize and openly consider the human relationships of those involved, especially as these relationships relate to other sub-groups in the organization. If the teachers in a school significantly alter their behavior, it affects established relationships with administrators, parents, and students. One cannot assume that all these groups will remain static and indifferent to any significant changes in this respect. Many researchers in this field (Dorwin

Cartwright and Ronald Lippitt, Sr. to name only two) have suggested that in any organization, attempts at change should not only be aimed at the largest group (that group receiving the major thrust) but at two other groups (to a lesser degree) as well—these groups being the one immediately higher and immediately lower on the hierarchical scale.

7. *Substantial influence for changes in the group can be instituted by the creation of a shared understanding by independent members of the need for the change, thus causing the focus of pressure for change to reside within the group.* A very dramatic case study which plainly illustrates this is reported in a work by Morrow and French.[9] A manufacturing corporation had a policy against employing women over thirty years of age because it was thought that they were more difficult to train, less likely to keep up with assembly operation, and more prone to be absent from work. The company's psychologist presented to the corporation's top management evidence that there was no basis for this belief and that to continue the policy within their company was unwarranted. Regardless of his findings, the psychologist's facts in the case were summarily dismissed and overlooked as a basis for further study and for action since they violated long term and commonly held and accepted beliefs—the findings were in direct conflict with the experience of the company's foremen. The psychologist then undertook a plan for bringing about the needed change considerably different from the usual reports, arguments, persuasion, and finally, pressure. He proposed to the company's management group that they conduct their own study of the problem and analyze the collected data. On doing this, the management group now had its own, rather than an outsider's, facts, and a study of the data caused a policy change which was immediately put into effect. The important factor here is that knowledge or information (as indicated on page 65) is not enough. The facts must be accepted and interpreted by the group if they are to provide a basis for effective and lasting change. Ample evidence indicates that where changes are actually implemented, in all likelihood there will be more resistance in those instances where an outside consulting firm undertakes a study and presents its findings, and those in which outside expert assistance collaborates with the group undertaking its own study and making its own findings.

8. *Relevant data relating to the need for a change, the plans for the change, and the consequences of the planned change must be shared and accepted by the appropriate people in the group.* Any planned change that a group takes under consideration requires that appropriate channels of communication must be opened. Most of us have observed that

---

[9]A. J. Morrow and J. R. P. French, Jr., "Changing a Stereotype in Industry", *Journal of Social Issues*, Vol. I, Number 3, 1945, pp. 33–37.

one of the primary causes of mistrust and hostility in a group is the existence of a void in communicating openly and freely about those things that can produce or are producing anxieties and tensions for group members. If we were to look more closely at a pathological group (i.e., one that constantly experiences difficulty in making decisions or in channeling the coordinated efforts of the members of the groups) we would most certainly discover many strong restraints therein working against the communication of important information between its members. It is not until these restrictions are eliminated (or at least substantially dispelled) that one can expect any significant and lasting changes in the group's functioning. Note well, though, that once restraints to effective communication are removed, that there will be a sudden rise in the level of anxiety, tension, and even hostility on the part of group members. It is a painful experience to communicate openly where open communication was thwarted or failed to exist for a long period of time. This pain, when accompanied by the resultant increased levels of tension, anxiety, and feelings that the new situation is "out of hand," can and often does cause a slowing down or stopping of the change process. Yet, though difficult, even a halt in the change process can be overcome and dealt with.

These eight principles represent a few basic observations that have emerged over the years from research in the dynamics of group interaction. Though useful to the change-agent, they should be viewed as tentative, for as the very nature of research is to revise and reformulate our conceptions, it is safe to assume that over a period of time they will be modified and improved.

A STRATEGY OF CHANGE

It would be absurd to imply that a set of universal recommendations can be set to provide the educational change-agent with appropriate strategies to govern all situations. Such recommendations become useless when taken out of their specific context. However, we have attempted to tentatively establish a set of general change strategies which should assist the educational change-agent in his client-system relationship. Hopefully, when these strategies are modified to meet the needs of the client-system, there is every reason to expect that the change-agent can provide an atmosphere where positive and significant change can come about. First, however, a word of caution. It has been the authors' experience that many educational leaders in the change-agent position have different experiential backgrounds and, quite often, different sets of values regarding education than those of the client-system. We have observed that the educational experience of many charged with the responsibility of implementing change in American schools is very dissimilar to that maintained by teachers—the client system. Usually the administrator has less teaching experience (in numbers of years) which makes him more vulnerable to "but what does he know about" criticism. He usually has better educational preparation, a masters degree or beyond, which may label him as a dreamy, impractical idealist. He is often younger than those who are expected to actually implement the changes, this too puts him at a disadvantage. Furthermore, he has usually undertaken his particular occupation because he is dissatisfied with education in its present form. Unless the change-agent is aware of these differences in experience, value, and personality, he is likely to subvert any positive relationship he might have with the client-system. Any planned change, therefore, must be designed to fit the cultural values and past experiences of those who are to be involved in it.

Educational change-agents should spend less time in the promotion of new ideas. More time should be spent in helping the client-system develop a more positive attitude toward change. Change should not be expected to come about until the client-system is disposed to or has been helped to realize the need for change on his terms. The authors believe that the change-agent would do well to consider helping the client-system develop a more favorable basic attitude toward new ideas and how these ideas will economically, personally, and socially, affect the individual and the group, rather than expending his efforts on promotional campaigns to gain superficial support for an innovative program.

At the outset, the educational change-agent should concentrate his efforts on the early adopters, the bulk of the opinion leaders in any group, when planning for change. His task will be much easier if he legitimately gains their support, enlists them to help sell the idea, and allows them to help diffuse the innovative idea among the larger group. Because this is such an important factor in achieving success for a planned change, it might be well to review what has been said about early adopters.

It might serve the purpose well at this juncture to focus our attention on the change-agent as a person, for in the last analysis it is the impact that the change agent has on his colleagues—the way in which he is able to work with them and the way in which he is perceived by them —that will dictate all the strategies conceived.

THE EDUCATIONAL CHANGE-AGENT

To this point we have been discussing the change process in a more academic tone, concentrating on such topics as why people resist change, how this resistance can be overcome, the group dynamics of change, as well as several others. We have indicated that change is inevitable and that the speed with which most change occurs is bewildering. But we have yet to direct our attention to the responsibility for change. And when we do, the entire change process becomes frightening and each person charged with an educational leadership role must inevitably face some serious dilemmas. For this reason alone it might be well to look at the change-agent as a human being and focus on how he might work with people in a humane way.

One approach to change involves the knowledge that the change-agent can help a group of people to perceive their problems more clearly, and this process of examination may lead to change of a planned and systematic nature. But the reader must ask himself if we should approach change by helping people to examine their problems.

On the other hand, change may arise from the necessity to adapt to a new situation, for example the need for us to do something about the overcrowded conditions in our schools, which heretofore have been operating in a fairly conventional manner. Such a condition may require that we rethink our school's program in broadly conceived terms. This may result in our experimenting with the use of large classes, better planning of space utilization, the use of new media such as television and programmed learning, the use of teacher aides, team teaching, grouping, and many other things. Should we use this knowledge to create crises with which we may work? Should we wait for this type of situation to develop and use it as our vehicle?

We have all witnessed, and perhaps experienced first hand, still a third way in which change may begin. Given certain sets of conditions it may become fashionable to reorganize classes or schools, teach in a new and different way, or introduce an entirely new program. It is then decided by administrative fiat to make a requirement of the fashionable change. There may be initial resistance to this intrusion, but gradually people will adapt to and may eventually welcome the change. The question that the reader must ask himself, though, is should we initiate change by leadership, deciding what should be done and then making moves to see that it is accomplished? Forced change of this type involves some rather obvious problems—not only those related to people's resistance to the change but, also, that of deciding whose right it is to determine what other people should value and what we value for ourselves. Forced change, although hazardous, at times appears to be the available alternative. And it may be that schools have existed in their present fashion for so long that they will never change without the application of some sort of external force.

Forced change of the imitative type is also dangerous and too often ineffective. This can be seen most vividly when we observe the problems encountered by many schools and school districts as they have attempted to become more "progressive" without any real understanding of what this means or implies about the views people must hold of human rights and behavior. It goes without saying, then, that attempts at change for excellence through imitation seem from the outset almost completely doomed to fail.

Yet, on the other hand, we must question the first alternative of growth and change through improved problem perception. Can we realistically afford to wait for people to perceive a problem and then desire a change? The experience of many educators seems to imply that to so wait means that no significant changes will ever occur. But since waiting is not the sole alternative to the seeming dilemma, the authors would like to share their position in regard to one of the alternatives above. This position is considerably supported by psychological research and experimentation conducted over the past three decades and offers a solution to the dilemma and a method of judging if change is merely change for change's sake or if, in reality, it is change for progress.

One conclusion readily reached from the growing amount of research evidence is that change is a normal aspect of human growth and development and that a condition of "no change" represents the atypical or the abnormal state of affairs. How such a conclusion could have eluded educators for so long is, to say the least, astonishing, for what is known of human growth and development tells us that, normally, people grow, develop, and make the most of their capacities. This can be observed most noticeably among people who are physically ill: if at all possible they progress toward health; the same appears to be true of people's psychological states.

A second conclusion is that maladjustment and maladaptive behavior is most often the result of adverse evaluation or of a requirement that people behave in a manner which is at odds with their understanding of their own experience. Most people are accustomed to being evaluated according to what they might class as important to other people. Starting with this in their homes and continuing it as they move outside, they are deluged with comments which suggest that they are right or wrong, good or bad, true or false. As a result they begin to deny their own experiences and to seek to behave in ways which will bring forth favorable evaluations, instead of remaining true to the meanings their own experiences hold for them. The stronger the evaluation, the longer it continues, and the greater its breadth of meaning, the greater will be the amount of distortion or lack of growth they will experience. So people learn to deny their experiences much like the young child who has pulled his baby brother's hair. His experiences may have been, depending on his feelings about his brother, "It is pleasant to pull brother's hair." But mother intrudes herself on the scene and informs him that he is bad. He now has a new meaning, "I am bad because I pulled brother's hair." Note that the original meaning of the experience is now denied and meanings are no longer relevant to the child's experience. He begins to doubt his own experience as a guide to behavior. If this process continues, maladjustment is inevitable.

A third conclusion is that to reverse the movement toward denial of experience and defense against adverse evaluation requires only that important other people—people in responsible leadership positions, for example—attempt to provide a climate in which it becomes possible for people to become our experience. This provided, the inevitable outcome is growth, unless, before these have been provided, the organism has been too severely damaged.

It might prove useful to the reader to take a look at the question from an entirely different point of view—the psychotherapeutic relationship between doctor and patient.

It is widely known that in the early stages of therapy the individual is characterized by fixity and remoteness of experiencing. Most characteristic of this stage are things such as negative attitudes toward self, negative attitudes toward other people, dealing with the small and peripheral aspects of problems, concern with external aspects of problem, locating the responsibility for the problem outside of oneself, a concern for the symptoms of the problem rather than with the problem itself, and an overconcern for the past.

As therapy progresses, problems become more central. There is a gradual owning of experience. The client even begins to feel that perhaps he has some worth and certainly that other people have worth. He begins to own his own feelings and internal communication becomes much more possible. Gradually, he comes to see himself as somewhat responsible for the solution of his own problems. He begins to deal more with the central aspects of problems and he becomes focused first in the present and later toward the future.

If therapy is successful, these directions continue to develop and the client eventually arrives at a point where new feelings are experienced with immediacy and with a richness of detail never before possible for him. Furthermore, his own conscious experiencing becomes a clear point of reference in acting and deciding. The client accepts ownership of himself and of his feelings and he is proud to claim them. In this later stage, experiencing has lost almost completely its structure-bound aspects and has become process experiencing—that is a situation is experienced and interpreted in its newness, not as the past. For the client at this stage, the self has become simply the subjective and reflexive awareness of experiencing. The self has become more frequently something confidently felt as in process.

This conception of psychotherapy has been called a process conception. In it people are arranged along a continuum from an end called "stasis" to an end called "process." At the stasis end, people are unchanging and in effect are running in the same place. At the process end, people are continuously incorporating new experience and changing. They are changing to become what it is their experience tells them they are.

Let us here reflect on the relevance of all of this for the type of school with which most educators are dealing. Visualize, reader, the kind of school which is "set in its ways," that shows little or no evidence of changing from the status quo, in which, to some of its faculty and staff, "progress" is a dirty word—the kind of school that seems to be going nowhere. The concerns of the faculty are quite similar to those of the client entering therapy. Attitudes toward self, if ever expressed, are negative. Comments such as these are frequently heard in the faculty lounge. "Teachers don't count for anything around here." "This community doesn't recognize our worth." "You don't have to be crazy to teach here but it certainly helps."

Attitudes toward other people are equally negative, "How can you do a job here with parents like these?" "The kids run this place and they're going to run it into the ground." "The kids are more interested in having a good time than they are in learning." "The principal is more concerned about public relations than he is about teachers."

Concerns are more likely to be peripheral and deal with only the symptoms. One of the authors recently visited a school such as this and when he asked the principal what his most pressing problem was, was told, "You know if I could ever get the lunchroom problem solved, I'd really have this job whipped." Symptoms of problems rather than the problems themselves are often the central concern. As an example, the concern with the fact that some youth are chronically absent or tardy have occupied the minds of administration and faculty for generations. Countless committees have been formed to study the question and countless suggestions have been made but seldom has the central issue been raised —"What should we do to make our educational program and institution so meaningful and so attractive for youth that they will not want to stay away?"

The locus of responsibility is considered outside of the self of the teachers of this school, and is revealed by statements such as, "I would like to try something significant but they won't let me." "They" may be the teachers down the corridor, the principal, the supervisor, the superintendent, the patrons, the state laws, the state board of education, the state course of study—anything other than the teachers themselves.

And the final symptom—a concern with the past rather than a projection into the future, that is, looking to the past for the solution of tomorrow's problems, is often expressed by comments such as: "I wish we would do away with our non-academic courses." Or, "Why don't we

cut out the fat and go back to the fundamentals of a good education?"
Or, "Why can't we get the kind of student we used to have?"

But some faculties sharply contrast to this. The members are strik-
ingly like the person who emerges from successful psychotherapy. These
people show positive attitudes, central concerns, a willingness to accept
responsibility, and a concern for the future. To illustrate: "My most
pressing concern is continuing to develop new and better ways of getting
students to participate and to enter into classwork with their fullest attention." Or, "My major problem is how to keep abreast of new knowledge and materials in order that I can continue to improve my teaching."
Or, "I am concerned with continuing to change my teaching practices to
fit the needs of individual students." Obviously, these teachers represent
people with positive attitudes, central concerns which are future oriented, who are willing to personally accept their responsibility for
change.

This latter group, it seems, represents the normal healthy personality. It is a well known fact that this is the type of person who emerges
from healthy families and from schools which appear to be "going somewhere." The more stasis-like person—child, teacher or administrator—is
one whose growth processes have been stunted, one who defends himself
in what he views as a more or less hostile world—a point of view far from
the truth when we consider the total experiences of most people.

For our purpose, let us look at the qualities of the "process" person,
who, because of his positive attitude about himself, has available to himself without distortion or denial the data of his experience. Because his
attitudes toward others make it possible for him to share in their experiences, he increases the totality of his own experience. Because he feels
no need to defend himself, he can in the light of much experience incorporate and examine. It is not surprising, then, that the fourth conclusion is that process people are in a continuous process of change. This
change represents progress, since it involves an internalization of new
experience and a potentially more intelligent and creative response.

If the process person becomes both the ideal and the central goal of
our efforts at change, one has a basis for deciding how he will attempt to
begin change. We have seen how forced change and mimicry fail to produce process people. (In fact, both forced change and mimicry often
cause people to move further from process. They require that people
ignore or deny their own experience, and act as if it told them something
different from what it does.) We now have a basis for examining those
conditions necessary to help to accelerate change—they should be similar
to those which yield process people. Can they be described? The authors
believe that they can.

The first condition for helping people to move toward process is
that they must desire to change. Although difficult, this is almost axio-

matic. All people desire to change in directions which are generally profitable. One way the educational change-agent can help them move in directions which all may feel profitable is to help them assess how they now perceive their most present and pressing needs.

A second condition relates to the change-agent. He must be able to accept without anxiety or falsehood the concerns of other persons. Not always easy, it can be done if the change-agent understands that this is where the other person is in his stage of development.

The educational change-agent must, thirdly, experience a positive and unconditional regard for the worth of the people, the teachers, pupils, and parents with whom he works. He can never assume the attitude that says to people, "I believe you have worth only if you display this kind of behavior or if you are interested in these kinds of things."

A fourth condition requires that the change-agent experience an empathic understanding of how the other person feels and what he is experiencing. This is most difficult—our culture conditions us to an evaluative relationship with other people and not a relationship in which we attempt to "walk in the other person's shoes." In this role there is no substitute for practice. Most people find that with practice they are able to become more empathic.

Fifth, the change-agent must attempt to communicate his positive, unconditional regard and empathic understanding for the other person to him. This, too, is not easy. It cannot be done if the change agent does not truly experience these feelings. But consistent effort on the part of the change-agent usually results in the other person receiving this communication, unless he has been so seriously damaged by previous contacts with the change-agent that he is unable to receive this kind of message.

The last condition is that the other person must receive the change-agent's communication of positive and unconditional regard and empathic understanding. As we have already pointed out, this is not easy. But consistency is the strongest tool that the change-agent has. Over a period of time he should be able to communicate with others. When his message is received in its fullest, the other person will be in a position to begin to change.

These, then, are both the necessary and the sufficient conditions for promoting growth in other people. And they say a surprising thing which leads back to the fifth conclusion. To help another person the educational change-agent must attend less to what he does to or for him and more to what he is in the relationship. When the change-agent says that the other person is not growing or changing, he is often saying he cannot be in some way helpful to him. Actually, by placing the blame on other people the change-agent may be merely attesting to the fact that he is not in the process himself.

We have said that change is normal. It appears whenever a person is not blocked in his being. It appears, also, to the extent that one can be authentic in his relationships. It is an outcome of his own being. But this has been known for a long time. Have you, the reader, ever seen a truly effective teacher without these qualities? Have you ever seen a truly effective leader without these qualities? When have you felt most successful in your work and believed that you have been most helpful to the other person?

But more things can be done and the authors wish to mention them briefly. First, it is necessary to organize in such ways that it becomes possible for the other person to become more self-expressive. Second, it is necessary to remove many unessential details which face the client and consume his energies. Third, the educational change-agent can help the other person to have the resources and support of his community through the ways in which the change-agent works with his community.

To us, the important thing seems to be that change can be evaluated as progress or lack of progress only by asking ourselves, have we enabled people to become more in process? Do they now have more personally internalized experience available to them and are they incorporating experience more readily? Are their concerns shifting from those of the stasis person to those of more process-like people? Have we enabled them to move into a position in which their normal growth urges can be expressed? If so, we have progress. This is our responsibility. What the people are with whom we work is in large part a reflection of what we are in our relations with them.

SUMMARY

The authors have attempted to give the reader a thumbnail sketch of the many facets of the concept of change. We have defined change as the perceived phenomenon which occurs when the balance and stability of a situation is altered; when there is a variation or modification in the procedure or object; when there is a substitution of one thing for another. The relationship between the change-agent and the client-system was discussed, along with the reasons why individuals choose to resist change. Several principles were advanced which are designed to assist the educational change-agent to become more aware of individual and group needs. A strategy for change was advanced to help the educational change-agent realize the enormity of the task of attempting to implement innovative ideas. With this change-related conceptual framework behind us, let us now consider the planning and implementation of a program of differentiated staffing.

5. Mission Analysis:
The Superintendent
and
the School System Staff

Differentiated staffing is both something old and something new. Imagine the shock of a kindergarten or first grade student who comes from the following differentiated staff:

Mother
Father
Sister
Brother
Grandmother
Grandfather
Aunt
Uncle

Such a student enters a typical school room with one other adult. He leaves a staff interested (generally) in *him*, for a relatively disinterested mono-staff, one teacher. Though this is said with tongue in cheek, it calls attention to the common element, the old and familiar in differentiated staffing.

True, many schools have for some time utilized specialized staffing patterns relating to art, music, and physical education. They have often had head teachers, lead teachers, or influential teachers in language arts, math, science, and other fields in the elementary schools, and assistant principals in charge of curriculum and instruction as well as departmental chairmen in secondary schools. To this extent they have become differentiated, and much of the data contained in Chapter 1 points toward the familiar of differentiated staffing. Yet there are other aspects of differentiated staffing which are *less* familiar.

When we mention accountability, Program Evaluation Review Technique (PERT), Program Planning Budgeting System (PPBS), and other popular terms in management sciences, we frighten many educators away. Yet more and more school systems are entering this new domain of management. Such an entry is conceived of as a framework in this chapter.

One of the new entry points in a systems approach to staffing in educational institutions is *mission analysis* (See Fig. 5–1), and when in a given school system we speak of it, we speak of the mission or purpose of the educational institution itself. To determine the overall mission or purpose of the school or school system, thousands of schools have participated in self-study programs arranged by such agencies as the North Central Association of Schools and Colleges, the Southern Association of Schools and Colleges, and various state accreditation programs. Germane to such studies are such questions as these:

What is the overall *philosophy* of the school?

What are the broad *goals* which determine a framework for implementing the school philosophy?

What *objectives* are specified in order to attain these goals?

Such words as philosophy, goals, and objectives are key terms in our overall *mission analysis*. Current sociological inputs as well as new theories in political science have much to say about the conduct of community-school teamwork in determining a broad but relevant *philosophical base* on which are structured *goals*, which lead to *objectives*. In addition, much theory of how groups work in a democratic atmosphere, based on the earlier explorations of Kurt Lewin, has developed into elaborate theories of change, some of which have been discussed in Chapter 4.

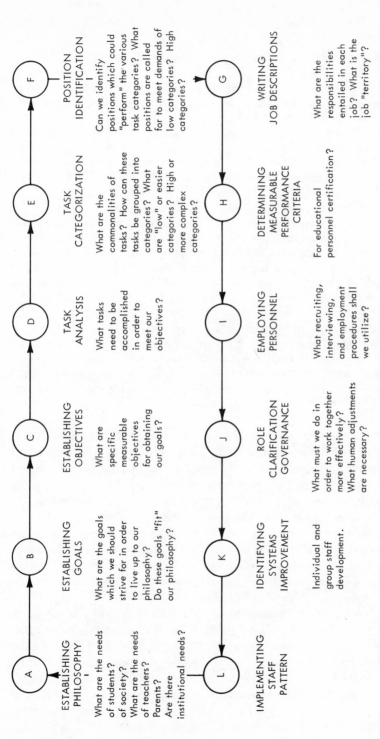

A — ESTABLISHING PHILOSOPHY

What are the needs of students? of society? What are the needs of teachers? Parents? Are there institutional needs?

B — ESTABLISHING GOALS

What are the goals which we should strive for in order to live up to our philosophy? Do these goals "fit" our philosophy?

C — ESTABLISHING OBJECTIVES

What are specific measurable objectives for obtaining our goals?

D — TASK ANALYSIS

What tasks need to be accomplished in order to meet our objectives?

E — TASK CATEGORIZATION

What are the commonalities of tasks? How can these tasks be grouped into categories? What are "low" or easier categories? High or more complex categories?

F — POSITION IDENTIFICATION

Can we identify positions which could "perform" the various task categories? What positions are called for to meet demands of low categories? High categories?

G — WRITING JOB DESCRIPTIONS

What are the responsibilities entailed in each job? What is the job "territory"?

H — DETERMINING MEASURABLE PERFORMANCE CRITERIA

For educational personnel certification?

I — EMPLOYING PERSONNEL

What recruiting, interviewing, and employment procedures shall we utilize?

J — ROLE CLARIFICATION GOVERNANCE

What must we do in order to work together more effectively? What human adjustments are necessary?

K — IDENTIFYING SYSTEMS IMPROVEMENT

Individual and group staff development.

L — IMPLEMENTING STAFF PATTERN

* What makes this a closed loop rather than a linear format? When we arrive at Ⓛ Implementing Staff Patterns, we must begin again the ESTABLISHING OF A PHILOSOPHY Ⓐ ad infinitum. This is a structured form of self renewal, leading to a constant refinement.

Fig. 5–1 Education: Suggested Format for Mission Analysis* Emphasis on Staffing Pattern

Let us expand these early steps of mission analysis.

1. We must determine the overall philosophy of our school or school system. In this regard there will be a body of literature: teacher handbooks, student newsletters, teachers contracts, board of public instruction notes, past records, formulated policies, and varying amounts of data based on previous self-studies. It will be possible for community-school teams to draw on this data. However, the philosophy must be scrutinized from time to time so that it may address itself to current felt needs. Out of all this study comes a refined *philosophy*.

2. Both long and short range goals must be set, which will lead the system toward a purposeful philosophy. Goal setting is not an exercise once done and then forgotten. In our time, social goals change even more frequently than the umbrella-like philosophy of educational endeavors. One way to set continuous goals is through the establishment of periodic task forces led perhaps by a school steering committee. Such studies should provide a wide strata of lay citizen and student input as well as the collective vision of professional educators.

3. Almost sequential objectives are then determined to see that *goals* are met. The present trend toward performance objectives or so-called behavioral objectives, as well as the present movement in performance contracting, indicate current public interest in determining measurable objectives leading to preconceived goals. These ideas alone have been the subject of several recent treatises.

Following the establishment of philosophy, goals, and objectives in this *systems approach*, the next step, *task analysis*, is of great importance to any concept of school staffing patterns. (Here *systems* is used as illustrated in Figure 1–1 and accompanying text in chapter 1.) By task analysis is meant the process of ascertaining those categories of tasks needed to meet objectives. Once these categories have been determined by task analysis, then the hundreds of tasks may be grouped according to a high and low categorization. Later we can observe how a school system might progress from *philosophy* through *goals* and objectives to *task analysis*. Though it might, at this point, however, be well to continue tracing the outer perimeters of this *systems approach*.

A ranking of the hundreds of tasks into high and low categories presents us the opportunity to group them into what might be called *position-identification-compartments*. These in turn lead to a further step, which entails the naming of jobs which the position-identification-compartments point toward. For example, do the tasks grouped into this or that particular position-identification-compartment seem to "dictate" a clerk's job, a master teacher's position, a curriculum research person, a community-school liaison, or other job categories?

After tasks and job categories have been determined, a school system moves to the next step, writing *job specifications*. What are the abilities needed by persons whom we hope to employ to fill the staff positions? Now that we have determined philosophy, goals, and objectives; after our task analysis has helped us to establish a staffing pattern through position identification; and after we have written job specifications and descriptions, and indeed have theoretically employed staff, what remains to be done?

In any newly instituted staffing arrangement, (and ample evidence suggests that this should occur in "status quo" staffs as well) a school system is faced with establishing clear working relationships among the staff. When one notices the recent tendency to utilize teacher aides in the classroom; or, in quite another way, when new faculty are introduced to an established faculty, emerging interaction conflicts almost always occur. In *role clarification*, one surmises that all of the present wealth of knowledge concerning small group theory would be put into play, thus making way for creative conflict, rather than the establishment of somewhat rigid formal structure which only gives rise to an informal structure running beneath, and oftentimes undermining, descending authority.[1] In this environment we see policies shaped by those members who wish to abide by those guidelines—involvement of the total staff in the governance of the school or school system.

Ideally, a school or school system hoping to move into new staffing patterns would intensively study perfecting something like a PERT network management scheme in order to make for more perfect orchestration, and maximum organizational strategies. Considerations toward this initial state are essentially problems in change, elements of which are discussed in detail in chapter 4. Here we shall assume that an overall strategy as mentioned above has been structured, and that the stage has been set for change. We are therefore ready to continue with a specific example of a systems approach.

A. *Philosophy* has been established: The school shall train students so that they may become contributing members of society.

B. *Goals* then must be devised to meet this rather general philosophy: Any student hoping to become a contributing member of society must be able to communicate his feelings, concerns, and rational thoughts to his fellow citizens. The school shall make every effort to instil an interest in communication, and to help the student gain many forms of communication skills.

C. *Objectives* then must be determined: Depending upon the wishes of the groups voicing consensus on *objectives*, such a list might include:

[1]Chris Argyris, *Personality and Organization* (New York: Harper and Row, 1957), Chaps. 3 and 4.

1. Students should so be able to read that they may comprehend current issues in the daily newspaper, leading national magazines, and incidental papers in areas which will affect their lives.

2. Students should be able to discuss and debate current issues presented in printed media by use of well developed oral language.

3. Students should be able to write compositions of varying lengths which relate to their own personal needs, as well as current social issues.

4. Students should have a working knowledge of mixed media such as audio records, video recorders, television as a cultural medium, and radio as a persuasive form of communication.

5. Students should understand techniques of advertising, fair and unfair "propaganda," and how newspapers, television, radio, billboards, store windows, and the like affect their life styles and both reflect and direct their cultural mores.

D. Task analysis now follows. What are the numerous singular tasks or jobs which need to be done in order that these *objectives* may be met? A few examples of tasks are given:

1. Diagnosing student's status and needs
2. Applying scientific educational research to enhance th. learning and instructional environment
3. Designing instructional material based on local research.
4. Adapting national curriculum models to fit local needs
5. Instructing faculty on new methods
6. Fulfilling classroom teaching responsibilities
7. Keeping up with records of attendance
8. Administering tests
9. Devising, adapting, or assigning commercial diagnostic tests
10. Scoring tests
11. Assigning students
12. Supervising programmed instruction
13. Counseling with students on learning problems
14. Counseling with parents and students
15. Counseling with students on interpersonal problems
16. Counseling with staff on interpersonal problems
17. Scheduling classes
18. Determining size of class for instructional task: independent study, programmed instruction, tutoring, small group, or large group instruction
19. Devising audio visual presentations

20. Running projectors
21. Scheduling use of audio visual equipment
22. Registering pupils

E. Task categorization is now called for. How would you group these tasks in high or low categories? What would you comment on the following groupings? Would they be logical or illogical? Would these categories be of a "high" or "low" order? What are other groupings? Do these groupings indicate staff positions?

1. Running projectors. Scheduling use of audio-visual equipment. Instructing faculty on use of new instructional media, electronic and mechanical aids. Registering pupils.
2. Writing and adapting curriculum to fit local needs. Fulfilling classroom teaching responsibilities. Counseling with parents and students.
3. Determining size of class. Scheduling classes. Counseling with students. Diagnosing student needs. Teaching responsibilities.
4. Administering tests. Scoring tests. Registering students. Supervising programmed instruction.

F, G, H. *Position identification* is now required leading to *job specification* or *job description*. For example, Task group (4) in item "E" identifies a position of relatively unskilled demands. A job description for (4) might be: Teacher Clerks—persons applying for this position should be adroit at following written instructions, possess average computational skills, write legibly, and be able to relate well to students in indirect supervisory tasks found in programmed learning laboratories.

I. Finally, assuming our job descriptions written, the positions filled, and that we have come to full differentiated staffing, our next step is *role clarification*. The whole idea of governance within this new staff is subject to question. When problems arise how will they be solved? When conflicts arise how will they be resolved? Who has direct leadership responsibilities with such new staff categories as teacher aides and clerks, audio visual technicians, teacher interns, part-time staff teachers, specialists, master teachers, research associates, and curriculum constructionists, to name a few? What is to be the source of power? What are the objectives and designs of management?

J. Now that we have designed approaches so that our staff is a more smoothly functioning team, we may utilize it to project ideas for future systems improvement, for individual and group staff development, and for career advancement within the system. Only then are we ready to put it to instructional tasks and further study, since it is then involved in a continuous recycling of the mission analysis process. Thus we maintain a closed loop system.

Is such a grand design possible? Obviously we should be able to accomplish these objectives of planned change, institutionalized change, when we are phasing in new schools. Is it possible to undergo a similar plan of self-renewal in schools already staffed with a status quo pattern and peopled with students? Schools, indeed, which are geared to perpetuate over and over a traditional pattern of instruction; one unwilling to change, and not adaptable to the more complex society than that in which its pattern was formed? Probably so. In the case of already established schools, would it be better to start with Step A? Step H? Step J? Step K? Where would you start and why? What would be the disadvantages and advantages of starting at these different steps according to chapter 3?

In the rest of this chapter, let us see what the superintendent, the principal, the teacher, and the school board member ought to know about differentiated staffing.

DIFFERENTIATED STAFFING
DEVELOPING A COMPREHENSIVE PROGRAM—
THE SUPERINTENDENT'S ROLE

The superintendent's role in developing and adopting new staffing patterns is crucial. For the school system which attempts to implement on a hit-or-miss basis is doomed to failure. The complexity of the problem is inherent in the sophisticated long-range planning which must occur prior to any full-scale employment of innovative differentiated staffing. Such a large-scale endeavor is illustrated in a process chart which clearly points out the difficulty and scope of the superintendent's management role.

As we have seen, a management plan consists of:

MISSION ANALYSIS

TASK ANALYSIS

JOB SPECIFICATION

All of which directly relate to the educational system under the superintendent's administration.

Other considerations are as follows:

1. How will the principals, teachers, lay public and students be involved so as not to be left behind?

2. How will nearby universities (or universities farther away on which the school system relies) be involved?
3. What will be the relationship of the superintendent's district to the state education agency, and to the legislature?
4. Will there be liaison with the USOE or with private foundations?
5. What will be the board of education's stand on providing money to bring in to the local system outside consultant help?

Another important consideration—how will a superintendent conduct a system-wide awareness campaign? Several school systems have used committees or task forces to do this.

A school system wishing to employ differentiated staffing may encounter resistance of several kinds. One typical question will be, "What research have we that says differentiated staffing offers better utilization of personnel? How do we know it is better than the old way?" The answer often given in reply is, "How do we know the old system is any better than the new differentiated staffing model until we test the two out together?"

Persons in leadership positions at one district which implemented the new system are said to have found more resistance at the elementary level than at the secondary level to differentiated staffing. One superintendent has said that some teachers fear that team teaching, use of paraprofessionals, resource centers, and flexible scheduling will permanently damage their children. He went on to say that they fail to recall that the present organizational structure established in 1870 at the Quincy Grammar School was designed for administrative convenience and that it rather callously ignored the needs of continuous educational progress for each individual student.

It has also been noted that secondary schools, accustomed to a wider variety of administrative and staff roles, are much more receptive to the idea of differentiated staffing than are elementary schools. This has yet to be proven.

The public as well as the teaching staff itself may equate differentiated staffing with pay raises. On the public side this will be seen as a newfangled scheme to pay teachers more money; whereas teachers are frightened that this may be merit pay in disguise. However, this may be avoided by a clear explanation of the difference between differentiated staffing and merit pay.

Merit pay provides more money for teachers who generally do the same things that other lower paid teachers do. The assumption here is that there are ways of determining who the better teachers are, and that these teachers should be rewarded.

In differentiated staffing, extensive planning leads to the setting up of jobs varying in complexity. Thus, there are different types of positions. In this differentiated system teachers are paid different salaries commensurate with their responsibility.

After differentiated staffing positions are set up teachers apply for positions which match their skills, training, and desires. Ideally, as well, there are training programs which lead to upward mobility all clearly spelled out—with decision making shared by teachers.

Superintendents should continually stress that it is inevitable that change will occur. Change is always happening. The positive approach is to get out in front of and direct change.

After a superintendent and board of education have decided to trial implement one or more phases of differentiated staffing, the following logical steps have generally been followed by school systems planning or implementing differentiated staffing.

Selecting a Pilot School

Either through implementing differentiated staffing in a new school, which is an easier way, or through having it selected by an existing school, plans must now be mounted to choose a pilot school, a trial ground for the testing of the new differentiated staffing model.

Starting With a New School

The total possibilities for planning a differentiated staff in a new school are almost limitless. There are probably not as many old patterns, traditions, or cliques to break. To begin in a new school is viewed as the better alternative.

Selecting a Staff in an Existing School

A second alternative is to work the pilot program in an existing school. One staffing possibility in an existing school is to accept transfer teachers who want to work in a differentiated staff, while others who do not want to work in a new staff could be allowed to transfer out. Attrition due to various aspects of teacher turnover would make room for additional interested teachers.

The following steps are related to and further develop those listed in chart form in Fig. 5-1.

Needs Assessment

STEPS A AND B. An educational needs assessment should be made. Students, parents, community members from all walks of life, and educational personnel should contribute to this assessment. This should lead to an educational philosophy and goals which will help to determine the *mission*.

Steering Committee

For direction, a small *steering committee* could be developed, composed of representatives from the superintendent's immediate staff; an elementary, junior high or middle school, and secondary principal, and several representative teachers.

Advisory Council

A larger *Advisory Council* could be formed based on the principle of *parity:* students, parents, community leaders, principals, teachers, university or college personnel.

Public meetings (one or two at most) could be held to complete this step.

Awareness Campaign

Note that throughout this phase a differentiated staffing awareness campaign should be started (perhaps using outside consulting services) with the objects the school board, principals' organizations, school faculties, and the general public. All media—newspapers, television, radio, bulletins to send home, memos to staff—should be utilized.

Student Performance Objectives

STEP C. Appropriate personnel, possibly principals and school faculties, begin to define and list appropriate student performance objectives for children in grades K–12. These should be broad general objectives leading to more specific objectives in sub-headings.

Task Analysis

STEP D.   Appropriate personnel define the skills, competencies, tasks, and theoretical framework (learning theories, scheduling, facilities, and the like) necessary to accomplish objectives listed previously in Step C. This process of Step D is referred to as task analysis.

STEP E.   Appropriate personnel will cluster the tasks mentioned in Step D into areas of commonalities and high and low competencies, so as to set up five or more levels of difficulties of tasks; undertake to develop in-service programs to train persons; and involve universities and colleges if possible. This process we refer to as task categorization.

Job Definition and Job Specification

STEPS F AND G.   Appropriate personnel will define the levels of positions required to accomplish the differentiated clusters mentioned in Step E, that is, they will write job definitions or job descriptions, write position questionnaires and job specifications and set salary levels. A next logical step would be to advertise position vacancies together with total job specifications and begin interviewing applicants for positions. The following steps use the newly hired people to staff the pilot school. Now we begin *operations* and *role clarification* for misunderstandings as to role conflict will naturally arise. It might be well to have already established contact with a consultant to help iron these problems out. However, through a well planned program it might be possible to handle role clarification from within with existing staff consultants. The important point is to plan for this phase.

Evaluation

It is assumed that evaluative criteria will have been developed before the project has begun. Carrying out the evaluation leads to further redesign.

CONCLUSION

The superintendent's role is seen as unilateral. Certainly in most cases these multiple responsibilities will be delegated to a task force or a project director and liaison staff. Although all of the steps as outlined are typical, the wise administrator will devise his own list unique to his situation.

THE SUPERVISOR AND CURRICULUM DIRECTOR— THEIR ROLE IN DIFFERENTIATED STAFFING

Ordinarily a major part of the central office staff but working in a unique relationship with principals and teachers, supervisors and curriculum directors are destined to maintain a crucial role in the evolving history of differentiated staffing. Supervisors and curriculum directors must know well what is contained in this chapter. They must know the superintendent's management role; they must support, advise, change, or consent to the superintendent's and board of education's plans. They must function as liaisons between central office and school, between superintendent and principal, between principal and teacher, between teacher group and teacher group. In short, both the supervisor and curriculum director must continue to be change agents, interpreters of broad sweeping innovation and diplomats extraordinary. Of all the factions in contemporary schools, their own professionalism must be on the highest plane. In the final analysis, the supervisor, in encouraging local internal commitment to innovation and controlled change, is ideally working himself out of a job. When most of the job of education is finally delegated to each primary school, and this unit is functioning with authority and responsibility at optimum levels, there will no longer be any need for any other than limited, outward supervision. Of course, the question is can a primary group keep up with all the ramifications of change in a society close to, if not in continual cultural revolution, and still attend to its own day to day business? It is in answering this question that one cannot help but note that if indeed the supervisor and curriculum director are working themselves out of a job it is not apt to occur soon. Why is this? Let us observe what we have referred to before as a systems approach, that is, putting it all together in the school system.

We have said that certain steps are necessary in any carefully thought out approach to differentiated staffing. Let us list these steps and then discuss the supervisor and the curriculum director in relation to these steps.

The steps are as follows:

A. Establishing a philosophy and constantly updating and refining it.

B. Establishing goals which fit the philosophy.

C. Establishing objectives which fall within the goal parameters.

D. Conducting task analyses to determine how to meet objectives.

E. Categorizing or ranking tasks.

F. Identifying needed positions to carry out groups of tasks.

G. Writing job descriptions and delineating responsibilities of the various positions.

H. Determining measurable performance criteria for the various jobs.

I. Recruiting, interviewing, and hiring personnel for the jobs.

J. Orienting personnel and clarifying roles.

K. Conducting inservice and staff development activities.

L. Implementing staff patterns.

Looking again at the *mission analysis* format in Fig. 5–1, let us consider the role of supervisor and curriculum developer in it step by step. First, not only are the supervisor and curriculum directors in a non-authoritarian role which allows them to naturally elicit open staff and community involvement as such a free and open environment may perhaps bring, but historically the non-line relationship of supervisors to principals and teachers has been most heartening for the improvement of instruction,[2] a major focus of differentiated staffing.

In many respects, philosophy setting for an entire school system has in the past been a standard job for such central office supervisory personnel. Thus, supervisors and curriculum developers have the most experience in this area, and would be apt to do a better job in coordinating the establishment and refinement of a philosophy. Too, the superintendent would be prone to turn to them; concurrently, principals and teachers, though maintaining their individual stances, would more readily accept supervisory leadership than the major leadership of either principal or teacher.

In establishing goals, for many of the reasons cited previously, it would be most simple for supervisory personnel to articulate what is volunteered by involved parents, students, principals, teachers, school board, and superintendent. Here again the unique, and sometimes unenviable job of silent encourager, listener, and go-between, establishes the supervisor as a major communication link.

In the establishment of objectives, expertise rests with the teacher and his interpretation of the learner. But here there are many vying disciplines, and it is here that all turn to the supervisory personnel as mediators, balancers, and impartial judges.

[2]Muriel Crosby, *Supervision as Cooperative Action* (New York: Appleton-Century-Crofts, 1957), 334 pp.

Ben Harris, *Supervisory Behavior in Education* (Englewood Cliffs, N.J.: Prentice-Hall, Inc., 1963), 557 pp.

Ross Neagley and N. Dean Evans, *Handbook for Effective Supervision of Instruction* (Englewood Cliffs, N.J.: Prentice-Hall, 1964), 274 pp.

Kimball Wiles, *Supervision For Better Schools* (Englewood Cliffs, N.J.: Prentice-Hall, Inc., 1967), 399 pp.

The busy world of schools leaves little time for organized task analyses. Here again, by historical accident, the supervisor finds himself not totally free, for every "odd job" which comes along is usually his, but additionally burdened with another major chore.

The supervisor and curriculum director are invaluable in the whole process of moving to differentiated staffing. Sensing their crucial leadership position, supervisors and curriculum directors would do well, if they have not already started, to read the sections in this chapter for superintendents, principals, teachers, and school board members.

THE PRINCIPAL: HIS CHANGING LEADERSHIP ROLE IN DIFFERENTIATED STAFFING

Differentiated staffing is such a new concept that there is still a "manageable" bibliography. In addition, by arranging to attend workshops on differentiated staffing, the principal will be pleased to find out that this is one innovation he can catch up with; and if he works at it and discovers one day that he, himself, is the leader of a pilot school planning to implement a differentiated staff, he can face this assignment with some confidence.

It has been said about the principal that his very survival as a top leadership person may depend on his learning of this new movement. For one differentiated staffing specialist speaking at an ESEA III PACE center has said that under differentiated staffing, the principal would "no longer dictate the curriculum, books, materials, or solely evaluate teachers, or adopt staff policy unilaterally, or be the single arbitrator of issues involving decision making."

The speaker, who might be taking an unfair stance on the present status of principals, was incidentally, a former principal. He went on to say that under differentiated staffing the principal would still be the top school manager, the command officer, the person legally accountable for the school, but that much of his authority would be delegated throughout a newly designed teaching staff—where the teaching roles change, too.

Principals who utilize departmental chairmen in their schools actually have a form of differentiated staffing. If, in addition, aides are used, a three-tiered differentiated staff already exists. The following provides an example:

Department chairman (*Principal*)

Staff teacher

Teacher's aide

What is missing here is a systems approach to the specification of this hierarchy. Not to say that there was no thought given to the establishment of departmental chairmen and the employment of teacher's aides; rather, it was, in most cases, a pragmatic arrangement.

A differentiated staffing arrangement is anything but casual. A casual glance at most differentiated staffing models could not begin to imply all the planning behind the rather simple looking stair step arrangement. Yet, before one arrives at the model which best fits his school, he must undertake a systems approach, which involves three major components:

MISSION ANALYSIS

TASK ANALYSIS

JOB SPECIFICATIONS

The principal must as well be the leader of a task force which gives in-depth consideration to some of the major variables in the process of differentiation.

Some of the major variables in differentiation are:

1. Content
2. Staffing
3. Facilities
4. Equipment resources
5. Self-instructional materials
6. Classroom organization
7. Scheduling

Classroom organization, scheduling, and *staffing* are vital to the process of differentiation. In classroom organization, for example, the solution must be actively sought to determine what learning can best be accomplished with various groups of students. This might lead to meetings of three hundred or more students for large group presentations, of small classes of nine to twelve for small group interaction, and of still others for individual consultation. Some teachers have talent and ability for large group instruction, others for small group, still others are better at one-to-one counseling and instruction.

Facilities and *self-instructional* materials offer even greater flexibility, for through large "quest centers," independent study laboratories, programmed instruction centers, libraries, and even computer assisted instruction centers, large numbers of students and their learning needs may be accommodated, freeing teacher time. The facilities where this learning activity can be housed is a prime consideration, and ideally necessitates long-range planning in the building program. Yet, even with the simplest facilities a great many variations can be tried.

Certainly *content* is a variable. Some subjects such as English and the language arts need be taught with a minimum of facilities (though this is quickly changing) while other subjects—physics, chemistry, even multimedia driver education centers—require greater material support. Content does matter. Notice, too, that content affects staffing—it is possible that trained teacher aides could supervise the organized content in a programmed instruction laboratory. However, only highly capable specialists could instruct large groups, or work with certain highly sensitive small group sessions.

For school systems to feel that in elementary and secondary schools all students must be in traditional classes all the time is a severe delimitation. In real flexibility, students should have some unscheduled time, and be free to go to a social area, or the library, or an open laboratory in or outside of the school. Of course, this degree of self-instruction implies self-discipline on the student's part. Such scheduling procedures are not to be undertaken without great planning, which will fit such activities into the total systematic program.

It is important for the principal to know what all professional and non-professional groups see as strengths and weaknesses of differentiated staffing. Many state education agencies and large city systems are viewing differentiated staffing as a way to improve the overall teaching-learning system. Some of the positive ideas are listed later in this chapter.

MISSION ANALYSIS FOR THE PRINCIPAL

Mission analysis is, simply stated, a synthesis of the philosophy and overall goals of the school crystallized into objectives. Many schools "inherit" a city or district philosophy, legal in nature, which generally says, in one way or another, that the children of the public will be provided with the best possible education. Mission analysis fashions vague statements of this sort into clear objectives.

Often, a school's written philosophy says something like this: Our goal is to provide maximum learning, based on the individual needs of our students. We shall take the child where he is and take him as far as he can go. This philosophy and these overall goals have not been arrived at arbitrarily, but through interaction within the faculty and within the larger community of lay citizens, students, university professionals, and colleagues from nearby schools and colleges.

Mission analysis in differentiated staffing follows exactly this process. But the new process of leading toward a differentiated staff experiences changes quickly after setting philosophy, goals and objectives.

What comes next is the arduous task of defining performance objectives for students. (Referred to often as behavioral objectives.) This process, still a part of mission analysis, is very important and will demand much of your staff. (You might consider bringing in a consultant to help in this step.)

Task Analysis

After performance objectives have been spelled out, the process of task analysis begins. What kind of tasks are required to get the job done? How will the students be helped to arrive at, or attain, these performance objectives?

Ideally, school principals and their faculties should approach task analysis as if they were designing the education system for the first time. The job of task analysis implies approaching the job creatively: opening the mind, accepting all new contributions large or small, and listening with critical patience to all ideas from all quarters.

For one national task force meeting sponsored by the USOE notice the following tasks, already ranked into job groupings:

PROFESSIONAL SPECIALIST (e.g., research experts, curriculum experts, media expert, testing and diagnosis expert, guidance expert)

    a. Diagnoses educational status of student.

    b. Prescribes experiences designed to remove deficits revealed by the diagnosis.

    c. Evaluates education progress.

    d. Participates in professional activities.

    e. Participates in learning activities to ensure professional and personal growth.

    f. Participates in planning and decision making relative to overall educational program.

    g. Keeps abreast with the latest information in each subject area field.

    h. Keeps abreast of developments in communication media and other aspects of educational technology.

    i. Participates in the ongoing inservice training program for all staff (this makes innovation a continuing part of the institution).

LEARNING ENGINEER (master or artist teacher)

    a. Diagnoses and prescribes.

    b. Adapts curriculum.

    c. Evaluates educational process.

   d. Helps establish the room or other environments conducive to learning.

   e. Assists in selecting instructional materials.

   f. Engages in professional activities.

   g. Participates in learning activities to ensure professional and personal growth.

   h. Participates in planning and decision making relative to the whole educational program.

   i. Supervises student teachers and interns.

   j. Identifies and helps recruit prospective teachers coming up through the system.

   k. Supervises supporting staff.

   l. Works with staff teacher in identifying learning problems and assists him in mobilizing resources to facilitate solution of problems and learning in general.

STAFF TEACHER

   a. Adapts curriculum to immediate needs of students being taught.

   b. Evaluates educational progress.

   c. Establishes learning environments.

   d. Provides for individual instruction.

   e. Selects a wide variety of activities designed to achieve learning objectives.

   f. Selects and uses method of instruction and use of different media.

   g. Selects instructional materials.

   h. Participates in parent conferences.

   i. Engages in professional activities.

   j. Participates in learning activities, to ensure professional and personal growth.

   k. Participates in planning and decision making relative to the total educational system.

   l. Identifies and helps recruit prospective teachers.

   m. Provides feedback on curriculum to learning engineer and professional specialists.

   n. Establishes and maintains a rapport with students and staff.

   o. Maintains discipline.

   p. Imparts information (curriculum content feedback to students on their performance—thinking processes, added to expression and skills).

   q. Functions as model of educated person.

   r. Assists in identifying learning disorders.

   s. Helps establish a love of learning.

   t. Advises and counsels.

   u. Participates in small group work.

v. Grades papers for evaluating performance of students.

w. Supervises supporting staff.

x. Acquaints the group with learning objectives.

y. Distributes rewards in order to facilitate the learning process.

ACADEMIC ASSISTANTS (volunteer help, college tutors, PTA's, interns, student teachers, club sponsors, etc.)

a. Participate in evaluating educational progress.

b. Supervise nonacademic learning activities.

c. Help to maintain discipline.

d. Impart information needed to carry out learning activities.

e. Participate in small group work.

f. Grade papers and provide feedback on performance of other kinds of learning activities.

g. Supervise study.

h. Supervise grounds.

TECHNICAL ASSISTANTS

a. Who deal with clerical items.

1. File
2. Type
3. Collect money
4. Take attendance
5. Keep records
6. Duplicate materials
7. Operate machinery
8. Take inventory
9. Keep certain kinds of records
10. Report
11. Police the room
12. Order supplies
13. Grade papers
14. Keep records on pupil progress
15. Participate in activities to ensure personal growth

b. Who work with students and other persons.

1. Supervise playground
2. Hall duty
3. Supervise study

4. Tell stories
5. Chaperon field trips
6. Supervise recreational activities
7. Help maintain discipline
8. Supervise nonacademic learning activities

SOME ADVANTAGES AND CAUTIONS OF DIFFERENTIATED STAFFING

The following "advantages" and "cautions," gleaned from a number of sources, are meant to serve as "thought" statements for the principal.

Advantages

1. Brings about a truly individualized teaching-learning program by identifying specific teaching-learning objectives.

2. Fashions a more effective curricular program leading to improved staffing patterns for implementation of a responsive, organic, living, curriculum, one subject to instant change to meet varying needs.

3. Identifies criteria for preservice and inservice training programs for educational personnel.

4. Leads to better manageability of educational variables.

5. Opens the educational system to new ideas outside the educational paradigm.

6. Attracts and holds talented teaching personnel.

Cautions

Most large system management experts caution against the following:

1. Care should be taken for assessment and planning.

2. Involvement in key planning is a major issue, particularly at the teacher and lay citizen level.

3. Trial or experimentation design should be horizontal, and should take approximately three years. Evaluation should provide both instant and long-range feedback.

CONCLUSION

Obviously the principal's role in differentiated staffing is important. He is the middle management key to top administration policy makers, to his superintendent and school board. In this, he can, as well, make that much easier and productive teacher efforts to make a better profession.

The principal is caught in a time of change which may lead to an education system as responsive to that change and as sophisticated in its approach as the well established and far advanced medical profession.

There is, in fact, a ripple, a hint, an intimation that education may hold the key to world betterment the likes of which we have not dreamed, for even doctors, space engineers, and astronauts are products of the schools.

All the future lies in front of education. The principal faces that future and gives shape to it like no other single administrator can.

DIFFERENTIATED STAFFING: WHAT CLASSROOM TEACHERS NEED TO KNOW

Differentiated Staffing is another term destined to join that growing glossary of new and innovative educational terminology. As a knowledgeable teacher, you have heard the term and you already partially know its meaning for differentiated staffing is both old and new. For example, the idea of teacher aides is certainly not a new idea. One or more teachers helped by a teacher aide is the beginning of a differentiated staff.

You may have served as a departmental chairman, or a part of a curriculum guide writing team, or a team-teaching person responsible for one certain phase of instruction. If so, you were involved in a form of differentiated staffing.

If you are a teacher in a secondary or elementary school and you have a knack for giving large group lectures so that other teachers have relied on you for this mode of instruction, or if you are better at working with small groups and other teachers wonder why, or if you are called on to talk to John or Bonnie because you relate so well on a one-to-one basis, then, you have been involved in a part of what differentiated staffing is all about.

Differentiated staffing is not just a series of arbitrary patterns. In this paper you will see that a great deal of thought and planning *must* go into any trial effort.

Nor is differentiated staffing a panacea, the answer to all our educational problems, though some of the growing publicity about this topic would almost have us believe this.

There are three questions often asked by teachers interested in differentiated staffing. What is differentiated staffing? Does differentiated staffing mean the same thing as merit pay? What is the purpose of differentiated staffing?

What is differentiated staffing?

Differentiated staffing is a new arrangement of school staff organization. Jobs, and the people who will fill these positions, are different in certain special characteristics.

Better, more discrete, definitions of job functions lead to varied teacher assignments.

In traditional staffing arrangements, all teachers are assumed to perform similar jobs. In a differentiated staffing arrangement the large job of the school is broken down into simpler components. The components, or tasks, represent different jobs. Persons apply and are appointed to these differentiated jobs based on their unique skills, training and likes.

Does differentiated staffing mean the same thing as merit pay?

No. Merit pay rewards some teachers who do the same things as other teachers based on a spurious scale which determines this assumed superiority. For example, if all U.S. history teachers have 150 students, five classes in a 30 x 30 room, the same adopted text, and no budget for additional material, what will merit pay be based upon? Probably personality! Differentiated staffing, on the other hand, through a process of mission analysis, task analysis, and job specification, sets up differing jobs with differing responsibilities and differing pay commensurate with the degree of complexity of the job. Thus, teacher performance becomes critical, as does performance evaluation. Here, however, our criteria become much more specific, a quality clearly lacking in the history teacher example.

There are many purposes for differentiated staffing. Differentiated staffing assumes that we can maximize the *human resources* potential in education—teachers, administrators, supervisors, paraprofessionals, everybody!

Teachers, independents, the NEA, and the AFT, have been talking of individual differences of students for a very long time. There are as well individual differences in teaching tasks, and individual differences in teachers, administrators, supervisors and paraprofessionals.

We know there are different individual jobs to do in American schools, and ability to carry out these task assignments varies. This is a major reason why differentiated staffing exists.

Differentiated staffing is, as well, a way of enhancing teaching as a career. It is no secret that one school system, which has recently implemented a differentiated staff on a trial basis, has offered a starting salary for at least one teaching position at a higher rate than the present school superintendent's position pays.

What, then, are some of the ingredients of a differentiated staffing recipe?

1. Increased learning leads to a better "educational pie."

2. Teachers themselves are the major ingredient, and the teaching profession is indeed a responsible, self-policing, self-evaluating body.

3. All teachers, being *teachers*, must do some teaching.

4. Teachers share in the decision-making process with top administrators.

5. Many nonprofessional tasks are given only to paraprofessionals, but we must remember paraprofessionals are human, too, not slaves.

6. In the ranks of any profession there are brilliant practitioners. More room at the top for better trained, more experienced, more capable practitioners must be made. Top teachers must make as much as or more than necessary administrators.

7. Teachers cannot arbitrarily be assigned to positions varying in responsibility. Just as mission and task analysis leads to a spectrum of job specifications, so teachers must apply for and be placed in these positions on the testimony of their stated wishes, capabilities, and training. Administrative hiring in schools must be shared with teaching peers. Some teachers will have a voice in personnel practices of schools electing differentiated staffing.

What should a teacher know about *mission analysis?*

Most classroom teachers have gone through mission analysis if they have participated in the evaluation and accreditation procedures of regional accrediting agencies such as the North Central Association of Schools and Colleges, the Southern Association of Schools and Colleges, and the like. In the Evaluative Criteria of these organizations, the first section always includes a section on arriving at goals and objectives. Essentially this is what we mean by philosophy and goal setting in mission analysis.

The idea of task analysis leading to job specification is a relatively new systems approach. Certainly the overriding consideration of this systems approach to differentiated staffing is to make the learning process easier for students.

Learning is a complex process, but even the little we know about it leads us to believe that by depending upon the varied strengths of teachers we can construct a better house of learning. In a real sense, education is the house that learning builds. If we do not rely on specialist-teachers here, on whom can we rely?

Consider one aspect of organized learning techniques—classroom interaction analyses. We have Bloom's *Taxonomy*, Flanders' *Interaction Analysis*, and an eclectic classroom theory of learning developing around these fragments. How might this determine a differentiated staff? Let us look again at mission analysis.

MISSION ANALYSIS	What are the objectives of the school?
TASK ANALYSIS	What are the numerous tasks required to meet the objectives?
JOB SPECIFICATION	How may the long list of tasks be grouped into specific job assignments?

Mission Analysis

Part of the mission of the school is to ensure that children receive free public school education up to a certain age.

Task Analysis

In order to meet the mission objective certain tasks are delineated. Let us take two tasks such as the following: 1. Certain community census statistics must be checked. 2. Rolls must be kept at school. Let us see to what job specifications they might lead.

Job Specification

1. Maintains lists of community census statistics such as head of family, median family income, drop-outs and the like.

2. Checks classroom rolls, and maintains lists of absences and average daily attendance.

In this simple illustration it should be easily seen that the person who performs task one is not the person performing task two. For one has a broader responsibility, affecting the total community and school population; while the second is less time consuming, and affects fewer persons.

It might also well be that the task one person, working throughout the total community, would need a greater degree of interpersonal skills than the person specified by task two.

Notice the following set of tasks:

Applying scientific educational research in the school system.

Designing curricula based on valid research theory.

Outlining biology to a large group of 350 students.

Performing demonstration teaching.

Working on a one-to-one-basis with a near-genius in math.

Explaining new innovations to the total faculty.

Helping small groups of students to write for publication.

Fulfilling full time teaching responsibilities.

Teaching Eskimo culture to a social studies class.

Filling out end of year reports of textbooks.

Demonstrating (for performance objectives) the guitar.

Accounting for pupil diagnosis and evaluation.

Helping students plan their future program.

Designing new technology to facilitate teaching and learning.

Suggesting ideas for better management of a programmed instruction course.

In this last set of examples of task analysis,

1. What kind of person would you want if one person had to perform all of these tasks?

2. If you could choose two, what kind of people would they be to divide all the tasks?

3. How many people would you need to ideally subdivide all these tasks?

In new staff organization models, use is made of teacher aides, educational technicians, teacher clerks who may have little or no formal college training, and people with a year or less of college training, as well as junior college graduates and university doctorates. Some categories might be filled only by a professional in the arts, or a competent scientist, a doctor, or a newspaper journalist, all teaching just a few lessons in a year.

Notice that MISSION ANALYSIS—►TASK ANALYSIS—►JOB SPECIFICATION does *not* work in reverse in a logical systems approach. For example, Fred is a good band master and he can teach social studies. Let's use him in these areas. Or, we want Sue, Sam, and Nick to do team teaching. How can we make this work? This is a pragmatic approach rather than the systems approach of which we speak.

LEARNING THEORY AND DIFFERENTIATED STAFFING

Learning theory is another factor that greatly determines differentiated staffing. Through great advances, since the Herbartian educational doctrine of the early 1900s, numerous schools of thought have been replaced by two contemporary learning theories:

1. The Stimulus–Response Bond or Contingency Management Theory, based on breaking learning tasks down into small increments and then by a reward system helping the learner to master a larger and larger scope.

2. The Gestalt–Field Theory, which assumes that motivation is of first importance and that learning must be approached in understanding "wholes" which suit the interest of the learner.

As an approach to setting up staffing patterns based on either or both of these theories, we can see how ideas such as stimulus–response bond and Gestalt–field theory begin to shape our thinking on staffing. Questions we might logically ask are, how would the staff differ if we chose to set up all learning on a stimulus-response bond theory where incremental learning and contingency management provide a dominant pattern, as opposed to a Gestalt-field theory where motivation and interpersonal relationships are so important.

Certainly the state of the art is such now that we would probably staff our school with specialists from both fields. However, with certain types of programmed learning (S-R Bond) a high level teacher aide might be used; while with a small group interaction unit undergoing "motivation therapy" a higher level professional might be called for. No attempt is being made to provide simplistic solutions to the demands of either of these prevalent learning theories, but obviously in a systems approach to education, learning theory does provide a dominant shaping force.

Regarding the various classification schemes of Bloom, Flanders, and Sanders as well as the thinking of many others, one can approach practically any learning endeavor and break it into distinguishable tasks which, in turn, specifies certain kinds of jobs. Let's look at this a little more closely.

Flanders, drawing on much research, has developed an interaction analysis system which isolates ten verbal elements. A trained observer following Flanders' format can note 1000 responses in a 45 or 55 minute lesson. The observer checks items of teacher talk: accepts feelings, praises or encourages, accepts or uses ideas of students, asks questions, lectures, gives directions, and criticizes or justifies authority. Student talk is measured by talk-response or talk-initiation. A third category is silence or confusion. Though there is insufficient space here to thoroughly explain the ratios of the interaction-analysis of what goes on in the classroom, certain kinds of "teacher talk" might be produced by various personnel. At present, this type of staffing design has *not* been tried. However, several school systems are beginning to consider such paradigms as Flanders'.

For an even closer look at such classroom research let us look at the Sanders "System for Analyzing Classroom Questions." Sanders divides his scale into

Low Level Cognitive Process
1. Memory

and

Higher Level Cognitive Process
2. Translation
3. Interpretation
4. Application
5. Analysis
6. Synthesis
7. Evaluation

These process categories can shape a differentiated staff. Let's consider how it could shape one simple lesson in an English language arts class in a primary elementary school classroom. For our purposes we have chosen the story "The Three Little Pigs." Here are some of the questions following the Sanders scale.

1. Memory—What are some of the things the three little pigs did?
2., 3. Translation-Interpretation—Why was one little pig foolish to build a house of straw?
4. Application—If the three pigs were really living today, what might they have used to build their houses?
5. Analysis—"The Three Little Pigs" is a make-believe story. What parts of the story seem most unbelievable to you?
6. Synthesis—How do you think the story would be different if told by Captain Kangaroo, or Sesame Street?
7. Evaluation—In this story do you think the "smart" pig was good or bad? Why? Was the wolf good or bad? Why?

Here are some questions we might ask ourselves. What kind of differentiated staff would it take to apply all of Flanders, Sanders, and Bloom to the total curriculum? In a lesson like the one on the "Three Little Pigs" could a teacher aide conduct some of the lesson? For example, question number 1—would a person with a higher level of classroom and children understanding be required for questions 5 and 6? Could an aide using the above as a pattern write learning activity packages? What kind of teacher could? The answers to these "learning theory questions" begin to shape the staffing patterns.

The Time Factor

Time is another important factor in any study of differentiated staffing. Thus flexible scheduling plays a part. Size of group is also a factor. In what time segments could types of learning be best accomplished? Can what now takes twelve years be done in eleven years or ten? Can what now takes five days be done in three? What could be done in twenty minute "Modules"? What might take 40 minutes, two hours? What about groups?

Can some things now done in an hour segment with 30 students be done in the same hour with 300? On the other hand, what things *not* now being accomplished with 30 students could be done with students on a one-to-one basis? What are some ways to use large, small, and one-to-one groupings so that the school day, week, year as well as the present curriculum, staff, and facilities accepts these new flexible groupings and schedulings?

With questions like these, a school faculty will feel most at home and be of most help in understanding how differentiated staffing can improve education.

Let us now look at some patterns of differentiated staffing which have been proposed. They are presented without specific comment. However, they have not been determined without paying considerable attention to *mission analysis, task analysis,* and *job descriptions.* Perhaps, in your own mind, you might work backward from these staffing patterns to see how they might have been determined. The patterns are given in random order with no alphabetical or best first order followed.

McKenna Model
1. A teacher of basic skills and knowledge
2. A liberal enlightener and master presenter
3. An identifier of talent who assesses interests and aptitudes
4. A developer of talents and aptitudes
5. A facilitator of attitudes and interpersonal behavior

Some of McKenna's terms are self-explanatory, for example "a teacher of basic skills and knowledge." But what is a "liberal enlightener?" Is this a person who can interrelate many specialized fields into one understandable whole? Is this why he is called a master presenter? Too, what is a "facilitator of attitudes?" Is this a person who helps to "establish" the right attitude toward learning? And what exactly is the right attitude? Does this presuppose a contingency management orientation? The terms are, in any case, interesting though speculative.

The McKenna Model could make an interesting discussion for a faculty considering moving to a differentiated staff. It is a revolutionary and creative model, and has yet even in part to be developed or attained in any place in the United States. This model and the following models should be taken as springboards to discussion and not "gospel."

Temple City Model
Master teacher
Senior teacher
Associate teacher
Teacher aides
Resource center assistants
Lab assistants

Head Start Model
Lead teacher
Assistant teacher
Teacher aides
Health services personnel
Parent advisors

Research And Curriculum Model
Teaching research specialist (doctorate)
Teaching curriculum specialist (masters plus 30 hours)
Senior teacher (MS, MA, MEd)
Staff teacher (BA, BS, BEd, plus 30 Hours)
Associate teacher (BA, BS, BEd)
Assistant teacher (associate degree—two years)
Educational technician
Teacher aide

Bruce Joyce's Direct Instruction Team
Team leader (group process specialist)
Assistant team leader (administrative facilitator)
Two "regular" teachers (specialist-interdisciplinarian)
Two interns (specialist *or* interdisciplinarian)
Two aides (clerks—typists)
A task oriented "crew" (task force approach)

Trump Model
(Revamping the present role structure through the "open plan" school)
Teacher specialists
Teacher generalists
Clerks
General aides

"Staffing specialists" (To Study the System)
Community consultants

The Family Style Differentiated Staff
(with tongue in cheek)
A mother
A father
Playmates
Two grandmothers
Two grandfathers
Friends of the family
Baby sitters

Ford Foundation Model
One Pattern of Team Teaching
A college professor
A male public school teacher
A female public school teacher
Student counselors
A psychologist
A psychometrist
A team facilitator knowledgeable in media
A health and recreation specialist
A teaching principal

CONCLUSION

Teachers and most other professional educators are generally familiar with the various patterns of differentiated staffing, but what they do not know is the thought and elaborate planning behind most newly proposed models.

From theory to actual classroom practice is a very long step which cannot be taken without the "seven league boots" of the teachers themselves.

DIFFERENTIATED STAFFING AS IT MIGHT BE VIEWED BY THE BOARD OF PUBLIC INSTRUCTION

It has long been suspected by the school boards, their professional agents and representatives—the superintendents, and many others, that the uniform flow of money into teachers salaries in so-called "across the board" raises would be threatened by a taxpayer revolt. That day has now arrived. No board member, or superintendent wishes to abolish the career aspirations and salary advancements of teachers. Across the board raises just no longer make sense to the public. If teaching is to become truly a profession, differentiated responsibilities coupled with differentiated salaries are now a must, if the kind of education the United States demands must survive.

One superintendent recently was noted nationally as paying one teacher on his staff $25,000—a few thousand more than he was drawing. Taxpayers, school boards, and superintendents are willing to overhaul the present pay scale *if* by pinpointing specific responsibilities a new pay plan can be justified.

What then is differentiated staffing? Does it really hold all that it is touted to hold in the way of revamping the present staffing and pay patterns in American schools?

The term differentiated staffing is such a new concept that there are still less than a dozen or so short papers which fully explain the subject. Some spurious comments and publications have even equated differentiated staffing with merit pay which is, of course, quite erroneous as will be seen later in the questions and answers of chapter 8.

An important concept in this new field of staffing has been stated very well by one university teacher training specialist who describes the present staffing system as "A teacher is a teacher is a teacher" parodying Gertrude Stein's "A rose is a rose is a rose" but also slanting an ironic comment toward a major problem in education today. Educators should recognize individual differences in the teaching tasks, just as education has for so long attempted to meet individual needs of students.

Obviously the tasks set out for the school staff range all the way from running a mimeograph machine, a relatively routine assignment probably not even requiring a high school diploma, to adapting some new theoretical hypothesis supported by research to classroom practice. Any definitive list of professional teaching tasks would include the following—some of a low order of skill, others of a higher degree, listed in random order as follows:

Applying scientific educational research to enhance the learning and instructional process.

Designing curricula based on valid research data.

Making the school faculty aware of a new instructional method.

Fulfilling full-time teaching responsibilities.

Keeping up with records and necessary paper work.

Accounting for pupil diagnosis and evaluation.

Selecting, or totally fashioning, designing and utilizing new instructional technology in the classroom.

These tasks differ greatly in degree of responsibility. It is probably not possible for any single person to perform all of these jobs. There simply is not enough time. In one month alone a person may look at a newly released bibliography and discover that there are several hundred articles, books, and theses which bear on his work of which he is unaware. What is called for is a comprehensive needs assessment of what society expects of its school system, followed by a task analysis and compendium of tasks, followed by specifications leading to job descriptions. The extensive skills required in a job which translates educational research into curriculum may demand high salaries. Such persons are usually found in higher education or in district, regional, state, or national consultant positions. If this person were found in a differentiated staff, however, he would be offering his service and series of skills at the immediate classroom or learning environment level. Such a person would, in addition, have *some* direct teaching responsibilities.

Differentiated staffing is many things. It is a design to attract manpower needs which our vast educational system will continue to need. It is a new personnel model designed to best use the different talents of not only the educational community, but of the greater community, what one recent educational writer calls the real world.

The new staff organization may make use of teacher aides, educational technicians, and teacher interns, clerks who have little or no formal college training, or for short periods of time a medical doctor in the community. Differentiated staffing utilizes people with a year or less of college training, as well as junior college graduates and university doctorates.

One of the strongest points for the differentiated staffing concept is the flexibility of assignment of staff and the resulting rewards for teachers, who are frequently unhappy with the status quo. A teacher looking for higher earnings will not find them in class. He either earns administrative or supervisory credentials and moves upwards *out of the classroom*, or he leaves education altogether. Studies of first-year teachers in some states illustrate that as many as 31 percent of first-year teachers leave teaching, never to return. Emphatically, teaching per se is failing as a rewarding career-oriented profession. Those who stay, stay in a system which pretends that all teachers are exactly alike, and which ignores their individual strengths or weaknesses, their unique experiential backgrounds, their great or limited interest in teaching, and the assessment of their performance in a specified job analysis.

One large school system cited a cost analysis of a single 2500 student school. Salaries for the traditional teaching staff totaled one-plus million dollars. Salaries for a differentiated staff came to approximately the same amount using job responsibility hierarchies illustrated in Figs. 1–2 and 1–4.

It is important to remember, however, that other variables are affected in the institution of a differentiated staff. Consider time and the schedule for example. We know that there are times in the learning experiences of students when a large body of students from 100 to 2000 can benefit by observing a film, or witnessing a dramatized lesson, perhaps listening briefly to a lecturer or team of stimulating lecturers supported by multi-media. With a large class lesson many teachers are freed. Teacher-time is gained. Additionally there are varying periods of time for student independent study, using varieties of programmed instruction, closed circuit television, dial-access learning, or any of a number of new technological tools. Again teacher time is gained.

A look at the existing schedule of most schools can uncover more ways to conserve teacher-time. There are still many schools which utilize the five-day-a-week class in English or mathematics when, no research to the contrary, one such class every other day for three weeks followed by a fourth week of inactivity proves to be just as expedient. Thus by rearranging modules of time we gain teacher time—which, superimposed over the traditional staffing pattern, gives us a surplus of teacher time and teachers.

Continuing with the elements of tasks, assigned job responsibilities, and personnel we discover that there are times when we need a highly trained communications and interpersonnel relations specialist with a small group of students, and other times when another student may lead the discussion, and so on and on.

There are several other factors to consider in understanding differentiated staffing. Phasing out of a traditional staff and gradually phasing in a differentiated staff, for example, or the whole problem of teacher training for a new era of differentiated staffing, or the new responsibilities of a truly professional teaching staff in its own governance and peer evaluation. Indeed, the whole problem of tenured and non-tenured positions (illustrated in Figs. 1–2 and 1–4.) has not been discussed. This question alone, though revolving around and insuring teacher tenure and security at lower paying levels, leads to higher rewards than tenure in the more responsible positions. It should be stressed, however, that even at the tenured level top performance is expected.

SOME GUIDELINES FOR IMPLEMENTING DIFFERENTIATED STAFFING

Note the new guidelines relating to implementing differentiated staffing, released from the Bureau of Educational Personnel Development of the USOE in relation to the Education Professions Development Act:

No unit smaller than an entire school staff should be differentiated.

The maximum salary of the highest paid teacher should be at least double the maximum salary of the lowest category of professional personnel.

All instructional staff should spend at least 25 percent of their time in direct contact with pupils.

All instructional staff in the unit designated as operationally differentiated should be on the differentiated salary schedule.

The differentiated roles of the instructional staff as well as the selection criteria for those roles should be clearly delineated.

The school district should agree to an external program audit annually, the results of which are to be made public.

Differentiated staffing generally accompanies other organizational and curriculum changes and usually includes specialization of staff, requiring the substantial development of new teaching roles.

Though it is not within the limits of this book to discuss all these points, of particular interest here is that "no unit smaller than an entire school staff should be differentiated." This allows a board and superintendent to deal with a discrete budget on salaries and provides historical base line data for future differentiating. What is found out at one entire school is, also, more easily adaptable or transferable to other single school units. Singularity of purpose and centrality of goals of a single school system also allows administrative decision makers to deal with the totality —the gestalt of the learning situation as regards staffing.

Of great importance, too, is the concept that "the differentiated roles of the instructional staff as well as the selection criteria for those roles should be clearly delineated." Let us underline *differentiated roles, selection criteria* and *clearly delineated.* These are key terms in any differentiated staffing one plans to undertake.

Consider as well new alignments of administrative echelons, the relocation of district or regional instructional administration supervision, the new role of the principal, and the dynamics and interpersonal conflict problems and solutions—these are bound to arise. However, these areas, though important, lie outside the scope of this chapter. The new system of differentiated staffing rests more firmly on philosophy and goals in part established by the tax-payer. On this base, the school board and superintendent, with his teaching staff can institute specific job descriptions, with varying responsibilities and varying pay.

CONCLUSION

School board members must be aware of differentiated staffing as it emphasizes the local democratic philosophy and goal setting. Citizens must be involved and it is the board's place to see that this takes place.

This section views the board as the appointed or elected representative body of the community. Theirs is an arena of policy making. This must be *informed* policy making.

SUMMARY

We have seen in Chapter 5 what is meant by mission analysis. We have approached it and seen it as it might be seen by management personnel in the American educational system. By management personnel is meant the school board, superintendents, principals, as well as classroom teachers.

How a school board might view new staffing patterns is influenced by community demand for accountability. A superintendent might look at differentiated staffing in the light of successive compromises leading to a smoothly functioning organizational unit. Principals might be prone to see differentiated staffing as an instrument of change in the immediate school unit, while teachers are most likely to view differentiated staffing in terms of learning theory.

Definitions and procedural steps for the superintendent, the principal, and the teacher are spelled out, each in a separate section for convenience of reference.

6. The Differentiated Staffing Model Becomes Operational

As the educational change-agent begins to move from the theory to the implementation of a differentiated staffing model, he should consider how to help his future coworkers in knowing as much about it as he. It is no mean task to diffuse an innovative idea—the change-agent has probably developed his beliefs about the values of differentiated staffing over a long period of time. To expect all others to accept the idea's complexities and immediately undertake the project's implementation is unrealistic thinking. But this is the mistake that so many American educational executives appear to make.

To diffuse any innovation, differentiated staffing, for example, from the dreaming to the doing stage one must move through four primary phases: understanding the innovation (it is unimportant if an idea is "objectively" new, as measured by the duration of time from its original discovery, for the newness of the idea to the individual determines his reaction to it); communicating the innovation to others; considering the social framework which the innovation may affect; realizing that changes, not instantaneous, occur over a period of time.

As the differentiated staffing concept moves toward the point where implementation is actually being considered, the educational change-agent should give careful attention to these four phases. The educator should seriously ask himself questions such as the following and be prepared to find realistic solutions to all of them:

The Innovation

Where did you first hear about the idea of differentiated staffing?

Can you trace your thought process from the time when you first heard about differentiated staffing to your present state of thought?

What or who is the force behind the differentiated staffing movement that you are considering (e.g., the board of education, superintendent, teacher groups, etc.)?

Are there any extraneous pressures for establishing differentiated staffing in your school or school district?

From where do these pressures come?

Is this the kind of change for which you wish to tenaciously fight or does it happen to be the bandwagon thing to do?

What are the "real" reasons for considering the implementation of the differentiated staffing model?

Can you list these real reasons?

Communication

Do you know enough about differentiated staffing to be able to tell others about it to their satisfaction?

Can you list those persons or groups to which you should convey the idea of differentiated staffing?

Can you rank this list in some order of importance (who should be told before whom) that may provide that final acceptance of the idea will be most fruitful?

Can you categorize the predisposed attitudes of the people on the above list (for it or against it)?

Social System

Can you describe the social system (defined here as a group of individuals working together for a common cause) in which this idea must work?

Can you identify and classify these individuals who will comprise the group (social system) with whom you will be working into the adopter category types discussed in chapter 4?

Can you identify any members of the group who tend to be excessively apathetic to change, who accept change for change's sake, or who reject all new ideas for no apparent reason?

Is there an apparent behavioral norm (along the adoptive category continuum) which seems to exist within the social system?

Over Time

How much time do you plan to provide for each of the following five areas:

> Awareness of the idea of differentiated staffing
>
> The generation of interest for differentiated staffing
>
> A study of evaluation of the concept of differentiated staffing
>
> Trial of a proposed differentiated staffing model
>
> To final and total adoption of the concept?

When the person responsible for the implementation of differentiated staffing has answered these questions with a high degree of inner satisfaction, he can see himself as knowing enough about the diffusion of innovative ideas to be able to consider the assessment and selection of staff to get the job done.

PLANNING FOR PLANNING

The educational executive and his immediate staff, charged with the responsibility of planning for and eventually implementing the differentiated staffing program, would do well to first consider the establishment of a project steering committee responsible for directing the development of a differentiated staffing pilot model. This group might then report to an elected committee drawn from a broad base of those directly or indirectly affected by the outcome of the steering committee. One might see the purpose of the steering committee as planning for the planning as well as directing the development of the project. It could give valuable direction and assistance in the planning for:

1. The selection of staff to carry out the new project.
2. The selection of the school or schools which will house the project.
3. Staff preparation and staff development activities.
4. The planning for the differentiated staffing model.
5. The organization form for planning.
6. The planning process for the differentiated staffing model.
7. The establishment of specific planning guidelines.
8. The establishment of a long-range planning calendar.
9. The planning for the allocation of resources.

SELECTION OF STAFF

Let us now direct our attention to the selection of the staff involved in the differentiated staffing model. The authors believe that the prudent analysis and selection of staff is the single most important component of any differentiated staffing model, the one which ultimately determines the success or failure of the effort. No other single factor is as essential during the planning and subsequent launch stages of the differentiated pilot model than the carefully selected, smoothly functioning team, each member of which operates with respect for each other and with a determination to see the cause succeed. It is vitally important, therefore, that the educational administrator proceed cautiously at this phase in his planning; a degree of caution here can do much to alleviate many future headaches.

It would be helpful to the educational executive charged with implementing the pilot differentiated staffing model to be able to select the team solely from volunteers. With a group of volunteers from which to choose the educational executive has a client-system that in all likelihood considers the innovative project as a challenge. It will be a group not resistant to change. The volunteer group will not harbor the same fears or possess the same social, economic, and personal needs and concerns as the larger majority. On the other hand, the individual volunteers should be carefully assessed to establish their reasons for volunteering. They may have a deep seated professional commitment to the concept of differentiated staffing as a means of improving educational programs in order that youth can gain greater benefits. There might also be certain social reasons related to the choice. For example, the teacher's fear of being transferred from the model project school if he does not become a successful member of the team, thus uprooting him and possibly severing some long established social ties. The volunteer may have some personal reasons for providing his services—the need for finding an environment where he might be less conspicuous than in the traditional classroom. Or the volunteer may view differentiated staffing as an answer to his economic needs. Regardless of what reason or combination of reasons there might be, the educational administrator's position is precarious if he does not try to determine what these reasons are for those individuals participating in the pilot study.

The reader will recall the discussion of adopter categories discussed in chapter 4, in which innovators were described as those who were willing to try new ideas. Because of this, they are sometimes characterized as being rash and daring in their ideas and, often, in their mode of operation, and are, because of this, generally viewed with alarm by their colleagues. They seldom command leadership positions. Those who comprise a volunteer group may include a number of innovators. Since the innovator's ideas often tend to isolate him from the mainstream, and, as indicated in chapter 4, the innovator tends to associate with like kinds, the educational executive must consider the individual innovator's effectiveness in a group situation. The educational executive must as well consider the ultimate worth of the volunteer innovator as an evangelist to convert others to the cause (should the project be successful), since innovator types may be viewed with alarm by their colleagues in the school district.

We have stated that the educational administrator who implements a differentiated staffing plan should give close attention to the analysis of those who may become part of a team. The first phase in the selection process are the interviews. The authors suggest that there be more than one interview session with each candidate and that there be more than one interviewer present at each session. Two is a reasonable number of interviews that could be conducted at two-week intervals for each candidate under consideration, with an additional interview scheduled if it is deemed necessary. The project director should probably organize two teams of two individuals each, whose judgments he respects, to serve as co-interviewers at each of the two sessions. Each group of two interviewers can then interview each candidate once. The project director then has his own opinion as a participant in both sessions, as well as the opinions of four others. Before the interview each candidate being considered should submit a statement explaining why he wishes to become a part of the pilot project. This process often provides a different perspective of the candidate than might become evident in interviews. People are usually more comfortable in writing about their interests, experiences, and strengths than they are in talking about them.

The interviews should be so conducted that, hopefully, they will yield the greatest possible amount of positive information about each candidate. For the primary purpose of the interviews is to give the interviewers data that will enable them to make correct decisions. An effort should be made to draw out information that will enable the interviewers to have more insight into the human qualities of the candidate. The interviewers should be able to make value judgments about the candidate's ability to live with the stress and ambiguity of new situations as well as his concern for youth, colleagues, and parents. Still other characteristics that should be looked for are empathy, initiative and openness to new ideas and ways of doing things. There are many other qualities that should be sought out. Those involved in conducting the interviews might do well to compile a list of them before beginning the interviewing process.

The second phase in the selection process, one that yields considerable information, is the development of a personal profile of each candidate being considered. Not new, the concept of a staff profile has been used for years by some educational executives to obtain, through the careful selection of certain kinds of demographic data, another picture or dimension of the staff. Generally, however, it has been used in making administrative decisions regarding the selection and recruitment of professionals to obtain a more balanced staff. Essentially, a personal profile is data first gleaned from records or a questionairre and then assembled in a series of meaningful charts or graphs. The kinds of composite data compiled on a staff usually include information about age, sex, years of professional experience, educational preparation, degrees received, marital and tenure status, salary, geographical location of birth, professional experience, and educational preparation, and other similar information conceivably helpful in developing a comprehensive picture of the district school staff. When armed with this information, the educator is able to make decisions based on fact rather than on guess.

The authors would like to show how valuable this information can be to the astute educational executive in a decision-making position. Recently one of the authors became familiar with a small Eastern suburban school district that, throughout the years, had never seriously considered the kinds of teachers it was employing. It knew that it had employed the best teachers available, but that is all that was known. When it did look at itself, it found that fifty-six percent of the faculty had more than fifteen years of experience (which obviously raised havoc with the school budget), nearly twenty-five percent of the teaching staff was either single or newly married and had less than two years' experience (a condition ripe for large turnover), and to compound the problem, nearly eighty percent of the administrative group were either very young and professionally mobile or were very near retirement. Assembled and charted, this data presented a picture that permitted the superintendent and his staff to make decisions and predictions based on fact. Why the average salary paid to teachers was significantly higher than in neighboring communities could now be better explained to the public. They could establish expectation tables of the number of people who would in all probability be retiring in subsequent years. They realized that they needed to emphasize recruitment of people with five to ten years of experience in order to effect a greater balance and, perhaps, greater stability, and they now had the impetus to begin a study of administration reorganization.

The example cited above clearly indicates why the authors feel that it is essential to consider staff profiles so that a different perspective can be gained on the key to the pilot project. When this information is coupled with indepth interviews of the candidates, the educational executive is in a better position to effectively establish the group with whom he is to work.

SELECTION OF SCHOOL

With staff selected, let us consider the school in which the model project will take place. The school and its contributing community must be carefully studied. Attention must first be given to determine whether the physical plant can facilitate an altered organizational pattern such as differentiated staffing. This does not imply that if the educational facility is not new all innovative ideas should be shelved—the authors have seen numerous instances where under seemingly impossible conditions excellent teaching and learning was taking place because the people involved wanted them to happen. Studies of the plant need merely be made to determine if there are some obviously overpowering limitations being imposed that could scuttle the best planned project.

The next factor that needs to be analyzed in the selection of a school is the community atmosphere that surrounds and permeates each possible school. What has been the history of school-community relations? Have they been tranquil? Have they been stormy, and if so, does a lingering hostility still exist? Is there a genuine feeling in the community that the professional staff is competent and can be relied upon to make sound educational decisions? Is there in the community a climate of support for the school's objectives and programs, as well as a feeling there that some change is good, and when adequately planned by competent professionals it can have a positive influence on the school's educational program? If the educational executive can express an unqualified positive response to all these questions, he is in a good position to move ahead. However, more than likely there will be innumerable degrees of shadings to each question, and the decision to proceed may be more difficult to make. Obviously, if the answers to all the questions are negative, then those in the position to make the decisions should admit that much work needs to be done and that to proceed would seriously risk the fruitful outcome of the best planned projects.

STAFF PREPARATION AND DEVELOPMENT

Staff Preparation

At this juncture we must assume that the school that will participate in the pilot project has been assessed and firmly established, that the staff of the school has been apprised of the differentiated staffing concept, that the interviews have been conducted and the staff profiles developed, and that the decisions have been made about the specific personnel who will comprise the team(s). It is at this point that the project director responsible for implementing the differentiated staffing model must begin to focus on staff preparation and development.

The change from the more traditional self-contained classroom with one teacher and twenty-five or thirty students to a differentiated staffing model can be frought with feelings of anxiety and insecurity for even the sophisticated professional. Unless these feelings can be adequately expelled and each person made comfortable in his new role, it is reasonable to expect that the ultimate outcome of the project will be substantially less than successful. Those readers who might be using this section of the book as a manual might reconsider the seven principles related to resistance to change developed in chapter 4. They are restated here to highlight their importance.

1. People change when they see a need to change.

How can the members of a team be assisted to look at the results of their labors and then look inwardly at their personal values, needs, and expectations? When people are helped to do this in an unthreatening atmosphere and when they do develop an honest rationale for the change, there is every reason to expect that the completed change will prove to be successful.

2. People will change when they know how to change.

In order to effect change one must modify his beliefs, attitudes, and values. The individual must look at himself from a different point of view and make some value judgments about himself in his present role. It is necessary for the individual engaged in change to have an insight into the process he must go through to successfully effect the change. It is also necessary for the client to be able to contemplate the outcome of the change. What things, then, can the educational executive do to assist individual team members in this process, in a manner that will not be threatening?

3. People change when they are actively involved in the change process.

If any significant change is to take place, the individual must see himself as an integral part of the change process. What steps can the differentiated staffing project director take to help individual team members to become in fact actively involved in the differentiated staffing change process?

4. People change when they are secure in changing.

People know how things were in the past and how they are in the present. They develop a sense of security commensurate with their understanding of the past and present. Insecurity often develops when the intervention of new processes are discussed and the individual is unable to see himself functioning within the prescribed framework. What can the educational administrator do to assist his staff to better understand their individual roles in a differentiated staffing process?

5. *People do not necessarily change on the basis of new knowledge alone.*

The educator who, for whatever reason, is implementing the differentiated staffing program must not be caught in the trap of merely disseminating information about differentiated staffing. If he does, he may find that the new knowledge *per se* may be threatening to the individual and do irreparable damage to the idea. How, then, can the educational change-agent find ways of providing new insights and new knowledge to those with whom he is working on the project?

6. *People change when they are encouraged and supported in changing.*

The individual who believes that those whom he respects are supporting him is more likely to undertake and carry through with a specific change. What steps can the project director take to alleviate the atmosphere of self-doubt, expectation of the worst, and unsupported risk to enable the individual to begin the most positive change?

7. *People change some attitudes slowly.*

One of the most significant factors as to why change occurs so slowly in education is that educational change-agents attempt to move an idea too rapidly and this, then, meets with resistance that slows down or stops new ideas. What kind of planning, therefore, should be undertaken by the educational administrator to fully implement an idea such as differentiated staffing?

The above principles, related questions, and subsequent answers and planning are imperatives in any staff preparation program. They should be considered and reconsidered. A plan of action should be developed to help each individual allay his specific fears.

Staff Development

Staff Development, often referred to as inservice education, is not only a means of making progress toward improved programs, but also encompasses the belief that the individual can improve and wants help in improving himself and his effectiveness as a teacher. A realistic definition of staff development is, ". . . inservice education as *planned activities for the instructional improvement* of professional staff members."[1]

Prevalent in the literature for at least three decades, the reasons for

---

[1]Ben H. Harris and Wailand Bessent, in collaboration with Kenneth E. McIntyre, *In-Service Education: a Guide to Better Practices* (Englewood Cliffs, N.J.: Prentice-Hall, Inc., 1968), p. 2.

inservice education are known to most educators. It might be helpful at this point, however, to review the salient points. Harris, Bessent and McIntyre, reviewing them, state them very succinctly:

> Fundamentally, inservice education programs are important for the following reasons:
>
> 1. Preservice preparation of professional staff members is rarely ideal and is primarily an introduction to professional preparation rather than professional preparation as such.
> 2. Social and educational change makes current professional practices obsolete or relatively ineffective in a very short period of time. This applies to methods and techniques, tools, and substantive knowledge itself.
> 3. Coordination and articulation of instructional practices require changes in people. Even when each instructional staff member is functioning at a highly professional level, employing an optimum number of the most effective practices, such an instructional program might still be relatively uncoordinated from subject to subject and poorly articulated from year to year.
> 4. Other factors argue for inservice education activities of rather diverse kinds. Morals can be stimulated and maintained through inservice education, and is a contribution to instruction in itself, even if instructional improvement of any dynamic kind does not occur.[2]

The authors feel that the importance of a well planned and well organized staff development cannot be taken lightly. This might in fact be the single most important facet on the differentiated staffing planning continuum. In planning for inservice programs, though, educators must be mindful that there are pitfalls which too often occur and, if permitted to go unheeded, can do irreparable harm to the very best of ideas. These pitfalls include the following:

1. Failure to relate inservice program plans to genuine needs of staff participants.
2. Failure to select appropriate activities for implementing program plans.
3. Failure to implement inservice program activities with sufficient staff and other resources to assure effectiveness.[3]

As we have implied the pivotal point upon which the success of the entire differentiated implementation program rests is with a professional staff that is prepared to accept the challenges of a new venture. In

---

[2]Harris, Bessent, McIntyre, pp. 3–4.
[3]Harris, Bessent, McIntyre, pp. 3–4.

order to be prepared, the instructional staff must be able to adapt to new roles, new responsibilities, and new methods of instruction. The only way to help in the reeducation of the instructional staff is to allow them to become involved with the planning process in the very early stages. Unfortunately, this in itself will not provide the staff with all of the special knowledge and skill necessary to function effectively from the outset. A well designed and carefully planned staff development program is essential to insure that the instructional staffing has all of the skills and knowledge necessary to get the job done. Perhaps an even more important factor is that a good staff development program that does nothing more than to provide a means of allaying and disspelling the anxieties and fears of the instructional staff is enough justification for its existence.

A well planned and comprehensive staff-development program should include:

1. The study of the group process and interpersonal relations;
2. The study of diagnostic and remedial techniques to provide for better instruction;
3. A study of the methods for providing individualized instruction as well as the ways for organizing the classroom to effectively implement an individualized instructional program;
4. A study of the preparation and the use of a variety of instructional media including a study of new techniques and new equipment;
5. A study of the testing and nontesting measurement and evaluation techniques.

Directly related to specific staff development programs is the need to establish continuity in programs for all staff members. If strategies such as the application of learning principles are to succeed over a prolonged period, there must be built-in provisions for continually training new personnel. Many school districts deal with a staff turnover rate of approximately twenty or more percent. This means that large numbers of new staff members will have to be continually and systematically integrated into existing programs. A well conceived program can easily fail after a year or two if this does not occur. Unfortunately, this is a major reason why seemingly successful pilot projects are too often not lasting and are not readily integrated into the school's operational programs. Schools usually do not have the wherewithal to maintain the type of staff development program necessary to insure success. A differentiated staffing model that is intended to work as planned over a prolonged period of time must have built-in structural and role provisions necessary for a smooth assimilation of new teachers into it. If it does not, it is safe to assume from the outset that the program is, at best, on shaky ground.

The school district planning both a move toward differentiated staffing and an inservice program to insure its success would do well to seek assistance from local schools of education and state departments of education. This is not to imply that the local school district cannot do an adequate job by itself in respect to planning and implementing staff-development programs, for many can. Rather, schools of education and state education departments contain a great wealth of talent. It behooves the thinking administrator to obtain all the assistance available to him.

PLANNING FOR DIFFERENTIATED STAFFING

Let us assume that the idea of differentiated staffing has now been diffused among all of those who will be affected by it, the staff selected that will participate in the project, and the staff development or inservice educational programs are now operational. The education executive piloting the model project is now ready to begin the active planning stage with his staff. It is important yet, perhaps, superfluous to mention that the final design model which will eventually be implemented should be the joint efforts of the entire team. The person responsible for the project must obviously undertake the initial work—diffusion of the idea, staff assessment, and staff selection and staff development—but when the time comes to plan the final model that will actually be used, it is necessary that it reflect the best in group problem solving and group planning. The following quotation from a resolution voted on and passed by the Connecticut Education Association will provide the reader with a rather concrete reason for the need for the advanced planning that involves people:

> The Connecticut Education Association recognizes many innovations designed to further the educational opportunities of children. One concept which purports to hold such promise and to provide for a better utilization of teacher time and talents is differentiated staffing. The Association believes that this concept must be carefully scrutinized and any plan for differentiated staffing be viable, flexible, and adaptable to keep pace with changing conditions in the schools and society.
>
> The Association insists that any design for differentiating staff, to be successful, (a) must meaningfully involve classroom teachers and the local associations from the initial stages of development through implementation and evaluation, (b) must clearly define roles and responsibilities of certificated and noncertificated staff so that the actual process of teaching rests in hands of individuals having sound educational preparation, and (c) must keep the community informed and seek its cooperation in order to prevent misunderstanding of the educational values to be gained from differentiated staffing.

Available funds must be sufficient both to assure maintenance of manageable loads and to guarantee remuneration for all staff-auxiliary personnel, teachers, and administrators—based upon well-grounded criteria and not bearing the characteristics of a merit pay plan for teachers.

The Association urges local associations immediately to initiate in-depth studies of the many ramifications of differentiated staffing. Local associations should prepare to act in full partnership and shall be accepted as full partners with their administrations in the consideration, design, authorization, implementation, evaluation and continuation of any plan for differentiated staffing. Any plan not so designed, implemented and evaluated should be rejected.[4]

If the reader is not convinced, perhaps the following resolution will bring additional insight into the concerns of professional organizations.

The National Education Association believes that, although differentiated staffing programs may offer hope for positive and real innovation in the future, they are subject to potentially serious abuses and shortcomings that are not in the best interest of students, teachers, and the public. The Association insists that no differentiated staffing plan should be undertaken or continued until (a) the classroom teachers and local associations are directly involved in decision making from the initial stages of development through implementation, evaluation, and continuation, (b) the roles and responsibilities of certificated and noncertificated staff are clearly defined and in the hands of certificated staff, (c) the community is kept informed and its cooperation sought, and (d) the funding is adequate to assure the maintenance of constructive teaching loads and to guarantee remuneration based upon the Association's principles of salary scheduling for all staff-paraprofessionals, teachers, and administrators—without the characteristics of a merit pay plan.

Local affiliates should be prepared to act in full partnership in the study of differentiated staffing and shall be accepted as full partners with their administrations in the consideration, design, authorization, implementation, evaluation, and continuation of any plan of differentiated staffing.

The Association strongly opposes adoption of unilaterally imposed differentiated staffing plans and will assist any local affiliate in its opposition to the same.[5]

The school district considering a pilot effort with differentiated staffing should realize that planning for this type of staff utilization requires

[4]Connecticut Education Association Policy *re* Differentiated Staffing adopted by the C.E.A. Representative Assembly, May 9, 1970. (Hartford, Connecticut: Connecticut Education Association, 1970.)

[5]National Education Association Policy (71.4) *re* Differentiated Staffing adopted by the NEA Representative Assembly, July 1971. (Washington, D.C.: National Education Association, 1971.)

long periods of time with considerable hard work. The model developed at Temple City, California, required approximately thirty-three months from its initial point of discussion to its final implementation in the first school. Sarasota County, Florida, drawing on the expertise of the Temple City model, was able to move through the same phases in approximately twenty-four months. Perhaps as more experience is gained and more models become available for consideration, the time needed to implement a model may be shortened. But the authors wish to caution the reader that the additional time spent in crossing all of the "t's" and dotting all the "i's" is not necessarily wasted time.

A review of the present planning and operational models of on-going differentiated staffing programs indicates that there are eight areas where decisions must be made and plans prepared. (The reader might wish to refer to page 10, figure 1–1 and the discussion of the process variables.) These include:

1. The levels and/or subjects to be included;
2. The levels or hierarchy of instructional responsibility with specific job descriptions which will clearly delineate what each person does on the differentiated staffing team;
3. Appropriate remuneration for each of the various levels of responsibility which will allow for attracting and holding competent professional and nonprofessional personnel (this item may have to be negotiated with the local professional association);
4. The necessary curriculum revision needed to accommodate individual students through multi- and varied instructional programs;
5. The role and degree which instructional support or ancillary systems (guidance, health instructional materials) play in the differentiated staffing model;
6. A consideration of the physical facilities necessary to accommodate the new program and a determination of which of the existing facilities will best lend themselves to it;
7. The organization of instructional personnel into a body which will permit group decision making;
8. The development of time flexibility necessary to accommodate new curriculum and instructional procedures as well as time for planning.

It can be readily seen from the above list that the movement from the traditional organizational pattern to differentiated staffing pattern will require more than merely listing positions or rank and attaching salary figures to them while hoping that everyone will do his "thing" correctly and adequately. If we think of a school district as being composed of an infinite number of flexible and constantly changing social subsystems, it is safe to say that most every one of these will be affected to a greater or lesser degree by a move to a differentiated staffing pattern. As an organizational innovation, a differentiated staffing plan can be attempted, perhaps achieved, even if mandated. But the reader who has carefully considered chapter 4 will realize that no one can bring change about in this manner and expect it to have a real and lasting effect. The educational executive responsible for the project must realize that with it as with any significant change there is a sociological dimension—only the teachers and staff can guarantee success of the project. This not considered, the project is doomed to failure. And a concentrated effort to telescope the time needed for appropriate planning, or any efforts to omit steps or omit involving certain people may as well prove self-defeating. For when the time that is required to plan adequately is viewed as an opportunity for self-examination and reeducation of an individual, then the time used is most worthwhile.

Pre-planning Activities

Before serious planning begins, the staff should consider conducting a series of meetings with those professionals not directly affected by the project as well as the public whose children will be affected by it to discuss differentiated staffing, the group's planning for it, and the expected outcomes. Nothing is more detrimental to the implementation of sound ideas and projects than to have them studied behind closed doors. Word eventually leaks out about what is being studied. This often elicits fears of anxiety and distrust as well as ignorant criticism of the unknown, at least on the part of those not actually involved in the planning. At a later date it is often difficult to overcome the hostility and distrust that has grown up merely because a study or planning group chose to work in a vacuum.

Planning meetings should be well thought out and well organized. The meetings should never be allowed to convey that those embarking on the planning do not know enough about the subject, nor should they imply that differentiated staffing is a *fait accompli* which will affect the lives of all without giving them voice. As an illustration, the authors would like to cite the case of a medium-size midwestern city which a few years ago attempted to undertake an innovative idea, a non-graded instructional program in their elementary schools.

A sizeable grant was obtained by this large midwestern school district and one teacher from each of the school district's thirty or so elementary schools was freed for one year for study, travel, and planning for nongraded elementary classrooms. At the end of this year of study, the groups returned to the respective schools and instituted a nongraded instructional program on a limited basis. These teachers were all given the newest materials and equipment, the benefit of expert help from the central administrative staff, and considerable recognition in the news media for their efforts. At the end of the year test results indicated that they had made splendid gains in their classrooms. During the summer a decision was made that all teachers in all elementary classrooms would immediately move into a nongraded program. One can readily imagine the hostility that arose when teachers returned in September and found that they had to alter or discard the planning they had done during the summer without having the benefit of a year of study and a year of exceptional support for their undertakings.

We have said earlier that the meetings held by the planning group for those indirectly involved should be well thought out. The planning for these meetings should not exclude consideration of the audience. Which groups of individuals should hear about differentiated staffing? Which groups should hear about it first, second, third, etc.? Should the community hear about the idea from the news media first? These are questions which only the individual school district can answer, but it is vitally important that they be considered and specific decisions made about them. The purpose of these meetings should be to provide the various groups with an opportunity to learn more about differentiated staffing so that they might raise intelligent questions which will serve as guidelines for planning the eventual pilot model. These meetings, also, serve the purpose of allaying some of the fears which can be generated when an issue as controversial as differentiated staffing is discussed. These meetings, too should be thought of as serving as a springboard for beginning to organize planning for differentiated staffing.

Organization for Planning

Any group planning activities that are engaged in will only be as successful as the organization for the planning allows. An organizational pattern, to be effective, must be well thought out and when it is, it can be a helpful aid to the planner, just as poor organization can grossly restrict the most experienced planners. We indicated earlier the need for the educator and his staff, responsible for planning for and implementing the differentiated program, to first consider establishing a project steering committee to direct the development of a differentiated staffing pilot model. We said, also, that this group might then report to an elected committee drawn from a broad base of those who would be directly or indirectly affected by the outcome of the steering committee.

The authors cannot stress enough the need for staff involvement of people in the change process. When Sarasota County, Florida, first considered differentiated staffing, a commitment was made to involve a large number of faculty and staff members as they undertook the study to evaluate and decide on the potential value of differentiated staffing to their school district.

There are still other considerations which should be thought through by the project director in order to provide for effective planning by the steering committee: it is essential, for example, that the board of education and central administrative staff be committed to provide ample released time as well as summer employment (preferably at full pay equivalent) for getting the job well done. All the necessary planning for a complex innovation such as differentiated staffing cannot be accomplished after teachers have worked a full day. Released time not only provides an opportunity for those involved in the planning to read, study, and observe at a less hurried pace but, also, it stresses the high priority of the concept and the board of education's and central office administration's belief in the project.

Also essential to the organization for planning is the provision for adequate resources needed to bring about the best possible planning. Both clerical assistance to get the planning committee's work completed in a reasonable time as well as space for individual study and small and large group meetings are both essential. Funds for consultant assistance and travel by the members of the planning committee should be provided by the board of education. There is nothing that gives an innovative idea greater impetus than the opportunity of talking to those who are knowledgeable about it and who have been instrumental in its implementation, especially when an individual or a group can travel to the location and make an on-site investigation of the innovation firsthand.

Planning Process for Staff Differentiation

The actual process of planning should occur at two levels—those of the individual school and school district. Even though only one school might be involved in the ultimate pilot project, the planning for that model for that school will have its effect at the central office administrative level and for that matter throughout the school district. In line with this, planning at two levels can make thinking regarding the ultimate impact at both the individual school and school district consistent. This is even more essential if several or all of the schools in a district are considering moving toward differentiated staffing. For while the central administrative offices are looking at the larger picture and its ramifications, freedom can be provided for building level idiosyncrasies as well as autonomy.

As the differentiated staffing steering committee begins to outline the problems and a means for solving them, it will immediately have to confront the components of the basic design model, which include the following:

1. The necessary qualification for each rank or level in the differentiated team hierarchy;
2. The policies and procedures which will govern the promotion on the career ladder which is built into a differentiated staffing model;
3. The policies and procedures which will govern tenure;
4. The methods of governing the supervision of the performance of those at the various levels or ranks;
5. The establishment of guidelines for the allocation of financial and other resources for the staffing and instructional materials in each of the pilot models;
6. The development of project goals for the whole district;
7. The development of differentiated staffing objectives for those who are involved in the pilot model.

Within these guidelines, each school planning for the implementation of differentiated staffing can then decide the appropriate staffing pattern and instructional program to allow for the achievement of overall school district objectives while meeting both student and staff needs.

In a special report, Dempsey and Fiorino[6] discussed the development of needs and cited some specific objectives:

Since the purpose of any innovation, including differentiated staffing, is to meet or satisfy the needs of the students and staff, the first step in the planning process should be the identification of needs. It is much easier to identify needs than to satisfy them. Recognizing this the Beaverton (Oregon) School District outlined these planning objectives:

1. To identify appropriate behavioral objectives for students from a wide range of economic and social levels.
2. To identify specific tasks that should be performed by educational personnel to help students meet these behavioral objectives.
3. To refine teaching tasks as they relate to:
   a. teaching skills, knowledge, and attitudes;
   b. utilizing procedural and organizational techniques for teaching; and,
   c. provide managerial leadership in allocating resources for teaching.
4. To correlate these specific tasks with the competencies and interests of educational personnel.

[6]Richard A. Dempsey and A. John Fiorino, *Differentiated Staffing: What It Is and How It Can Be Implemented* (Swarthmore, Pa.: A.C. Croft, Inc., 1971), pp. 36–37.

5. To develop criteria and programs for the training and retraining of the educational personnel required to perform these tasks.
6. To develop criteria and procedures for evaluating the results of Items 1–5 above.

Planning Guidelines

To assist the instructional staff in its planning, several guidelines have been developed for consideration. These guidelines were developed under a Federal project entitled, "More Effective School Personnel Utilization" which was administered by the Bureau of Educational Personnel Department in the United States Office of Education. The guidelines that were cited are:

1. No unit smaller than an entire school staff should be differentiated.
2. The maximum salary of the highest paid teacher should be at least double the maximum salary of the lowest category of professional personnel.
3. All instructional staff should spend at least 25 percent of their time in direct contact with pupils.
4. All instructional staff in the unit designed as operationally differentiated should be on the differentiated salary schedule.
5. The differentiated roles of the instructional staff as well as the selection criteria for those roles should be clearly delineated.
6. The school district should agree to an external program audit annually, the results of which should be made public.
7. Differentiated staffing requires other organizational and curriculum changes, and the substantial development of new teaching roles.

These guidelines should prove helpful to any staff which is planning for a differentiated staffing model. They raise sufficient questions to cause the group to fully consider the ramifications of their undertaking. It might here prove helpful to next consider the larger dimensions of the differentiated staffing model prior to implementation.

Long Range Planning

Everyone talks about long range planning, but no one does much about it. When in education long range planning is done, it usually takes the form of projected school facilities planning and projected budgets. Long range planning for curricular improvements, personnel projections, and the implementation of new programs is tragically almost nonexistent. However, when considering the implementation of an innovation as complex as differentiated staffing, long range planning is an imperative facet of the entire program.

In the special report on differentiated staffing previously cited, Dempsey and Fiorino suggested a planning and implementation schedule for differentiated staffing, extended over a six-year period as follows:

First Year

1. Workshops for administration, instructional staff, and community
2. Formation of a steering committee and begin functioning
3. Appointment of a project director
4. Formation of task forces and begin working on
   a. Communication
   b. Teacher task analysis
   c. Evaluation
   d. Finance
   e. Salary
   f. Legal aspects
   g. Objectives and curriculum
5. Accomplishment of planning objectives as listed on page 36.

Second Year

1. Completion of an evaluation model
2. Completion of a staffing model
3. Completion of a new organizational pattern
4. Preparation of a manual of policies and procedures
   a. Definition of roles and responsibilities of differentiated staff
   b. Policies and procedures regarding selection, promotion, tenure, salary, and evaluation of staff
5. Selection of a pilot school
6. Selection of a staff for school
7. Begin staff development education project
8. Gather benchmark data
9. Completion of curriculum revision
10. Completion of any building alterations
11. Conduct seminars for parents of children in the pilot school

Third Year

1. Implementation of differentiated staffing in pilot school
2. Plan for and develop a model for second pilot school
3. Evaluate model in first pilot school
4. Conduct staff development education program for staff of second pilot school
5. Identification of staff knowledge and skill deficiencies
6. Plan for and conduct staff development education program to overcome deficiencies

Fourth Year

1. Implementation of differentiated staffing in second pilot school
2. Plan for and develop a model for second pilot school
3. Evaluate model in first pilot school
4. Conduct staff development education program for staff of second pilot school
5. Revise policies and Procedures Manual as needed
6. Plan for and develop model(s) for school(s) to be differentiated the following year
7. Revise and continue inservice education for both new and experienced teachers

Fifth Year

1. Implementation of differentiated staffing in selected school(s)
2. Make necessary modifications of models in schools which have been differentiated
3. Continuation of data collection and evaluation programs
4. Make necessary revision in curriculum, policies and procedures, and staff development education programs
5. Plan for and develop models for remaining schools
6. Continuation of staff development education of both new and experienced teachers

Sixth Year

1. Implementation of differentiated staffing in remaining schools following established patterns
2. Continuation of evaluating and refining all dimensions of differentiated staffing models

The planning and implementation schedule presented above is purely suggestive in nature, for each school district must plan its own schedule. The recommended time for total implementation may be shortened for small school districts and expanded for large ones. Note, though, that the suggested activities are gross descriptions of a series of events.[7]

Planning for Resource Allocation

It was suggested earlier in this chapter that there should be a high degree of autonomy between schools and between the schools' instructional staffs in the local school district. To develop one model and copy it in all future endeavors is not sound thinking. If a differentiated staffing

[7]Dempsey, Fiorino, pp. 45–47.

pattern is to become successful, allowances must be made for the uniqueness of the individuals involved as well as the uniqueness of the individual school and its climate. This should not be construed to be uncritical
support or a do-as-you-please attitude on the part of the key educational
administration, but rather a recognition that there are numerous innate
differences between individuals, instructional staffs, and schools and that
variations on a theme should be the watchword.

If the concepts of unit autonomy is accepted and applied, it then
becomes necessary to recognize that there will be different resources
available, both human and physical, with which to work. Furthermore,
depending upon when the implementation of the differentiated staffing
program is scheduled, there may be a variance in fiscal resources. Recognizing this, the Sarasota County Public Schools have devised a system of
allocating fiscal resources to each school on the basis of each school's
needs.

A unique system of staff units has been devised whereby "staff units"
are allocated to each school according to a pupil-teacher ratio appropriate
for the level of the school. The ratio is determined by the County's central administrative section according to the total funds available for instructional personnel salaries, the mean salary to be paid during the
academic year, and the anticipated total number of instructional units
available to the school district. For example, if $9,000,000 are available
for salaries and the mean salary of each member of the instructional staff
is $9,000, then 1,000 staff units can be allocated to the school district
during the fiscal year.

The pupil-teacher ratio used in determining staff units may be the
same for all schools in the district or a lower ratio may be used where it
is deemed appropriate. In either case, the number of pupils anticipated
to be enrolled in each school is divided by the predetermined pupil-
teacher ratio and the resultant constitutes the number of staff units assigned to that school. If the enrollment in a school is 1,000 and the predetermined pupil-teacher ratio is 20.1, the school would be allocated 50
staff units. To assist in the planning for the appropriate mix of instructional staff members to effectively utilize the 50 alloted units, the following unit equivalencies have been assigned to each position in the hierarchy:

Consulting teacher	1.50	units
Directing teacher	1.25	"
Staff teacher	1.00	"
Instructor	1.00	"
Resident intern	.50	"

Instructional assistant	.50	"
Aide	.35	"
Student assistant	.03	"

The reader can readily see the amount of flexibility that this system provides. When this kind of flexibility is coupled with a high degree of building level autonomy, there is seemingly no end to the kinds of imaginative instructional and organizational patterns that can be developed.

SUMMARY

Differentiated staffing from the origin of the idea to the implementation of the program, is full of complex ramifications. The authors feel, as do those school districts where differentiated staffing exists, that the concept deserves careful consideration. However, it is imperative that any school district considering differentiated staffing realize the vast amount of planning necessary for it to come to fruition and function fully. Failure to do the essential planning necessary to insure successful implementation will, in most instances, result in an unfortunate experience, chaos, and futility.

7. Selected
Differentiated Staffing Models

We have selected several differentiated staffing models to provide the reader with not only a better understanding of the pattern of personnel organization but, also, to more clearly highlight the similarities and dissimilarities of each. We have not intended to apply a value judgment as to the effectiveness of the models discussed, but merely to examine the data available to us. We assume that the reader will more fully investigate any or all of the models in order to answer his specific question.

Whenever examples are selected, we are often questioned about those left out. We trust that the reader will bear with us—we could not have included all those models on the drawing boards, those nearly operational, and all those that are operational. Because a model was not selected does not mean that it is not effective. We, simply, did not include certain programs due to a lack of space. We sincerely regret that we could not include all.

The models selected include: the John Adams High School in Portland, Oregon; Anniston Educational Park in Anniston, Alabama; schools in Beaverton, Oregon; Camden, New Jersey; Dade County (Miami area), Florida; the Mary Harmon Weeks Elementary School in Kansas City, Missouri; the Louisville, Kentucky Public School System; the Marin County (California) differentiated staffing project; a proposed model in the Manhattan area of New York City; Venice Junior High School in Sarasota County, Florida; and the Temple City Unified School District in California.

Less complete descriptions of differentiated staffing projects come from Mesa, Arizona; Fountain Valley, California; Oak Grove Junior High School in Bloomington, Minnesota; the Mankato State College Laboratory School in Mankato, Minnesota; the Coatsville, Pennsylvania model; and the Menasha, Wisconsin, Public Schools.

The grouping of school information, some of it hypothetical, was structured in a question-answer format. The questions in which descriptions were framed follow:

1. What is the school size? Is it a city district, or county district school? What is the population at large? Discuss the student population.

2. Was there local media coverage of the differentiated staffing concept?

3. How did the differentiated idea start?

4. How were the general public and the school board convinced to support the differentiated staffing concept?

5. What opposition was there to the differentiated staffing idea?

6. What would be a brief description of the project?

7. What is the attitude of the persons involved in the differentiated staffing—the staff themselves?

8. What would be a comparison of what was to what is?

9. What were cost estimates involved in the implementation of the differentiated staff?

10. Does differentiated staffing require special facilities?

11. May the project director, or may the forces behind the project be viewed as agents of change?

12. Was a formal task analysis undertaken?

Both operational models and planning models, as well as conjectured models, are analyzed through the use of these questions. The numbers at the beginning of the following questionnaire paragraphs will refer to these questions.

JOHN ADAMS HIGH SCHOOL,
PORTLAND, OREGON
DIFFERENTIATED STAFFING PROJECT

1. The John Adams High School is an inner city school in Portland, Oregon and one of fourteen high schools in the twenty-seventh largest school district in the United States. The population of Portland is a half million in the 1971 census estimation. The student population of the school is 1750. The student body makeup is approximately 25 percent black, about 30 percent white from an economic lower class, with the rest mostly white middle class students. There is a small percentage of rural students, the rest are urban and suburban.

2. The differentiated staffing concept was not local news. Consequently very little, if any, local media coverage was given. However, due perhaps to the Charles Silberman book, *Crisis in the Classroom*, and coverage in the May, 1971 *Phi Delta Kappan*, considerable interest in the United States has been aroused.

3. Mr. Allen L. Dobbins and several other graduate students at Harvard University had constructed a theoretical model for an ideal school,[1] from which the differentiated staffing model in Portland was developed, under the leadership of Mr. Dobbins, himself.

4. Actually, much of the Adams point of view hinged around a needs survey, which led to a suggested new curriculum designed along the lines of an interdisciplinary or cross-disciplinary curriculum. Thus a single problem-centered course outline was developed which was very broad in nature. Traditional courses such as social studies, English, math, and the like were then joined to support the student-centered and problem-centered curriculum. The differentiated staff grew logically out of a need to implement this new curriculum, and it was the curriculum which required a "selling job." In general the public wanted to know if the curriculum was as good as the old. The general public really never questioned the staffing phase.

In all of this early designing, adapting, and implementation, the Portland School Board was very enthusiastic and supportive from the start.

5. Some opposition developed among a "second echelon" of teachers and administrators. One reason for this was that Mr. Allen L. Dobbins did "come from the outside" and true to the principles of group dynamics, local forces were suspicious of this outside influence. The op-

---

[1]These observations are based on a telephone interview between the authors and Mr. Dobbins.

position was sporadic, not really an organized force, and through the early stages of the differentiated project began to dissipate. There was no opposition from the public or the School Board.

6. The differentiated staffing project sprang from a needs assessment which led to a new curriculum (mentioned in question number four).

However, further development of this curriculum led to a team teaching approach in order to define objectives and methods of carrying out the objectives. This task led to a need for and employment of specialists in the various curriculum areas, who were called curriculum associates, and working with them, team leaders. Other categories which were needed were staff teachers, who worked more directly at teaching as distinguished from curriculum development, practice teachers, intern teachers (some working on master's degrees), and even student teachers.

A unique feature of the John Adams High School differentiated staffing concept is the horizontal groupings of team leaders, trainers of teachers, leaders who specialize in the development of a new "breed"—the clinical supervisor, and researchers, or research associates.

7. Starting in June of 1969 there was, generally, a feeling of being overworked and underpaid but nevertheless enthusiastic. There was and is a feeling of excitement at being challenged by something which seems destined to change the direction of American education.

8. What was and still is the traditional staffing pattern in most schools in Portland and elsewhere is that of thirty or so students with one teacher at a time in an instructional process. Of course, Adams School, fairly new, was opened with a new staff (described in question six). The more traditional grouping of teachers, department heads, perhaps an assistant principal, and a principal has given way at Adams to a differentiated staff—a clinical staff.

9. The costs involved were mostly in salary increments for increased responsibility. However, there were, previous to the project, salary increases in Portland for department heads and vice principals, so with curriculum associates, team leaders, research associates, and the like receiving these increments in their stead, the cost almost evened out.

Overall, however, over about a four year period including the planning phase roughly $250,000 was budgeted to include extra costs for planning, for some limited project staff, for salary increments. A large part of this, approximately $150,000, went for inservice training and other types of staff development associated with the differentiated staffing project.

10. The answer to this question at John Adams High School is clearly "yes." However, the Adams School is architecturally a traditional school with box-like classrooms designed for 30 to 35 students. *Staff members view this as a great constraint.* Such structural arrangements

inhibit one-on-one learning groupings, small group situations, large group instruction, learning lab activities, and other such flexible grouping and scheduling. The differentiated staff at Adams work around this by sometimes *crowding* 75 pupils into a classroom designed for thirty or so. At other times a teacher and a small group may seem oddly out of place in an otherwise large classroom. *Sometimes individual tutoring may take place in four corners of a classroom.* Most of these arrangements have been forced to work by a highly enthusiastic and creative staff. *Yet, all could function so much better in a different structural arrangement of facilities.*

11. Quite clearly most of the personnel involved in the John Adams High School differentiated staffing project do view themselves as change agents. One person, however, made the statement that the forces at work in Adams might possibly change other schools around the nation more so than local schools.

Most of the staff did view themselves as change agents in a very broad movement in American education.

12. No. Actually, a model was conceived outside and brought in. Through a needs assessment, a curriculum was developed to which the outside model was adapted. However, those involved in the planning for John Adams High School did see merit in a formal task analysis. Extremely complex pragmatic considerations, however, precluded a formal task analysis.

ANNISTON, ALABAMA, PUBLIC SCHOOLS DIFFERENTIATED STAFFING PROJECT

1. Phase I of the Anniston Educational Park houses the high school where a planning project for a differentiated staffing model was undertaken in 1970–71. At the time of this writing, the implementation stage had not yet occurred but was anticipated.

Anniston High School, a city or town school, houses a grade nine through twelve program with approximately 2000 students and a staff of 55 teachers. The population of Anniston, Alabama, is around 8000. The student body is composed predominantly of black students from Anniston and nearby rural areas.

2. There was local media coverage through both newspapers and radio. The general population of Anniston was generally receptive to information about its new school. In addition, there had been a citizen and teacher task force organized, and in a small community the size of Anniston much coverage was circulated by word of mouth. The community, teachers, and students all appeared to be well informed about the differentiated staffing planning project.

3. The differentiated staffing idea came about through what is perceived by the project administrative staff and other personnel as a natural evolutionary process. Within a regional boundary Anniston has since 1966 developed a reputation for innovation. A part of this innovative practice involved some rather well established patterns of team teacher and flexible scheduling. However, on reappraising their team teaching efforts, Anniston personnel discovered several practices which could be strengthened by a closer look at job analysis, large and small group instruction, and the overall coordination of a total faculty rather than the somewhat informal organization of the existing team teaching. Thus, the step to begin planning for a differentiated staff seemed natural to take, an answer to the question, "after team teaching what?" Throughout the differentiated staffing study Anniston personnel were reminded again and again of what careful thought must be given to staffing patterns, and came more and more to view the old method of team teaching as being extremely unsophisticated in comparison to the analysis which led to the differentiated model in their school.

4. The school board of Anniston has of recent years taken great interest in innovation. Through the school board, greater involvement of the general public has been sought. Actually, in this instance involving the planning phase of the differentiated staffing project, there was really very little convincing to do. The community was proud of its new school and had confidence in the school board and project staff; the community and school board were fairly eager to see new and better staffing designs tried.

5. There was no discernible opposition to the differentiated staffing idea. This may have been attributable to the high confidence of the community and school in the leadership and to the halo influence of a new school and the innovative atmosphere surrounding it. It may even be that opposition lies dormant and will emerge later during the implementation year, but at the time of this writing no opposition was reported.

6. The differentiated staffing design is based on a multilevel career lattice proceeding from paraprofessional through instructional specialist to school director. The developed model provides a method for retaining and rewarding experienced competent teachers who might otherwise turn to administration or some other occupation where salaries are greater and status more readily available. The retention and career ladder aspects based on varying levels and types of professional responsibility, coupled with compensation for increased responsibility, is a key element in Anniston and many other differentiated staffing projects. One point repeatedly made in the Anniston study worth noting here is that retention of quality teachers might not always be tied in with salaries, but has to do as well with the feeling of psychological success that leads from shared decision making.

The unique approach which has been taken by Anniston concerns what is called *tri-partite career ladders*. There are two separate but parallel tri-partite career ladders in the Anniston plan, one for instructional matters, the other for clerical concerns, as follows:

Instructional	*Clerical*
Instructional associate	Clerical associate
Instructional assistant	Clerical assistant
Instructional aide	Clerical aide

In addition to these roles, there are two other wide areas of staff differentiation. One has to do with professional teaching roles:

Professional Teachers

Instructional specialist
Senior teacher
Staff teacher
Junior teacher
Associate teacher
Apprentice teacher.

The final category with administration:

Administrative Differentiation

School director
Associate school director for administration
Administrative trainee II
Administrative trainee I.

Training programs have been designed to tie in with the career ladder, and a great deal of the responsibility for training as well as deployment of human and material resources will reside with senior teachers and instructional specialists. Additionally, the higher grade teaching positions are responsible for keeping abreast of research and development.

Governance within the Anniston High School faculty as well as shared strategy formulation is to be handled by the school decision-making body, the Instructional Council, composed of senior teachers from each subject area, the school director, a paraprofessional from each of the three levels of the instructional ladder, and the instructional specialists for the subject areas. The school director will have one vote as will each of the others on this council.

In summary, the Anniston model is based on the philosophy of personalized instruction. The goals are meant to give credence to the worth of the individual student. Objectives then become more specific as job responsibilities clearly become those of staffing for continuous, nongraded, highly individualized instruction. Various area career ladders including paraprofessionals (both instructional and clerical), professional instruction, and administration go to make up a fairly complex differentiated staff self-governed by an instructional council. Inservice training or staff development are self-contained in the system as is the responsibility for research and development adaptation and data gathering. Conceivably this could approach a closed loop model.

7. The differentiated staffing project in Anniston has only recently completed the planning phase. However, the various task force members who have been involved with the planning and development have high morale and great expectations for the implementation of the project.

8. For many years systems such as Anniston have "rocked along" leading almost from a hand to mouth existence. The recent emergence of planning and development has involved the whole system as well as surrounding systems in a new era, one based on a calculated strategy for change. There seems to be coming from this a new professionalism, one which leads to a better learning environment akin to specialized clinical treatment in even small town education.

9. The cost element involved concerned merely the planning stage in the neighborhood of forty thousand dollars.

10. Anniston believes that the development of unconventional and innovative staffing patterns ought not to lead to a product housed in traditional surroundings. In this regard earlier educational specifications task forces had helped to develop and build an open plan school to provide a maximum of flexibility. Such a specialized facility provides room for individual tutoring, small group work, and large group instruction.

Space is also provided for each of the professional staff members with an emphasis on the role of teacher as counselor and resource person.

Special facilities, then, are seen as being required by the Anniston planning staff. Flexibility should be provided for now and for the foreseeable life of the school plant.

11. The project director, administrative staff, and involved faculty all view themselves as agents of change not only in their own community but in the surrounding region.

12. A Task Analysis leading to specific job descriptions and further governance of the differentiated staff was carried on through the planning phase.

BEAVERTON, OREGON, SCHOOL DISTRICT
DIFFERENTIATED STAFFING PROJECT

1. The Beaverton school district is around fifty-seven square miles in size and has a population of 65,000. Beaverton District #48 is the fourth largest school district in Oregon with a total student enrollment of 18,000. In the total system there are over 900 teachers and around 70 administrators. There are in all thirty schools in the district.

There are three schools involved in the differentiated staffing project: Aloha High School, Mountain View Junior High School, and Cooper Mountain Elementary School.

Aloha High School has a student population of approximately 1000 from a wide variety of socio-economic backgrounds. The professional staff is just under 40; the community itself is a part of the greater metropolitan district of Portland and a rapidly growing suburban area.

Mountain View Junior High School started operating in 1969–70 with a faculty of 26 and a student body of around 500 in grades seven through eight. In late 1970 the population rose to around 800 students when a ninth grade was added. The student population represents a broad spectrum of socio-economic levels.

Cooper Mountain Elementary School has around 500 students in grades one through six, and is presently staffed by 24 certificated persons.

2. There was considerable press coverage of the differentiated staffing project in Beaverton with a local newspaper, the *Valley Times* providing a full page special on the project in one issue.

3. The pilot program on differentiated staffing in Beaverton was conceived in August of 1968. Well before this time, however, Beaverton District #48 had attempted to readjust traditional staffing patterns, to drastically change curriculum and methodology to make it possible for student self-pacing and continuous growth in student achievement. In the effort to more deeply individualize the school program, Beaverton had engaged in a number of exploratory studies involving peer teaching, cross-age tutoring, student-teacher assistants, college-student tutors, interns, summer enrichment programs, teacher aides, laboratory assistants, and the like, all pointing toward an evolving differentiated staff. However, with the advent of USOE funds, Beaverton decided to launch a full scale systems plan of approach to differentiated staffing on July 1, 1969.

4. The local public and the school board were encouraged to support the planning phase for differentiated staffing by an energetic and young administrative staff, by interested and innovative teachers, and by outward forces espousing differentiated staffing.

5. Some resistance to change, though not severe, came from practically every quarter. There was some concern on the part of many: by lay citizens that new staffing patterns might upset this or that child's education; among school board members that the system might too quickly immerse itself in costly and unproven programs; among teachers that rigid hierarchies and merit pay plans loomed on the horizon; among building administrators that outer forces were moving to abrogate their authority. Each of these arguments were countered by a rather elaborate planning phase which involved all of these groups in helping to determine a future course of action which the times seemed to demand.

6. A total description of the staffing project could best be seen in surveying some of its administrative plans. The Beaverton District planned to design a differentiated staff model through total community cooperation and to field test it. Data would be generated for design of educational personnel training and retraining programs. Under this general administrative mandate differentiated roles were developed, based on task analysis associated with educational objectives. Great involvement of teachers, community, and nearby colleges and universities was included.

The district differentiated staffing project contained several steps. The steps were as follows:

1. An educational needs assessment was called for, in which students, parents, various community members, and educational personnel participated. National, regional, city, and state needs assessments were also taken into account.

2. Behavioral objectives for a wide range of social behavior were developed for the total education program.

3. Lists of cognitive, psycho-motor, and affective skills, and understandings, and appreciations were developed which would lead to measurable objectives stated in number two.

4. Responsibility levels were determined for educational personnel to accomplish completion and implementation of a system to lead to the accomplishment of steps two and three.

5. Job descriptions were written based on considerable action research, development, and data gathering.

6. Hypothetical models were developed.

7. Training programs were conceived.

8. A pilot program was implemented.

9. Evaluation and redesign were to be ongoing parts of the project.

From this planning came a number of differentiated roles, some new and some traditional, which included new assignments for principal, vice principal, director of pupil personnel, director of research and development, instructional consultant, curriculum domain specialist, team coordinator, media specialist, various librarian roles; numerous counseling roles such as orientation counselor, college counselor, counseling intern and testing intern; an activity director was also proposed.

To these various supporting roles a teacher hierarchy was proposed and added:

Teacher
Associate teacher
Teacher assistant
Intern
Practice teacher
Consultant
Teacher aide

The emphasis on those traditional positions would have to be on learning and instruction, on assisting the total teacher staff, on research and development all with a total commitment to the student and student needs.

The retention of the traditional job description of a principal with more emphasis on faculty interaction facilitation and instructional leadership is a combination of old and new. The vice principal's position oversees administrative services to the total staff, emphasizing building management, student accounting and control, and budget management. The total counseling aspect of guidance and pupil personnel is designed to permeate the system giving maximum help to teachers and students.

Taking the three participating schools one by one, we may observe more specific outcomes of the differentiated staffing project in Beaverton.

For Aloha High School the following new kinds of differentiated staff positions have been identified:

Domain chairman
Skills program specialist
Supervisor of teaching assistants
Team leader
Associate teacher
Business and industrial consultant
Technicians
Teaching assistants

The domain chairman provides leadership for the development of interdisciplinary curriculum and gives impetus to better teaching processes. The skills program specialist diagnoses and prescribes at all skills preparation levels in math, science, reading, and writing; he also develops materials, and supervises teaching assistants in their use. A supervisor of teaching assistants both designs and conducts staff development workshops and longer programs for teaching assistants. Team leaders work with interdisciplinary teams, organizing, coordinating, and implementing core course type programs for students. Associate teachers have no responsibility for curriculum design, but instead work under the general direction of one of the aforementioned personnel categories.

The district, plus a local business or industrial concern, together appoint a business and industrial consultant. This person teaches, counsels, and advises students and school district personnel in matters closely related to the business world.

Technicians take inventories, do minor accounting, order materials, prepare experiments, and do some demonstrations designed by others more expert in curriculum demonstration.

Teaching assistants are noncertificated staff who are under direct supervision by certified professional staff members. They come in various categories such as teacher intern, practice teacher, student assistants, clerks, aides, as well as community resource personnel.

Mountain View Junior High School is concentrating on large and small group instruction, independent study, cross-discipline laboratories, resource rooms, and media instruction. Use of Aloha High School students as specialty teachers and teacher aides is being tried. Various categories of differentiated staffing roles which are a continuation and adaptation of those used in Aloha High School are being tried as well.

Some recommended categories for piloting are:

Principal
Vice principal
Instructional coordinator
Methods specialist
Area leader
Master teacher
Team leader
Staff teacher
IMC director
Associate teacher
Intern teacher

Activity director
Special program instructors
Production and audio visual specialist
Community resource coordinator
Independent study facilitator
Classroom assistant

The principal not only serves as administrator but is free each week for two hours to devote specific time to the instructional program. The vice principal, among administrative hours, also works directly with students in planning school activities. The instructional coordinator manages curriculum development and facilities and also teaches part time. The methods specialist must keep up to date on curriculum, trends, techniques, and materials of a general methodology nature. Area leaders are to provide expertise in specific curriculum areas. Master teachers teach, and supervise, assist, and train interns, associate teachers, and student teachers as well. The team leader works closely with the area leader and helps promote interdisciplinary cooperation. Staff teachers assume a greater share of student leadership and increased instructional responsibilities. The IMC Director continually disseminates information to and for students and staff, and is in charge of the Instructional Media Center, a sophisticated "super" library. Associate teachers are first-year teachers who may be promoted to staff teacher any time after the first year. An intern teacher may remain in this position, where duties performed are essentially those of associate teacher. The activity coordinator manages all student extracurricular activities and works with the student government. Special program instructors primarily work with exceptional children. The production and audio visual specialist assists faculty and students with media production. The community resource coordinator is actually a career counselor for students, while the independent study facilitator helps students teach themselves through independent study.

The Cooper Mountain Elementary School presently operates with various organizational patterns composed of three teams, one team each for grades one and two, grades three and four, and grades five and six. Each team has an appointed team leader. The following supportive staff is fairly traditional: principal, resource teacher, counselor, reading teacher, speech clinician, music teacher, physical education teacher, and instructional materials center coordinator. Some innovative practices being used are peer teaching, cross-grade teaching, cross-grade grouping, use of high school and college students as teacher trainees, use of parent volunteer aides, and various large and small group learning practices.

Plans for the future at Cooper Mountain Elementary School include vertical differentiated staffing with a minimum of levels, more use of aides, clerks, and community resource persons, and the institution of role clarification programs and staff development. The present proposed positions are as follows:

Principal
Instructional coordinator
Curriculum team coordinator
Instructional team leader
Instructor
Associate instructor
Part time instructor
Intern

Here as in the Aloha High School, the role of principal has changed to reemphasize instructional leadership and interaction processes. The instructional coordinator teaches 25 percent of the time but also coordinates functions of all teams. The curriculum team coordinators differ by subject specialty and supervise curriculum development in their area. In addition to teaching, the instructional team leader serves as chairman of his team meetings. The instructor is responsible for the instructional program for a given number of children and also contributes to curriculum development. All first-year teachers are associate instructors who may be promoted to full instructor any time after the first year. Part time instructors are certificated personnel under the general direction of instructors. Interns may be from colleges or other agencies; they are responsible to an instructor.

Some additional categories are teacher aides, student teachers, and high school aides as early entries.

7. There is, overall, very high morale, great interest, and deep motivation among the staff at the three pilot schools. Personnel work harder than ever before and seem to enjoy it more. There is a spirit of cooperation, of seeking further change.

8. In previous years the Beaverton District had tried many instant innovations but to little avail. There seemed to be little hope of moving off dead center. This left a relatively efficient but not outstandingly notable school system. Then, as social forces demanded relevance, the interest among laymen and educators alike spurred a new look at the Beaverton system, and differentiated staffing emerged as a national idea, and seemed to have come of age. A new experimental interest, a livelier and more forward looking school district has come about.

9. Extra costs were in the neighborhood of two or three hundred

thousand, all factors considered. Beaverton got its big boost with the original EPDA grant of around $90,000 with a District #48 allocation of $40,000.

10. Beaverton personnel seem convinced that special facilities, which will provide flexibility for independent study, large and small group instruction, and space for multidisciplinary groups of differentiated staff to plan with peers and counsel with students, are needed. Special facilities for multimedia instruction are also a major need.

11. Certainly, all of the educational personnel who are involved in the Beaverton project view themselves as change agents. They have seen themselves become a center of national attraction. They have felt themselves change, and observed the change process at work. They want to remain a part of change.

One of the overriding goals behind the Beaverton project is the desire to be constantly involving generation after generation of new and better staffing patterns with no real commitment to any one static pattern. In a sense, Beaverton is looking for controlled organic change.

12. A formal task analysis was made and is continuing as a part of an ongoing self-renewal program.

CAMDEN, NEW JERSEY DIFFERENTIATED STAFFING PROJECT

1. The Camden, New Jersey, City School System contains grades K through twelve. Thirty-six schools are operated by the district, including two senior high schools, five junior high schools, and twenty-six elementary schools. The total number of students is almost 21,000. The differentiated staffing project itself began in the 1970–71 school year in three inner city schools—one senior high school, one middle school, and a K–3 elementary school, all medium to large size, in a city of 140,000.

2. There was a considerable media coverage, perhaps because the combined federal funds totaled almost a million dollars. In addition, one of the large local industries (Radio Corporation of America) was destined to play a big part in the project.

3. The differentiated staffing idea started over felt needs. Camden was a large urban district with such problems as outdated curriculum and teaching methods, poor student performance, excessive teacher turnover, an increasing dropout rate, all of the problems of an urban school in the twentieth century. However, community support groups, RCA, the New Jersey State Department of Education, the USOE, nearby Rutgers University, Glassboro State College, and several creative people on the administrative staff of the Camden School System sufficiently read in differentiated staffing helped start the program.

4. The support came from all ranks of citizens in the city. Citizens were aroused and were aware that steps needed to be taken to improve the schools. The school board was from the start enthusiastic and supportive. Naturally, the million-dollar support for a total program involving Model Cities and other school programs helped.

Later, as the project got underway such groups as the Community Advisory Council and grass roots neighborhood school advisory teams, the Office of the Mayor, Model Cities, The Camden Educational Association, the City Zone Parent Teachers Association, Camden City Administrative Council, and other groups became involved and gave support.

5. There was some opposition. Some persons were fearful that a predesigned model of differentiated staffing would be imposed on them, and some parents were suspicious of something new. The picture presented, though, was one of taking a hard look at the system and coming up with something better. The idea of involvement and discovery of new models through this process was stressed, as opposed to the idea that something new and untried would be forced on all concerned.

6. A brief description of the Camden project is difficult because the differentiated staffing project is a part of a total and unique program. One of its most unusual aspects is that the management phase has been divided and partly given to private industry. This is not a performance contract, but a purchase of outright consultant help and expertise from RCA in the area of management techniques, a systems approach to problems, and short-term expertise in many areas including curriculum and instruction. It is possible for RCA together with the Camden School System to write performance contracts with other people, for example, training programs for teachers, administrators, school board members, even maintenance personnel. In this regard, during the summer of 1970 training courses were established for new teachers, substitute teachers, security guards, paraprofessionals, and lunchroom aides. In addition, all faculty members of one inner-city high school received training in decision making and communication.

The differentiated staffing itself is found in three inner-city schools. All three schools use the same carefully planned model, a seven-man team consisting of one master teacher, two regular teachers, and four paraprofessionals, responsible for 100 students.

Pay for master teachers will be about what it was for high-school department chairmen. Other salaries are proportioned in scale to this.

Working with these teams are 25 parents, 25 students, a full time representative from the New Jersey State Department of Education, and select administrators. Much of the planning and decision making is left up to this total combination and to the differentiated staffing team.

7. The attitude and spirit are generally high. The differentiated staffing teams see themselves as members of an important new order of

things. The parent and student involvement is touch and go; however, this too is working out toward a better than average interest and attitude.

8. Now Camden School System personnel really have a chance to see differentiated staffing in action and to know what it can be. Before there was little knowledge and less interest in new staffing patterns; now the teachers themselves and administrators are talking about and planning for new methods and patterns of staff utilization.

9. A total of around $300,000 went into management, training, and systems analysis considerations in the first year of the project. This left about $600,000 to go into other phases of the program involving new programs, new curriculum, the differentiated staffing teams themselves, evaluation studies and the like.

10. The Camden, New Jersey School System is discovering that careful planning and a systems approach actually does legislate special facilities. Present facilities are working, but more flexibility in architecture could allow greater adaptability of the differentiated staffing models, could produce a generative effect to further expand, alter, and improve the experimental staffing pattern.

11. Certainly there are several echelons of force and influence behind the Camden differentiated staffing project. All of those forces view themselves as change agents. The differentiated staffing teams themselves as well as the parents and students involved in the advisory teams view themselves as change agents.

12. A formal task analysis was undertaken utilizing a systems approach. The emphasis was on management of programs, however, and not necessarily a subcategory analysis of tasks leading to specific job description and role clarification of the differentiated staffing team.

DADE COUNTY, FLORIDA PUBLIC SCHOOLS DIFFERENTIATED STAFFING PROJECT

1. The Dade County, Miami-Miami Beach area of Florida, is a metropolitan community of well over a million people, a county district with a central office county staff for general county administration. The school district, the seventh largest in the United States, is subdivided into six districts. It is in one of these, the Northeast District, that two schools have implemented differentiated staffing projects. The first, Norwood Elementary School, has a student population of approximately 600 students which is organized into four general areas or "little schools": these are preprimary (ages 4, 5, and 6), primary (ages 6, 7, and 8), junior (ages 8, 9, 10), and senior (ages 10, 11, and 12). The second, North Miami Beach Senior High School, has a student population of 2400 which is also

organized into "little schools" of around 600 to each unit. The population is representative of Dade County with predominantly white population and small minority groups, of which both black and Cuban predominate.

2. The Dade County school system has its own television station; there are other public television stations in the vicinity. All stations carried some information on the project, as did the local press. In addition, a number of in-house information newsletters went out from the school system and from the local Classroom Teacher's Association. One fairly extensive booklet has also been printed which describes both differentiated staffing projects in great detail. Many conferences, consultations, and general meetings have been held concerning the project. The project is known by many persons interested enough to have written or visited the system.

3. Exploration and inquiry into differentiated staffing began in late 1967 and throughout 1968. Formal study was initiated and approved by the Dade County Board on September 17, 1969. After this a one-year study found personnel throughout the system continuing to review the literature, attend meetings, and discuss the concept.

In June, 1970, Dade County's Northeast District was designated as the representative district for involvement in the Florida State Education Department School Staffing Study in cooperation with the U.S. Office of Education under the Education Professions Development Act. Later, both Norwood Elementary and North Miami Beach were selected, with faculty approval, as pilot schools and charged with the responsibility of writing individual designs to be implemented in September 1971.

4. The Dade County School Board, the superintendent of schools, and his central staff, as well as the Dade Classroom Teacher's Association all played a part in early county support of differentiated staffing. Their motivation was that of interested professional concern directed toward exploration, research and development into an innovation which seemed to hold promise for improving the system.

5. Opposition to the idea of differentiated staffing manifested itself mainly in terms of slow deliberate study, which is perhaps inevitable in a large system. What might be overcaution in a smaller system might merely be warranted concern in a larger more complex system. Nevertheless, as early as 1968 two nationally known consultants in differentiated staffing worked with the Dade County School Board and administrative staff and well over a year later the first formal action was taken.

There was other opposition to differentiated staffing among administrative groups and teachers as well, which mostly dissipated through a year of excellent communication and study.

At the time of this study Dade County was just beginning implementation of its two models, and teaching and administrative personnel were still evidencing a wait-and-see attitude.

6. Associated with the differentiated staffing project at the district and school level is a Review Advisory Committee composed of an instructional representative from the Dade County central staff, the Executive Secretary of the Dade County Classroom Teacher's Association, the principal from each participating school, a classroom teacher from each project school, the Northeast District Director of Elementary Education, and the Northeast District Director of Secondary Education. This advisory committee as well as school steering committees have emphasized an open school climate which allows all professional staff members to participate actively in the decision-making process.

Goals and objectives for the project are listed by the Dade County Board of Education as follows:

Goals

1. To develop and implement a more flexible staffing model, that can be adapted to the uniqueness of each school and that meets the following criteria:

    a. Student centered (roles are based on defined student objectives and are centered on tasks to be accomplished from defined student needs)

    b. Creates a model in which roles are fluid (that can be changed in relationship to one another as the tasks change–students need change)

    c. Fosters a humanistic school climate inducive to learning

    d. Promotes a shift from teaching per se to the management of learning

    e. Provides career incentive for instructional personnel

2. To establish a system of accountability whereby all those responsible to the public for the education of children may be related to the growth and development of the student.

3. To develop and initiate a training program that relates to numbers 1 and 2.

Objectives

1. To develop and implement an organizational structure that provides for various points of entry and flexibility for the change as the need may be.

2. To demonstrate that teachers will develop greater commitment to the profession and to the task by greater involvement in the decision-making process.

3. To demonstrate that differentiated staffing provides excellent training opportunities for the student teacher, the intern, and the beginning teacher and will tend to develop a committed and mature professional.

4. To change the role of the principal and other administrators so as to provide for a greater emphasis on instructional leadership and some direct involvement in teaching.

5. To create a learning environment that provides for continuous progress learning for every individual.

6. To develop an organizational model which provides for greater self regulation within teaching staffs.

As it can be seen from the county's goals and objectives, the emphasis is on a management design for a learning system. They believe that only through using more and different manpower resources can a truly individualized learning environment be established and maintained. It is in the allotment and management of this manpower that Norwood Elementary School makes its own unique contribution.

The staff organization at Norwood Elementary is unusual in its superficial structure.

Principal

Team coordinator

Master teacher

Teacher

Instructional aide

Clerical aide

Senior intern

Junior intern

Yet in the distribution of this staff, the innovative element is seen. As has been mentioned, the total school has been divided into "little schools" of various age levels. The entire professional staff in any instructional area, however, is responsible for planning and implementing the total instructional program for all students in that area. In the primary, junior, and senior areas, a team of four to six professionals will be working together to manage all available resources (time, personnel, materials, and the like) in as effective a way as possible for approximately 200 students. The specific distribution of personnel, professional, and paraprofessional, is the decision of the team members of each instructional area. Personnel arrangement will be determined by decentralized decision making and vested in those respective "little school" teams which are responsible for actually implementing the instructional program.

The tentative organizational structure is illustrated in Figure 7–1.

Responsibilities of the differentiated staff are as follows: The principal has a fairly traditional role. However, there are in his job makeup strong emphases on management and organizational development, as well as staff training and retraining. The team coordinator orchestrates all team objectives and is directly accountable to the principal. The master teacher's role lies in diagnosis, prescription, implementation, and evaluation, and is also directly responsible to the principal. Other responsibilities include the teacher's to the team of master teachers to whom he is assigned—he instructs under their supervision; the instructional aide's to the master teachers of the instructional area to which he is assigned; both senior and junior interns to a supervisory teacher and a university supervisor from his home college or university; and clerical aides to master teachers.

The Miami Beach Senior High School has a much more diversified differentiated staffing model. Some of the roles which follow are more traditional than other, newer, coexisting roles.

Principal

Vice principal

Business manager

Community relations specialist

Human relations specialist

Inservice coordinator

Psychological service consultant

School social worker

Media technician

Coordinating librarian

Teaching designer

Teacher prescriber

Resource specialist

Facilitating teacher

Instructional intern

Instructional aide

Clerical aide

The principal, together with the staff, is responsible for establishing and implementing the school's general philosophical guidelines and long-range goals. The vice principal is an extension of the responsibility and authority of the principal and as well provides liaison among the various instructional components of the school. The business manager is charged with maintaining financial processes and accounting. The Community Relations Specialist promotes, facilitates, and coordinates all ac-

PRINCIPAL

SECRETARY
CLERK

PRE-PRIMARY (25 per session)	PRIMARY AREA (170)	JUNIOR AREA (200)	SENIOR AREA (205)
1 Master Teacher	3 Master Teachers	1 Team Coordinator 3 Master Teachers	3 Master Teachers
1 Instructional Aide	1 Teacher	1 Teacher	2 Teachers
1 Senior Intern	1 Clerical Aide	1 Clerical Aide	1 Clerical Aide
1 Junior Intern	5 Senior Interns	5 Senior Interns	5 Senior Interns
	3 Junior Interns	3 Junior Interns	3 Junior Interns

The faculty senate is composed of one pre-primary master teacher, three master teachers from the primary area, one team coordinator and three master teachers from the junior area, and three master teachers from the senior area.

Fig. 7–1   Norwood Elementary School—Tentative Organizational Structure

tivities directly involving school and community. Human relations specialists create and maintain a harmonious climate. Inservice coordinators, psychological services, school social workers, media specialists, media technicians, and the coordinating librarians, have titles which are self-explanatory. Teaching designers help other teachers find and determine suitable student learning modalities, whereas the teaching prescriber diagnoses and prescribes in a continuing assessment program for students. Specific learning situations are handled by resource specialists while the facilitating teacher guides students in their independent study. The intern and aides have no major instructional responsibilities but instead assist in various instructional and clerical matters.

7. Anticipation is the predominant attitude of the personnel involved in the differentiated staffing project as startlingly new concepts are tried. Morale is generally high. There is some anxiety.

8. From what was to what is is generally captured in the new role of teachers as shared decision makers. Originally, teachers were little involved in major decisions which could turn staff arrangements around, rearrange schedules, plan and manage determined change, and totally coordinate instructional activities with considerable assistance from aides and clerks. These are the main differences.

9. Dade County operates on a multimillion dollar budget and many parts of the system were directed toward planning, research, and development for the project. A total funding figure is not available, but the general figure of $250,000 covers a considerable amount of direct expenses. Implementation itself is confined to the instructional salary limits of the two pilot schools involved. There will be, however, sizeable ongoing research and development, planning and evaluation programs.

10. There is a general feeling, unsupported as yet by research, that special facilities designed specifically for alternative models is desirable. In any case, facilities for teacher planning offices and meeting areas, large group, small group, and independent study, lounging and recreation and reading rooms for students are almost mandated.

11. Some involved were reluctant to describe themselves as change agents, but instead preferred the term, *change managers.* Others did view themselves as change agents.

12. A formal task analysis was undertaken in Dade County.

MARY HARMON WEEKS ELEMENTARY SCHOOL, KANSAS CITY, MISSOURI DIFFERENTIATED STAFFING PROJECT

1. Mary Harmon Weeks Elementary School is designed for 1000 pupils with ages that range from five to eleven years, and is a part of the City district of Kansas City, Missouri. The at large population of Kansas

City and surrounding Jackson County is well over a million. Not only is it located in an urban center, but Mary Harmon Weeks is classified by the Kansas City system as a central city school. Its population is largely black and its concerns are with the needs and readiness levels of the inner-city child.

2. Only very limited media coverage was given the Mary Harmon Weeks Elementary School Differentiated Staffing Project. However, considerable interest has been shown nationwide and hundreds of letters, over a thousand brochures describing the differentiated staffing project, and local guided tours have been a part of a larger national interest.

3. There is no doubt that the Education Profession Development Act and the personal charisma of Dr. Don Davies of the USOE gave great impetus to the Kansas City project. However, the germ of the idea originated in Kansas City needs studies of an ongoing nature several years before the actual funding of the project.

Certainly one of the assumptions leading to differentiated staffing concerned the idea of *innovation*—that in order to be dynamic and effective a profession must have members and groups which create. This idea was the seed bed for the Mary Harmon Weeks project.

Another generating factor was the Kansas City philosophy and objective paradigm. Since the central city school students to which the system was directing its experimental efforts were culturally different from the middle class mean, and that their needs as well were different, the question arose as to how traditional staffing patterns, designed primarily for middle class and suburban children, could satisfy inner-city needs.

In addition to cultural, and socio-economic differences, the philosophy-goal-objective entity addressed itself to the vast differences between young students of any one cultural or ethnic group. There were the differences of physical growth, intellectual development, social maturity, and other multiplex interrelated personality areas concerning the individual elementary school pupil, all of which factors condition and influence the nature of learning, the modality of instruction, and the overall and limitless gestalt of the learning-instruction environment. Of all of this thought and study given to staffing considerations in Kansas, the uppermost question was how can the instructional-learning program be individualized?

It was in the midst of these deep problems that differentiated staffing emerged nationally, and Kansas City picked it up. How Kansas City adapted to this new innovation will show more clearly in a description of the Mary Harmon Weeks project which follows later.

4. In many respects earlier Federal programs such as the Elementary and Secondary Education Act of 1968, Title I for disadvantaged children and Title III for innovative programs had paved the way. The public

was not only accustomed to change but was demanding change. The school board, as well, was change oriented and forward looking. All were eager to experiment. There was little in the way of selling which needed to be done, except for a laying out of careful planning.

5. There was limited opposition from organized ranks of elementary principals throughout the Kansas City system, most of which stemmed from a speech by a well-known proponent of differentiated staffing heard by one of the principals, which had been titled, "Is the School Principal Obsolete?" Odd how one small coincidence like this could have started some minor but well organized opposition.

Too, there was some opposition among teachers, but this diminished as they became more involved in the program.

6. The differentiated staffing project at the Mary Harmon Weeks Elementary School can best be described by the following simple outline:

Philosophy
The system plan
Staffing description
The personnel model
Program highlights

In philosophy, the school is committed to certain beliefs: that inner-city children be accepted and attended to by a sophisticated learning team, that each child receive the most highly developed learning environment, that each child experience an individualized curriculum, and that each child realize continuous progress.

In order to meet some of these needs a systems plan incorporating large group, small group, and individualized or independent study was evolved. Non-grading and team teaching components were added. Flexible scheduling, resource centers, materials centers, and open plan building facilities were added to assemble a total system.

The staffing arrangement at Mary Harmon Weeks specifies several different levels of responsibility and assigns titles to the staffing pattern. It should be understood that each of these titles has been defined through rather studied analysis of function and job description.

Position levels are as follows:

Level 1   Coordinating instructor
Level 2   Senior instructor
Level 3   Instructor
Level 4   Associate instructor
Level 5   Intern

Level 6   Student teacher

Level 7   Paraprofessional

Certainly, one of the most outstanding features of the Kansas City project is the total organizational model, which graphically illustrates all aspects of the organic system. The following illustration serves to point out the consideration given by the Kansas City system to careful planning.

One of the noticeable features of Figure 7–2 is the versatility of its use. Such a chart readily illustrates communication lines as well as a strong focus on technology. Quite clearly, the chart demonstrates a well-structured advisory complex, and a sharply defined democratic (as opposed to a laissez faire or authoritarian) atmosphere—an arena for shared decision making.

The program highlights of the project are manifest. Such an arrangement insures developing and field testing of instructional methods and materials. Shared decision making is a major part of this project. With teachers involved in developing system-wide strategies, and the engendering of a professional tone, the project tends to attract highly competent teachers. In keeping with this professional setting, new teachers are helped by organized supervisory assistance and staff development programs which involve all staff members.

Near and at the bottom of the chart one cannot help but notice the input of community resources, non-credentialed staff, into the system.

7. The attitude of the differentiated staff at Mary Harmon Weeks Elementary School in Kansas City is good. The staff has a good feeling about the organization and their place in it, their involvement in planning, in development of instructional strategies and materials, in scheduling, and in their meaningful part in the operation of the system.

8. The Weeks School in Kansas sets an entirely new pattern of instruction. Before there was frustration and almost hopelessness felt by the individual teacher in the face of great environmental odds. Today, the pattern of team work, of capitalizing on individual teacher strengths is a trademark of the Kansas City model.

The rather extensive use of paraprofessionals in the Kansas City model is also something that has come about through the differentiated staffing project.

In addition, there is real teacher involvement in decision making, a real commitment to practical research and development, and planning, that did not exist before.

9. Although total cost dollars are difficult to project because of total system commitment to such large items as school plant, sustaining salaries for teachers, planning, and support, the rough estimate would be around

CABINET

Principal

Primary Coordinating Instructor
Intermediate Coordinating Instructor
Administrative Coordinating Instructor

INSTRUCTIONAL COUNCIL

Senior Instructors
Instructors
Associate Instructors
Interns
(Both primary and intermediate)

SUPPORTIVE SERVICES

Personnel in: AV Resource, Physical
Education, Art, Pupil Services, Instrumental
Music, Health, Vocal Music.

NON-CREDENTIALED STAFF

Clerks, Student Teachers, Resource Persons,
other Paraprofessionals as needed

FIG. 7-2 DIFFERENTIATED STAFFING MODEL

$80,000 as an in-house figure for specific development and early implementation of the model.

10. Kansas City does subscribe to the idea of customized facilities for customized programs. As have other school systems, Kansas City built open plan for the Weeks system and continues to build open plan schools in anticipation of future staff development.

Adjoining rooms without walls, or the open plan school, encourages greater interaction between teachers and students, teachers and teachers, and students and students. There are no artificial barriers to compartmentalize teachers and students, no self-imposed strictures to an otherwise open and heuristic curriculum, and no pat lock-step boxes to enclose an artificial learning environment about which every theory knows very little.

Such an open plan is well suited to differentiated staffing.

11. The project directors, teachers, and supporting administrative staff may all be viewed as change agents. Each feels a keen interest in bettering American education through careful planning and innovation.

12. A task analysis involving philosophy and good setting, objective determination, and projection of staff was undertaken in Kansas City. Though the differentiated staff was implemented perhaps in advance of desired further study, nevertheless the Kansas City model stands as an example of early rudimental task analysis.

LOUISVILLE, KENTUCKY, PUBLIC SCHOOL SYSTEM DIFFERENTIATED STAFFING PROJECT

1. The Louisville, Kentucky Public School System is a city district with 55,000 students in 70 schools. The differentiated staffing project is located in the city district. Of the total schools in Louisville, fourteen schools are involved in the differentiated staffing project, nine elementary schools, four junior high schools, and one senior high school. There are 700 staff members involved, and over 11,000 students. Many of the students are inner-city, with a large proportion of black students. The population of the Louisville metropolitan area is a little less than one million.

2. There was extensive media coverage of the differentiated staffing idea in the Louisville media, which was solicited in order to inform as much of the public as possible. As one of the administrative officials connected with the project has said, the project officials did not want to hide anything "under a bushel basket." Thus it was thought by all of the administrative staff that total community involvement, even in a city as large as Louisville, would be sought.

3. The major reason for starting a differentiated staffing project in

Louisville was the real necessity for change. Personnel in leadership positions here were seeing traditional programs which did not seem to work. Both lay citizens and school personnel were seeing achievement scores go down, the dropout rate increase, rising school student suspensions, inability to attract top teachers to inner city schools, and rising delinquency, a number of problems which seemed insolvable through traditional means.

The differentiated staffing project grew out of a total look at the educational process in Louisville and was a part of a wide task force outcome associated with many other facets of the system.

The leadership of the superintendent, the school board, and the total Louisville Central Office staff led to the further appointment of an advisory group. Grant requests were written for projects under the Education Professions Development Act, the More Effective School Personnel Utilization program, the Teacher Corps, and the Career Opportunities Program. Louisville was also incorporated into the Federal Government Site Concentration where many Federal programs could be brought to bear.

4. The general public was aware of the need to change, and expected and wanted change. The large advisory group which worked early with the project accepted this challenge, and looked for better new ways to do what the public expected of education.

There was, of course, total support from the Louisville School Board from the start, and strong interest and leadership from the change-oriented superintendent of schools. Media helped to get the project off the ground and also helped to get greater public acceptance of the idea.

5. There was some opposition to differentiated staffing, mostly from teachers who felt more comfortable with the older, traditional patterns—the single classroom, tenure in an unchanging milieu. These, and even some otherwise fairly innovative teachers, were opposed to ideas of working cooperatively and sharing responsibilities with teams of people. Some teachers were afraid of new roles.[2]

6. The differentiated staffing project in Louisville is subsumed under a very large overall mandate for change in the system. There are several different models, mostly organized around the important idea that the principal is the principal learning facilitator, supported by a business manager. The general design of a typical differentiated staffing team could be listed as follows in a team of eight to twelve adults: one coordinating teacher, one staff teacher, four special teachers who work with for interns, two paraprofessionals. Working with these are student teachers and parent volunteers, with the total staff working with from 100 to

[2]Generally, the symptoms of opposition to change were classic. For a general discussion of these, see chapter 4.

110 students in many instances. This particular staffing arrangement is referred to in Louisville as the Teacher Corps Model, or Project Focus.

Another model, the so-called Impact Model, has one teacher co-ordinator, two staff teachers, three paraprofessionals and a variable number of student teachers and parent volunteers.

Paraprofessionals in the program do everything their skills and abilities will allow them to do, from clerking and typing to full time teaching. The Louisville system expands the role of what is normally thought of as a paraprofessional.

7. The general attitude of the staff is positive. Working on the differentiated staffing teams and being associated with such a far-reaching pattern of change is exciting and meaningful to the participants involved in the project.

8. One important factor has to do with the recruitment of teachers for inner-city schools. Before the project began, it was very difficult to attract and retain teachers to these tough jobs. Now teachers stay and morale is high.

Another difference is in the increased interest of the principal and staff in the learning process.

In addition, student suspensions are down. General delinquency and vandalism has diminished. In some models, but not all, achievement levels have increased.

One overall thrust of the differentiated staffing project was to introduce a philosophy to all the schools of the system that "it would be all right to be different." This encouragement of change has created subtle variations, and some major variations in the differentiated staffing modules. Before change was difficult to come by.

9. It is difficult to sort out all of the programs associated with differentiated staffing in the Louisville schools, for the system is undergoing considerable change in a number of areas involving several major multimillion dollar programs. However, under the Education Professions Development Act there is a More Effective School Personnel Utilization grant for $130,000; the FOCUS program under the Teacher Corps is approximately $700,000, and the Career Opportunity Program grant is for approximately $250,000. Thus, considerable expenditures have already gone into the program in its first phase.

10. The differentiated staffing project in Louisville is operating in existing buildings not specifically planned for new ideas in flexible staffing. Here and there in the system some walls have been knocked out. Greater use is being made of all available large areas, and rearrangements in traditional classrooms have been made to allow different kinds of teacher leadership.

It is granted by those directly associated with the project that open space buildings would facilitate the new staffing arrangements and allow the flexibility which would be required in second and future generation staffing patterns.

Special facilities for large group and small group, that is for 200, 300, or more students, space for five to eight students, and rooms for individual teacher and student, and other individual student arrangements are definitely needed.

11. There were many change agents working in the Louisville School System. Certainly the members of the School Board and the Superintendent himself were oriented to and actively seeking change. With the Superintendent's leadership his entire central office staff supported and encouraged change. This environment was also reflected at the project staff level and among the teachers on the firing line.

The Louisville differentiated staffing project represents an example where the total commitment at the top opened the way for creative change below. Here there were no rigid guidelines or hampering rules. Rather different and creative ways of doing things were solicited and accepted by the top echelons.

12. The Central Office Staff organized and maintained a task force effort for analysis of the system. A sizeable Research and Development Component within the Central Staff composed of well-qualified research practitioners gave considerable support to the task force. Consequently, the Louisville project undertook a system-wide analysis, and developed rather sophisticated data gathering instruments for future analysis of results.

MARIN COUNTY SCHOOLS
201 TAMAL VISTA BOULEVARD
CORTE MADERA, CALIFORNIA

1. The differentiated staffing project within Marin County encompasses three local school districts out of twenty-two autonomous districts. In addition to these, which work with the intermediary county office, some San Francisco City schools are involved in the project. In all, there were originally seventeen schools involved at the project's start in 1969, but by 1971, the number was reduced to eleven because of budgetary restraints. These eleven schools comprise seven elementary schools, three middle schools, and one high school.

The student makeup of the Marin County Schools is predominantly of affluent middle and upper middle class suburbians. The San Francisco schools' students, however, are of mixed socio-economic and racial background.

The Bay area, the locale of this differentiated staffing endeavor, has an overall population of well over two million people.

2. Media coverage of differentiated staffing was not actively sought or really stressed in the Marin County project. The general administrative staff felt that coverage might be too much influenced by the Temple City Model, which had had much press coverage, particularly in California.

There were the usual reports of school board meetings. Materials produced mainly for and directed toward teachers was widely disseminated throughout the area.

In general, communication within the school system was encouraged as opposed to publicity releases to the public at large.

3. The impetus came from a USOE grant request under certain guidelines of the Education Professions Development Act. At that time, the project writer, Dr. Hollis Moore, was finishing his work at Stanford University. Under one section of EPDA, Dr. Moore was seeking staff development funds. However, he found that under another section tied in with School Personnel Utilization (SPU) the USOE provided a more helpful framework for what he hoped to accomplish in Marin County.

Whereas earlier Dr. Moore had hoped to develop a paraprofessional training program, he now found that the emphasis in this earlier program on minority groups, more closely associated with urban areas, could not apply to his own situation in a relatively affluent suburban district. Thus, Dr. Moore shifted his thinking from the section or part of the Education Professions Development Act which emphasized minority employment, to a more experimental part of the EPDA which emphasized new staffing patterns.

In this shift, the original ideas were almost completely revised, in accord with SPU guidelines, in the direction of exploring teacher leadership talent and teacher support areas.

Quite clearly here the start of the Marin County Differentiated Staffing idea sprang from a combination of local needs and broad, innovative, stimulating federal guidelines.

4. The fact that the USOE was willing to invest money in the experimental concept of differentiated staffing provided a major focus for school board interest and involvement. Not to be overlooked, however, was the interest among school board members and lay citizens stimulated by the possibility of greatly enhancing a planned staff development program. That a training design could be instituted which would improve the calibre of professional staff, provide for innovative teacher leadership, and improve overall staff structure and staff utilization, were the motivating factors for the support of school board and citizens.

5. In varying degrees, there was a considerable amount of opposi-

tion. Much early opposition faded as opponents of differentiated staffing came to know more. In fact, a ratio or proportion might probably be shown to exist to the effect that those who understood the least opposed the ideas the most.

Much of the early opposition came from those who thought a model such as Temple City's would be imposed on the Marin County system. As these opponents discovered that there would be no static "perfect model" forced on them, but that the process in which they would be involved would provide their system with unique differentiated staffing models that would meet their own situation, opposition began to fade. In this respect large numbers of personnel needed to know that differentiated staffing did not mean the imposition of a model, but instead pointed to the process of assessing needs, determining philosophy, goals, and objectives, and setting priorities. They needed to know that all this would be done through them, that is through work with the total staff. That there would be no preconceived notions, but explorations instead, and with a broad range of personnel, had to be stressed and understood.

As the Marin County project reached its third year in 1971, however, there was still residual opposition from teacher groups still set against the idea of hiring and utilizing uncertificated personnel, aides, clerks, and other paraprofessionals. Especially considering the surplus of certificated teachers in many areas, and the dearth of available jobs, were organized teacher groups resisting new differentiated staffing models. They seemed to view the hiring of paraprofessionals as preempting their own jobs.

There was, in addition, a third area of opposition. Building administrators were reluctant to see shared decision making, not to mention broad teacher involvement in what had heretofore been their exclusive domain.

What had been sizeable opposition at first diminished to smaller pockets of resistance as understanding grew.

6. The project in Marin County is basically a differentiated staffing plan exploring role categories of teacher coordinators, resource teachers, team leaders, staff teachers, and such special paraprofessionals as student teachers, interns, instructional assistants, clerical aides, and community volunteer resource persons willing to give limited time in their area of expertise such as law, medicine, architecture, and other professional areas. Also, the use of regular parent volunteers for small group help, library assistance, and preliminary checking and grading of papers, as well as exploration of cross-age tutoring between high school students and elementary children.

7. Attitudes cover a wide spectrum, in that the Marin County project incorporated into its design existing schools and inherited staffs. Such

an eclectic program is bound to present different viewpoints. Staffs range from the most conservative self-contained classroom modality to those more interested in team teaching, flexible scheduling, and intergrouping. There is a mixture of younger and older teachers. In a sense, this staff could be said, if we might use the term, to be representative of a sample of middle America.

On the whole, there is a good attitude with no staff rebellion or lost schools. Those who started with the project wish to remain with it. Other schools not in the project have expressed a desire to join it.

There is an exceptionally good feeling among various leadership personnel such as team teachers, resource teachers, and coordinators who, to be of real service, are anxious to expand their sphere of influence throughout the staff teacher ranks.

There are some negative feelings, some who wish not to want to become involved. Once staff gets involved, it shows high interest.

8. Previous to the start of the project, teachers had a tendency to remain isolated, each individually pursuing his own interests with a minimum of staff-school relationships.

Now teachers, with enlarged perspective, generally seek involvement, and are interested in analysis and planning. These increased efforts in planning and development are the most startling changes.

There has been a shift among building administrators as well, who are now more willing to share in decision making, to discern and use the strengths of teachers. There is less "seat of the pants" administration, and more thought-out management, and an interest in such innovative practices as flexible time, flexible space, and new arrangements of students and teachers.

No longer do teachers try to be all things to all students. Teachers know they cannot be all things. They recognize their own strengths and build on them.

9. Here, as in most differentiated staffing projects, cost analysis is not exact because of the tendency to overlap in old budgets and new grants. However, the budget from March 1, 1969 to June of 1972 can be estimated at $309,000 for 17 schools (March, 1969–June, 1971) and 11 schools (June, 1971–June, 1972).

10. It has been possible in the project to do many things just by knocking holes in walls to give flexibility. It is estimated, though, by the project staff that there would be greater achievement with open space schools, which would give mobility to teachers, aides, and students in a way not now possible.

11. The director of the project and many involved in the staff do consider themselves change agents who are trying to encourage and facilitate change, to find new and better ways of doing things.

12. There was incremental planning, that is, planning from step to step, but no formal task analysis or really long-range planning was done. The system is now rethinking the project and undertaking task analysis.

PROPOSED NEW YORK CITY
DIFFERENTIATED STAFFING MODEL—DISTRICT THREE,
NEW YORK CITY BOARD OF EDUCATION[3]

1. Activity in differentiated staffing in District Three of the New York City Board of Education is postulated on a project proposal submitted to the United States Office of Education under the Education Professions Development Act. At the time of this writing, the model is purely speculative and the following statements conjecture.

The original proposal entitled "Careers in Education" directed itself to the construction of a prototype differentiated staffing model for inner-city, metropolitan school systems.

At the time of this writing it had not been ascertained where the differentiated staffing project was to be placed, whether at Public School Number 11 or Public School Number 130, both medium-sized city schools in the Manhattan Borough, New York City.

The population, both student and community at large, reflects the inner-city around Public School 1, located in the lower east side of Manhattan. This is a special service school area of economically disadvantaged, essentially minority groups with ethnic distributions of Blacks (4%), Oriental (65%), Puerto Rican (25%) and other ethnic origin (6%).

2. There was local and some national coverage of the differentiated staffing project proposal, entitled "Career in the Classroom."

3. Need for system renewal seems to have been an early impetus to the New York City differentiated staffing project. There seems also to be interest in New York City among several groups of persons, what the project proposal refers to as "multi-institutional linkages," in establishing more viable organization models for a large metropolitan inner-city system. In fact, a unique feature of the present proposal is the interorganizational coalition formed which includes

1. The United Federation of Teachers in New York City
2. District Three, New York City Public Schools, and
3. New York University

[3]This project report is based on a conjectured model fashioned through an analysis of project proposals and other releases from the New York City area.

All of these groups were instrumental in developing the differentiated staffing model which is presented later in this section.

4. Several letters of support from various parent groups, as well as school board personnel, indicate that there was considerable communication and involvement in the New York City project. This was the key to support.

5. What opposition there was centered mostly around whether or not differentiated staffing was some form of merit pay. This opposition diminished as teachers began to understand the concept defined in the project proposal as a career model, or career lattice. The restriction of the pilot project to one or two schools in lower Manhattan may have dampened broader criticism and opposition, but this assumption must wait for proof on a wide application of the differentiated staffing model to other parts of the city.

6. The project description is based on the EPDA proposal mentioned earlier and is based on a number of premises:

1. That there is a need for a metropolitan differentiated staffing design for inner-city schools.
2. That such a model ought to meet the direct needs of the city schools.
3. That the professional role of the teacher ought to be enlarged particularly in the decision-making area.
4. That career entry and career development ought to be associated with preservice and inservice training.

One point well established in the project proposal concerns the high turnover rate among teachers in larger metropolitan systems. The New York City Board of Education indicates that of the teachers who enter teaching each year, 50 percent will leave for other occupations by the end of the second year. This accounts, then, for the emphasis in the project on career entry and career development.

Professional aspects of the project deal with the status of teaching and with the tendency of the present educational system to behave paradoxically. As it is stated in the EPDA proposal, "Paradoxically, education is one of the few social enterprises that rewards excellent performance by promoting the individual away from the client he is trained to serve."

Community needs are met, in the project proposal to develop and implement, through interaction of community groups, the New York City Public Schools, and professional personnel from New York University.

Finally, the idea of developing a prototype differentiated staffing model for inner-city schools was stressed in the proposal.

Objectives of the proposal are listed as follows:

1. To develop and implement two staff structures—one for a five level professional teacher staff, and one for a three level paraprofessional "career lattice."
2. To provide for lateral entry points in the career structure.
3. To develop a career model which emphasizes instructional change adaptable to a variety of inner-city school settings.
4. To demonstrate how teachers can be more significantly involved in decision making.
5. To demonstrate that the experienced teacher can function as a university adjunct professor.
6. To demonstrate that the differentiated staff can be employed in screening, selecting, and training of career possibility individuals for teaching.
7. To develop new types of teacher-administration roles.
8. To develop an organizational model, self-regulatory for the teaching profession.
9. To provide a model responsive to the minority, inner-city child.
10. To create a new learning environment based upon varying individual learning rates.

A further part of the well-organized plan for differentiated staffing relates to the several groups of variables which would bear on the total school systems. The units listed are:

ORGANIZATION
Team teaching
Nongraded instruction
Flexible scheduling
Large group-small group instruction

CURRICULUM
Continuous progress curriculum
Individualized learning materials
Instructional behavioral, or performance objectives
Independent study

TECHNOLOGY
Computer assisted instruction
Programmed instruction (paper, print)

Other hardware, software, teaching machines
Audio
Audio-visual, other media

FACILITIES
Instructional resource center
Instructional materials center
Independent study carrels
Large group-small group instructional space
Team planning and teacher office space.

Considerations listed for training modules in the proposed program of differentiated staffing were as follows:

Instructional management concepts
Organizational behavior
Community relations
Community analysis
Systems monitoring
Evaluation
Research methods
Educational change and the change process

Figure 7–3 illustrates the career levels as listed in the EPDA project proposal.

A description of the varying roles which offer upward mobility for all personnel follows:

Intern teachers are viewed as those who are seeking entry as a professional, a beginning or apprentice teacher. There is a minimum of responsibility in teaching. A probationary teacher has completed a year of satisfactory service as an intern and his level of performances in content and methodology would represent an increase over that of the intern. He would require further training under the adjunct professor, as he proceeds with full time teaching and membership on an instructional team. The staff teacher has completed all probationary service and is tenured in a professionally demanding position emphasizing diagnostic skills, sophistication in curriculum design, understanding of the appropriate use of technology and media and general teaching expertise. A coordinating cluster teacher has demonstrated competencies in leadership skills. He would assume responsibilities for proper application and implementation of total instructional programs in the classroom. He provides assist-

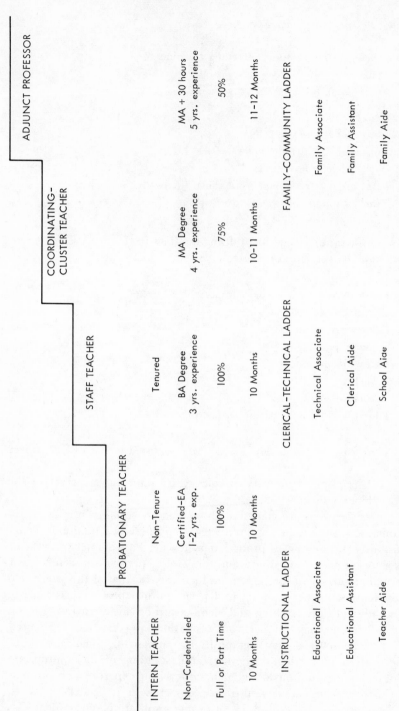

FIG. 7–3 PROPOSED DIFFERENTIATED STAFFING MODEL-DISTRICT THREE, NEW YORK CITY, EPDA PROPOSAL

ance and direction to the teaching staff under his general direction. He is as well a master practitioner. An exemplary teacher with depth in experience, and ability to train others may become an adjunct professor. His strengths are manifold in the science and art of teaching and in his subject or skill area. He teaches students as do the other members of the differentiated staff, but he also has major responsibilities in screening, selecting, and training interns and probationary teachers.

The paraprofessional ranks also have upward mobility, and the roles may be defined as follows: There is the *instructional ladder* composed of personnel who work in activities related to the instructional process in special study areas, libraries, and in the general classroom. For example, the teacher aide with no previous experience or paraprofessional training may prepare instructional materials under teacher direction, score objective tests, or monitor halls, playground, lunchrooms and the like. Educational assistants and educational associates assume more and more responsibility.

A second part of the paraprofessional ranks includes the *clerical-technical ladder* of school aides, clerical assistants, and technical associates, all of whom perform clerical, secretarial, and technical work of increasing complexity.

Finally, there is the *family community ladder:* the family aide to serve as liaison between home and school; the family assistant who helps families understand school homework, school goals and organization, and generally works in school community relations; and the family associate, who assumes a greater responsibility in community-school relations in such related and complex areas as the school lunch program, and general homemaking as it affects the student. His responsibility is to raise the level of home environment.

7. This question is not applicable at this time. No data was currently available at this writing.

8. Any number of books on ghetto schools are readily available. The descriptions may be more or less applicable to the school district in consideration. However, even so, the plans and projections of the differentiated staffing project in the New York City Model show great promise to drastically change the total picture of inner-city schools for the better. Such items as better facilities, more personalized learning, retention of a highly professional staff with community service, and the like might be listed as what now is promised.

9. Cost studies were not available at the time of this writing.

10. Consideration in the project proposal was given to several facility and space problems. It seemed readily apparent that such things as resource and materials centers are almost mandatory, as are areas for large and small group instruction, independent study carrels, space for team and cluster meetings, and office-counseling space for individual teachers.

11. Certainly all of the many individuals in the coordinating institutions view themselves as change agents helping to create a more meaningful differentiated staffing model for inner-city schools, one which may, in fact, be a prototype.

12. The interorganizational coalition mentioned earlier in this report provided much incremental planning for the project. Parts of the project itself will provide further task analyses.

SARASOTA COUNTY SCHOOL SYSTEM DIFFERENTIATED STAFFING PROJECT

1. The Sarasota school system is a county district system in which the chief city and county seat is Sarasota. The name of the county is Sarasota County. The population of the county at large is slightly over 100,000, with the City of Sarasota having a population of around 50,000. There are in the county eleven 1–6 schools, one kindergarten school, four K–6 schools, one 3–9 school, two 1–12 schools, and three 10–12 schools, in all a great variety of organization reflecting the philosophy of the county—local options for local needs. To date six schools are participating in the differentiated staffing project, and of these three have implemented the Sarasota process model partially or in full. One selected school, the Venice Junior High School, and its differentiated staffing project are discussed later in this section.

The student population of around 4000 students is largely of a white middle socio-economic background with around 10 percent of the total population representing minority disadvantaged groups. There is considerable achievement spread among the student population. In general, the senior class achievement scores (based on college entrance exams) often rank at the top of Florida's total scoring.

2. There was press, radio, and television coverage of the Sarasota staffing project. In addition, there was wide dissemination of mimeographed material and printed brochures among Sarasota faculty and community members. Numerous speeches were made as well at local civic club luncheons and dinners concerning the project.

3. The Sarasota school system has for several years carried on programs in study for system improvement. As an innovative system, personnel in the Sarasota County district have regularly examined new ideas and approaches which seemed to hold promise. In May of 1968, the Sarasota School Board, administrative staff, and teacher associations began to study the potential of differentiated staffing, which had then recently come to national attention. Initial interest led to further data gathering, much reading, discussion, and further planning, which led to a

county administrative directive organizing a continuing study of differentiated staffing. Following this, members of the administrative staff and faculty conducted on-site visits of existing programs in Temple City, California, and Kansas City, Missouri.

Concurrently with the Sarasota County School Board Administrative Study, the Sarasota County Teachers Association appointed a representative committee consisting of all levels of instructional personnel to study differentiated staffing in order to assess its value to Sarasota County Schools. At the end of seven months of study, this committee recommended to the Sarasota County Teachers Association that differentiated staffing should be endorsed for further study and possible implementation.

On March 11, 1969, the Sarasota School Board approved the concept of a differentiated staffing steering committee composed of the following proposed voting membership:

6 Classroom teachers (1 elementary and 1 secondary from each senior high school area)
1 Counselor
2 Department or grade-level chairmen (1 elementary and 1 secondary)
1 Representative of educational media services
1 Representative of pupil personnel services
1 Subject area supervisor
1 Supervisor of intern teachers
1 Representative of vocational-technical and adult education
1 Aide
1 Representative of business services
2 Principals (1 elementary and 1 secondary)
1 Director
1 Assistant superintendent for instruction
1 Representative of Sarasota County Teachers Association
1 Representative of the citizens advisory committee
1 Director of staff development (to serve as "executive secretary")

Much of the rest of the start of differentiated staffing in Sarasota concerns voluntary initial involvement and utilization of State of Florida Educational Improvement Funds and United States Office of Education Funds to further and crystallize the idea.

4. The general public and the school board were convinced to support differentiated staffing by close communication with the school administrative staff and faculty. An informed administration fully explained to the school board what was to be attempted and recommended

a method to follow. Clearly outlined procedures were followed from the start; this system design and good lines of communication insured the support of differentiated staffing in Sarasota.

5. Hesitations and concerns were voiced in Sarasota by several groups and individuals. There was, however, school board, administration, and faculty commitment to the idea that *no* model of differentiated staffing would be *imposed*. In this regard the central administration joined with the Sarasota County Teachers Association, and interested staff members of several schools for a two-year study which led to eventual implementation of models in volunteer schools.

6. Study in Sarasota led to the central idea that any differentiated staffing model designed, or other outcomes, would be subservient to the unique philosophy, goals, needs, and objectives of each school. In addition, certain minimum school system standards of staff allocation, job specifications, salaries, and instructional programs would need to be maintained. The outcome was to produce a process and a *System Model* which would be broadly applicable to the entire school system of Sarasota County.

This overall paradigm then would be subdivided into two sub-models—the staffing sub-model attained by process, and the implementation sub-model obtained by county-wide formula based on allocation of school personnel.

The staffing sub-model is best seen in Figure 7–4, which shows horizontal differentiated tasks—four broad function areas.

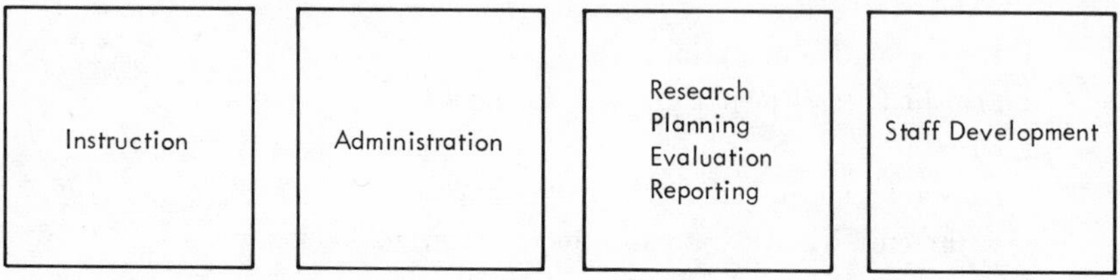

| Instruction | Administration | Research Planning Evaluation Reporting | Staff Development |

These are all viewed as co-equal functions. In practice, a directing teacher, for example, might have 60% instruction, 20% administration, 10% research, planning, evaluation reporting, and 10% staff development, for which component-percentage time is paid.

FIG. 7–4   HORIZONTAL DIFFERENTIATION

Vertical differentiation is evidenced by a hierarchical rank as follows:

Vertical Differentiation

Principal or principal-teacher

Consulting teacher

Directing teacher

Staff teacher

Instructor

Resident intern

Paraprofessional personnel

   a. Instructional assistant

   b. Teacher aide

   c. Student assistant

   d. Adjunct teacher

   e. Volunteer assistant

The relative placement of these differentiated staffing positions may be seen in Figure 7–5.

FIG. 7–5 VERTICAL DIFFERENTIATION

Principal teacher	A = 55%	R = 20%	S = 15%	I = 10%
Consulting teacher	A = 20%	R = 10%	S = 10%	I = 60%
Directing teacher	A = 25%	R = 25%	S = 25%	I = 25%
Staff teacher				
Instructor				
Resident intern				
Instructional assistant	All percentages would be allocated as			
Aide	demonstrated above			
Student assistant				
Volunteer assistant				
Adjunct teacher				

I = Instruction, A = Administration, R = research, planning, evaluation, reporting, S = Staff development.

If one uses both the horizontal differentiation and the vertical differentiation paradigm it would be possible to illustrate graphically the horizontal and vertical responsibilities and placement on *levels* of responsibility. Thus the unique conceptualization of the design enables us to overlay a horizontal differentiation graph over a vertical differentiation graph and come up with a graphic functional position chart on each member of the staff.

Responsibilities of each of the various vertical positions can be described briefly. The consulting teacher has primary responsibility for leadership in a broad area of instruction. His responsibilities might include supervising of grade levels, managing a particular subject throughout a variety of grade levels, coordinating staff developments, or planning research evaluation—reporting work, together with administration. The directing teacher is responsible for leading a limited part of the instructional program, and is among other things a master teacher who should be expert in one or more of its areas. Staff teachers are comparable to the traditional classroom teacher with tenure, and are assigned to work in a single team or to one single duty in a specified function area. The instructor is a beginning teacher who remains probationary for three years, and works with and assists staff or directing teachers. Resident interns are college students who are in their final year of preservice training, supervised in instructional situations by various senior staff members. The three levels of paraprofessionals perform limited work on a full time assignment. For example, an instructional assistant instructs, but only under continued supervision. Aides and student assistants perform work of a clerical or technical nature and are sometimes called on to supervise small groups working, for example, with programmed materials. The adjunct teacher is a lay citizen who is expert in some field of the arts, sciences, business, or technology. Perhaps drawn from the ranks of Sarasota's retired community, he or she works on a daily demand basis. Volunteer assistants are from the community at large working as their ability and skill is called on. The principal, or principal-teacher, is the person in the school having ultimate legal responsibility for the instructional program. His authority is delegated by the district superintendent whose duties are prescribed by law. Note in the Sarasota plan that the principal or principal-teacher may still, in transition, be viewed as a "final authority figure," but, as is happening in some Sarasota schools, may perhaps evolve into *one* member of a faculty governing board, in which each member has an equal vote in decision making and school management.

Freedom to implement any part of the vertical and horizontal differentiated staff is theoretically and practically possible in Sarasota schools. Essentially, though, formulas are at work which

1. Specify a process for staff allocation
2. Divide county schools into several classifications according to size and type
3. Assign unit values to each requested position in the vertical hierarchy
4. Specify a procedure for determining needs and approximating number of job classifications needed at a particular school
5. Prescribe by standard index and chart which job specifications may be collated for each staff member
6. Finally, there is a handbook of general criteria by which the total staff is held accountable for performance.

Venice Junior High School provides us with an example of a typical pilot school in Sarasota County now under differentiated staffing. Located in suburban Venice, Florida, it houses grades seven, eight, and nine with an enrollment of 900 students. Venice Junior High School has been allocated 44.7 staff units based upon a student-teacher ratio formula of approximately 20 to 1. Using the various procedural formulae, the school's faculty board proposed the following staffing pattern:

Differentiated Staffing Pattern for Venice Junior High School

Department	*Staff*
English	1 Directing teacher
	4 Staff teachers
	1 Instructor
	2 Aides
Mathematics	1 Directing teacher
	2 Staff teachers
	1 Instructional assistant
	1.5 Aides
	8 Student assistants (one hour/day)
Science	1 Directing teacher
	4 Staff teachers
	2 Aides
	1 Student assistant
Social Studies	1 Directing teacher
	2 Staff teachers
	2 Instructors
	2 Aides
Physical Education	1 Directing teacher
	4 Staff teachers
Foreign Language	1 Directing teacher
	3 Staff teachers
	1.5 Aides
Electives	1 Directing teacher
	2 Staff teachers
	2 Part-time staff teachers
	3 Instructors
	1.5 Aides
Instructional Media	1 Part-time directing teacher
	1 Staff teacher
	3 Aides
Counseling and Administration	1 Staff teacher
	1 Principal
	1 Directing teacher (research-evaluation-staff development)

7. There is an overall feeling of confidence and assuredness which comes from a job well understood and well done pervading both staff and involved persons associated with the differentiated staffing project in Sarasota.

8. Sarasota has for a long time been able to attract highly qualified teachers. The school system in the county has consequently flourished. Differentiated staffing has provided new systems of organization that are up to the professional grade and calibre of the advanced personnel which Sarasota continues to attract. Most of those associated with the differentiated staffing project view the present period as the end of one epoch and the beginning of an outstandingly new age, an age with a sense of urgency about it, a new evolutionary plateau for education.

9. It is interesting to note that though planning, research, and development costs were about $200,000 (training, staff development, total involvement of the system in allied or tangential operations being considered), actual implementation of models, once formulae are developed, is rather low.

As an example the following chart shows a comparison of traditional salary costs to differentiated staff salaries:

COMPARISON OF SALARY COSTS AT VENICE JUNIOR HIGH SCHOOL

Department	Traditional Staff Salaries	Differentiated Staff Salaries
English	$ 58,755	$ 58,302
Mathematics	49,720	45,558
Science	53,500	52,844
Social studies	46,482	44,556
Physical education	43,326	44,834
Foreign language	40,764	40,010
Electives	50,659	53,887
Instructional media, counseling, and administration	61,434	60.973
	$404,640	$400,964

However, ongoing research and development, planning and evaluation, and the like are phase-in costs which remain with a progressive minded system wishing to maintain and improve its differentiated staffing models.

10. Many different types of facilities are being tried in Sarasota and at the time of this writing no evidence fully supported one type of facility over another.

11. Those associated with the differentiated staffing project in Sarasota do view themselves as change agents.

12. A formal task analysis was undertaken in Sarasota County.

TEMPLE CITY UNIFIED SCHOOL DISTRICT (CALIFORNIA) DIFFERENTIATED STAFFING PROJECT

1. The Temple City Unified School District is about seventeen miles from metropolitan Los Angeles. The district comprises four elementary schools, an intermediate or pincer high school, and one high school. The district is a bedroom suburb composed almost entirely of homes and apartments. Its total population is around 33,000, with a student population of around 5,000. Public records dated in late 1969 indicated the following staffing in the district: 170 certificated personnel including one superintendent, two assistant superintendents, one coordinator of instructional technology and materials, one director of secondary education, one elementary guidance coordinator, one music coordinator, one school psychologist, one speech therapist, six building principals, and six school counselors. Also during this period 1968–69, the district had also employed seventeen senior teachers and one master teacher, along with a number of paraprofessional aides.

2. The Temple City model has been cited in a number of reports.

3. The initial funding for the Temple City project was received in December, 1966, from a private grant. Since that time other private grants, state and district monies, as well as a considerable amount of U.S. Office of Education funds have gone into the project.

4. The general public and the school board of the Temple City District are generally receptive to the leadership opinions of the district superintendent. This trial attempt of differentiated staffing was well thought out and well presented. Generally, all concerned were eager to involve themselves in a thorough study of the concept.

5. Temple City encountered resistance of several kinds. One typical resistance question was, "What research have we that says differentiated staffing offers better utilization of personnel? How do we know it is better than the old way?" The often given reply to this resistance play was, "How do we know the old system is any better than the new differentiated staffing model until we test the two out together?"

Persons in leadership positions are said to have found more resistance at the elementary level than at the secondary level. One superintendent has said:

Some teachers fear that team teaching, use of paraprofessionals, resource centers, and flexible scheduling will permanently 'damage' their children. They fail to recall that the present organizational structure established in 1870 at the Quincy Grammar School was designed for administrative convenience and that it rather callously ignored the needs of continuous educational progress for each individual student.

It was also noted that a larger proportion of women than men object to teachers assuming different roles of professional hierarchy. It has been said, perhaps unfairly, that the primary level especially offers great resistance because the "protective" environment at this level with the principal as the dominant "father" figure often legislates against strong teacher decision making and frequent collegial dialogue toward reshaping the curriculum.

On the other hand the secondary schools accustomed to departmental chairmen, assistant principals and a wider variety of roles is much more receptive to the idea of differentiated staffing.

Some of the public as well as the teaching staff at first equated differentiated staffing with pay raises. On the public side some saw this as a newfangled scheme to pay teachers more money; whereas, some teachers were frightened that this was merit pay in disguise. This fear was answered by an explanation of the difference between differentiated staffing and merit pay.

6. The Temple City Unified School District contributed several innovations, not only differentiated staffing, but flexible scheduling, provision for instructional student time, use of paraprofessionals and aides particularly to provide teacher time for planning and diagnosis, use of resource centers managed by paraprofessionals, team teaching, concept of school managers involved in classroom teaching, change processes, teacher behavior and classroom interaction analysis, performance objectives, teacher satisfaction measures, pupil satisfaction measures, teacher pupil interaction and learning modality, classroom teacher support and service categories, organization aspects of scheduling, teacher assignment, plant use, pupil management, articulation, and financing, and community support.

Efforts of the system have centered around changing the school schedule by instituting a flexible schedule which would allow for greater utilization of staff and for large group, small group, individual, and tutorial study—all of which is called modular scheduling. In addition emphasis has been placed on curriculum revision founded on performance based criteria, or performance objectives. In this regard LAP MATERIALS or learning activity packets have been a form of programmed instruction greatly utilized. Attention has been paid to media centers, laboratories, and libraries in relation to SOUST or the scheduling of unscheduled student time in an effort to improve student independent study. Finally, a major emphasis has been placed on changing the traditional decision-making structure through training programs in group processes, leadership styles, interaction analysis, and allied areas of study.

The Temple City system approach to differentiated staffing led to the following implemented and anticipated *strands* of study: scholar-teacher arranged study, instructional management, organizational analysis, evaluation, survey of model or innovative school buildings, disadvantaged adult studies, associate teacher training, group dynamics, staff teacher training, community career ladder studies, master teacher training, senior teacher training, school system progress studies, and training for aides.

Several variant staff patterns are often associated with the Temple City project. One, reported in the January, 1968, issue of the *Phi Delta Kappan*, presented a ranking as follows:

Teaching research associate
Teaching curriculum associate
Senior teacher
Staff teacher
Academic assistant
Educational technician

A second variation was noted in an April, 1968, presentation to the Faculty of the School of Education, the University of Southern California, where the staffing pattern was viewed as follows:

Teaching curriculum research associate
Senior teacher
Staff teacher
Associate teacher
Academic assistant
Educational technician
Clerks

Croft Educational Services, Inc. (New London, Connecticut, 1969), lists the Temple City model in yet another way:

Master teacher
Senior teacher
Associate teacher

Teacher aides
Resource center assistants
Lab assistants

However, the most recent information from the superintendent's Office of the Temple City Unified School District gives a listing which is accurate to the now existing pattern in that district:

Master teacher
Senior teacher
Staff teacher
Associate teacher
Teacher intern

At the time of this writing (Summer, 1971) the district was advertising applications for teaching curriculum associates, but currently had none. The position was thus still hypothetical.

Since late 1971 all of the schools in the Temple City Unified School District had moved to a differentiated staff. There was only one master teacher in the district, but all schools were staffed with senior teachers, staff teachers and associate teachers, while most schools had teacher interns as well.

The master teacher is a lead teacher with great expertise in some subject area. He has as well a broad understanding of methodology, learning theory, and a grasp of curriculum theory. He would be a well-trained and respected master of his field, and would spend three-fifths of his time in direct instruction to students.

The senior teacher is primarily responsible for the application of curricular innovations to the classroom. He subjects them to modification. From his work emerges refined, sound, and practical curricula.

The point to be stressed here is that since the senior teacher has demonstrated excellence as a teacher he continues to teach. With manifested leadership capabilities, he is a master practitioner, who, with a great deal of experience and training, still remains vital and imaginative. He must know of the most recent developments in teaching and in his subject/skill area.

It is proposed that these people spend most of their time doing what is most needed—teaching effectively. The senior teacher would be on a ten-month contract and would spend four-fifths of his time in a classroom. He would be responsible for inservice classes, workshops, and seminars. He would give assignments to student teachers, develop pilot programs, perhaps function as a teaching team leader, planning with his team schedules and programs. He would aid the staff teacher in meeting student needs, develop creative techniques and materials, serve on an academic senate and be responsible for the educational assistants in his area.

The staff teacher is the core of the education program. His strength lies in his ability to communicate with students, work with parents and effectively implement the goals established by the county and the state. He is given a ten-month contract and receives a salary based upon a regular schedule in the current range. All his time is spent in classroom teaching. He must be able to plan daily for groups, meet individual needs, keep classroom control, maintain pupil rapport, select and organize materials, confer with pupils and parents, effectively use educational assistants, function as a member of a teaching team, and utilize opportunities to grow professionally.

Teachers indicate that they do quite a few things not listed above. We only mentioned jobs which are closely related to instruction. The staff teacher is freed from both curriculum development and nonteaching clerical tasks—he can devote more time to teaching. He must have teaching credentials, and at least a bachelor's degree.

It is a goal of the differentiated staffing concept to utilize the special qualifications of all teachers by allowing them to work with others in more efficient management of talents, space, time, and materials. Team teaching becomes one excellent method of achieving organizational flexibility, but this is not necessarily mandated in a differentiated staffing plan.

The *associate teacher* is a beginning teacher or provisional teacher with full time teaching duties, which do not, however, require responsibilities which call for mastery of an area of study or advanced learning, or great expertise in a subject field or skill level. The associate teacher functions as a partner on a team of staff teachers, perhaps headed by a senior teacher.

The *teaching intern* works with teachers in the instructional program involving the use, preparation, and evaluation of materials, and in related work with students. He maintains physical materials, leads small group discussions, grades papers, and gives specialized instruction in remedial and enrichment areas. He supervises student study and resource center activities.

Various *aides* perform the routine tasks of an ongoing classroom, thereby relieving the teacher of many clerical duties. Their functions vary, depending upon the subject area or grade level in which they work. Their job might include routine ordering of supplies, bulletin board displays, mixing paints, record keeping, duplicating materials, typing, grounds supervision, and related duties.

Many teachers estimate 25 percent of their time is spent in clerical tasks. The proposed plan would cut this to around 4 percent. It is impossible to eliminate it entirely since the technicians must be supervised and this takes time too.

The *academic senate* serves as an integral part of the differentiated staffing project in Temple City. A policy-making body, this group lends support to the involvement of the teacher in decision making.

7. The general feeling and attitude and as well, an overall evaluation of the Oak Avenue Intermediate School differentiated staff faculty was assessed in a late 1968 survey and was reported in the document, "An Interim Evaluation of Oak Avenue Intermediate School—Differentiated Staffing, Flexible Scheduling."

In the report successes leading to high morale were reported in areas of individualization of instruction, the open climate and collegial atmosphere, an enriched school environment, teacher participation or decision making, pupil and teacher enthusiasm for school and teacher satisfaction with the program.

However, emerging problems were also listed such as teacher fatigue, trends toward cliquish groupings of higher echelon teachers, faculty separation, trends toward a new elite in decision making, conflict due to role ambiguity, disappointment over an incomplete media center, and students who won't assume responsibility for independent learning.

8. Though the general educational level of the Temple City District has always been above average, the institution of differentiated staffing for research brought the area almost instant national acclaim. Such attention could not help but change, almost overnight, the attitudes and practices of any number of people in the system. The fame was not always helpful, but overall the system became more attentive, and more conscious of the need for further improvement. The major difference was the experiment in teacher decision making. This forms a notable comparison.

9. Because of the multitude of special grants and projects in addition to local and state funding formulas, it is difficult to assess the exact dollar figure. Funds exclusively directed to differentiated staffing per se during the planning and implementation stages could roughly be estimated at somewhere around $100,000 per year average for five years out of the total district budget of 4.7 million.

The total operating budget for Oak Avenue Intermediate School, where the original differentiated staffing study was undertaken, is approximately $420,000. It has been estimated that under traditional staffing the present differentiated staffing budget would vary only slightly.

10. Learning laboratories, resource centers, adequate and special facilities for large group, small group, and tutorial study add immensely

to the differentiated staffing system. Whatever the excellent traditional facilities might have been there would be a need to alter or adapt them in some way for new flexibility.

11. The project director, the district superintendent, and certain staff members definitely view themselves as agents of change.

12. A formal task analysis was undertaken in the Temple City District.

ARIZONA
MESA PUBLIC SCHOOLS

Those familiar with the early development of differentiated staffing and the Temple City model will recognize Fenwick English, who fashioned the differentiated staffing project at the Mesa, Arizona, Public Schools.

The Mesa model is touted as a client centered staffing project because the base of the project rests on a base of learner needs. Thus, the staffing pattern is not conceived as an arbitrary model into which students must be fitted, but instead as a fluid or flexible model.

Stressed in the Mesa model are both horizontal differentiation and vertical differentiation which are best illustrated in the following charts.

It can be seen that in Figure 7–6 instructional goals are first defined. The horizontally differentiated staff then further professionally delineates these goals, and by its working with the student, the learner helps in determining student goals. Thus, the term *client centered*.

Should the horizontally differentiated team wish to go outside the system to bring in short-term contracted expertise in its mission, it has the flexibility to do so.

In vertical differentiation one may observe both the flexibility and fluidity of the task force approach. As illustrated in Figure 7–7, a teaching team helps the student learners reach student goals based on overall instructional goals. The order and expertise of the vertical staffing arrangement then determines how to successfully complete, or help students to complete, student goals.

One may easily see how the staff may at one time be vertical and at another horizontal. It is this instant manipulatibility which allows the staff to attend to the learner, the client.

Based on a description of the project design in an EPDA project proposal the administration arranged for a planned program of communication and considerable school-community involvement in a consortium scaled to cooperate with other schools in Arizona.

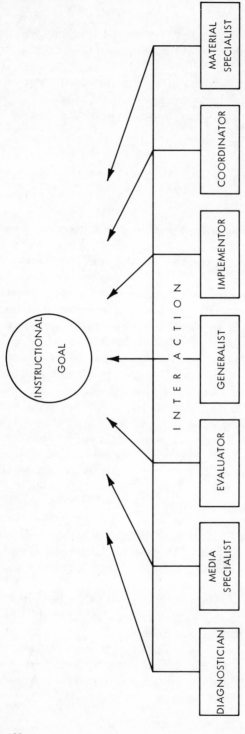

Instructional goals are connected with student learning by a professional staff which is horizontally differentiated. It is the instructional goal which knits the differentiated staff together. The group is, in this case, oriented toward a certain instructional goal discovery.

FIG. 7-6 HORIZONTAL DIFFERENTIATION

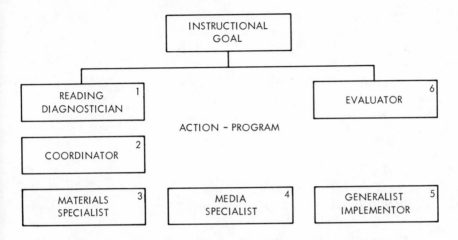

THE NUMBERS INDICATE THE RANKING OF ORDER AND THE FLOW OF
TASK IN THIS CLOSED LOOP DIFFERENTIATED STAFFING MODEL.

FIG. 7–7   VERTICAL DIFFERENTIATION

OTHER PROJECTS

Some additional descriptions of differentiated staffing projects are
listed in the following sections. More explicit information is not readily
available on these newer projects. However, the interested reader might
seek further information by ascertaining the names of the school superintendents in these areas and contacting them.

CALIFORNIA
FOUNTAIN VALLEY SCHOOL DISTRICT,
FOUNTAIN VALLEY, CALIFORNIA

There are twelve schools in the Fountain Valley School District.
The organization of each school is built around a learning center for
each of three groups of students in K–3, 3–5, and 5–8. Thus teams of differentiated staff find themselves housed in clusters of six or eight classroom pods around the central resource room.

The differentiated staff may be listed as follows:

Coordinating teacher
Classroom teacher
Teacher-aide
Teacher assistant

"Work study" college students
"Work study" high school students
Volunteer parent aide

The differentiated staffing listing illustrates a team or cluster. The coordinating teacher functions as the cluster leader. A principal and a *learning analyst* work with different clusters and combined clusters in turn.

ARIZONA
SCOTTSDALE PUBLIC SCHOOLS,
PUEBLO ELEMENTARY SCHOOL

Continually seeking better means of staff utilization is a primary idea underlying the Pueblo model. To this end the Pueblo model fully subscribes to no set design, but has come up with its present alternative model.

The unifying concept is the cluster. There are clusters for language arts, math, social studies, and science. There are allied to this specialized staff additional members in psychology, music, foreign languages, art, home economics, physical education, industrial arts, and library. The school itself is headed by the senior cluster leader or principal who is assisted in routine office management by a business director.

The hierarchical ranking of the differentiated staff is as follows:

Senior cluster leader
Business manager
Cluster leader
Team leader
Instructional manager
Instructional assistant
Instructional aide

Some of the features of the project are found in student involvement, special building facility and instructional materials, independent study, and student accessibility to the staff. In addition, team teaching as well as the concept of the little school of around 200 students to each unit is used.

All definitions of specific roles, responsibilities, and interstaff relationships will be delegated as an overall task to the team members themselves.

ILLINOIS
UNIVERSITY HIGH SCHOOL,
COLLEGE OF EDUCATION,
UNIVERSITY OF ILLINOIS,
URBANA, ILLINOIS

The Developmental Staffing pattern being developed in this laboratory high school believes that if the educational climate of the school facilitates and motivates adult-teacher growth and development, so it will for the youngsters the school serves. To create and maintain a healthy and facilitative climate, the model utilizes the humanistic professional involvement of its staff and makes them active members in its bureaucratic structure as opposed to the "traditional" educational structure that limits or excludes such active participation. This model views the use of educational "hardware and software" for the purpose of meeting educational objectives as only secondary and supplemental to the utilization of the school's existing human resources.

The University High Model combines the major philosophical points of view that all differentiated staffing patterns must confront as they allocate responsibilities to roles and roles to individuals. These points of view are found in the *educational model* and the *engineering model*.

University High School's Developmental Staffing draws from the "educational model" in that the work of the school is examined in terms of a hierarchy of objectives, the most important of which require more sophisticated skills. The model calls for the best qualified teachers to be assigned the responsibilities in pursuit of the more sophisticated objectives.

The model draws also from the "engineering model" in that responsibilities are allocated to roles based on detailed job analysis.

But, the University High Developmental Staffing Model goes beyond these two thrusts. Its primary aim is consideration of human potential and relationships. The model, therefore, is classified as a *behavioral science* model. Responsibilities are allocated on the basis of motivational potential and the commitment level of the teacher. As a teacher expresses an interest in and a capacity for increasing his commitment and investment in the school and its work, he receives more challenging opportunities and inservice training for more challenging and responsible roles.

This is an investment/return model. It is hypothesized that heavy financial and inservice training investments in the adults will return dividends in the form of concerned and growing students.

MINNESOTA
BLOOMINGTON, MINNESOTA
OAK GROVE JUNIOR HIGH SCHOOL

In a comprehensive program attempt to provide individualized learning for every student, the Oak Grove differentiated staffing project concentrates on six major objectives:

1. Flexible scheduling—instructional learning activities need different time patterns for greatest efficiency.
2. Differentiated instruction—variable grouping arrangements from independent study to large group instruction are needed to provide match with instructional objectives.
3. Differentiated staff assignments—staff should be assigned so as to maximize their professional strengths.
4. Flexible use of space—we should strive toward a maximum potential from space in meeting the demands of the teaching learning process.
5. Students must internalize the commitment for learning.
6. Comprehensive communications and involvement—teachers, parents, students, all need to *know* and to be involved in the educational process.

The differentiated staffing project has been outlined on a departmental basis as follows:

Differentiated Teaching Staff

ART DEPARTMENT
Team coordinators
2 Certified teachers
1 Certified graduate intern
2 Certified undergraduate
  interns
2 Student teachers
2 College paraprofessionals

INDUSTRIAL EDUCATION
DEPARTMENT
Team coordinator
3 Certified teachers
1 Certified undergraduate
  intern
1 Student teacher
1 Teacher-aide

HOME ECONOMICS DEPARTMENT
Team coordinator
2 Certified teachers
1 Certified graduate intern
2 Certified undergraduate interns
2 Student teachers
1 Paraprofessional

LANGUAGE ARTS DEPARTMENT
Area leader
9 Certified teachers
6 Certified graduate interns
2 Certified undergraduate interns
2 Student teachers
2 College paraprofessionals
2 Teacher-aides (part-time Social
  Studies)

FOREIGN LANGUAGE DEPARTMENT

1 Team leader
2 Certified graduate interns
2 Student teachers
1 College paraprofessional
2 Amity aides

MEDIA SERVICES DEPARTMENT

Area leader
1 Resource center specialist
2 Library specialists
2 Certified graduate interns
1 Secretary
1 Graphic artist
1 Resource center clerk
2 part-time production clerks

PHYSICAL EDUCATION

Area leader
4 Certified teachers
4 Certified graduate interns
1 Certified undergraduate intern
2 Student teachers
1 College paraprofessional
1 Paraprofessional

HEALTH DEPARTMENT

1 Team leader
1 Certified teacher

STUDENT PERSONNEL SERVICES

Area leader
3 Counselors
2 Deans
2 Learning disability specialists
1 City-school coordinator
1 Social worker
1 School psychologist
1 Nurse
1 Secretary
1 Attendance clerk
4 part-time supervisory aides

MATHEMATICS DEPARTMENT

Area leader
7 Certified teachers
2 Certified graduate interns
3 Certified undergraduate interns
2 Teacher-aides

MUSIC DEPARTMENT

Team coordinator
2 Certified teachers
3 Student teachers
1 College paraprofessional

SCIENCE DEPARTMENT

Area leader
7 Certified teachers
2 Certified graduate interns
2 Certified undergraduate interns
1 Student teacher
1 Paraprofessional
2 Teacher-aides

SOCIAL STUDIES DEPARTMENT

Area leader
8 Certified teachers
3 Certified graduate interns
2 Student teachers
2 College paraprofessionals
1 Paraprofessional
2 Teacher-aides (part-time Language Arts)

The Oak Grove model has a number of unique features. The method of instruction, for example, is changeable on a day-by-day basis, week to week, and ranges from 1 to 1 tutoring to 500 to 1 large group instruction. Great attention is paid to multi-materials, multi-tests, student learning packets, and mixed media presentation such as the Oak Grove random access learning system, and a rather massive closed circuit television system for *student* or *peer* instructional programs, as well as teacher prelaboratory instruction. The entire instructional system is a continuous progress curriculum.

MINNESOTA
WILSON CAMPUS SCHOOL,
MANKATO STATE COLLEGE,
MANKATO, MINNESOTA

A laboratory school of Mankato State College in Mankato, Minnesota, the Wilson Campus School is a K–12 continuous progress, or nongraded, institution.

Several differentiated staffing theories are at work in the Wilson model. However, the two ideas most central to the differentiated staffing movement are the consultant concept, and the hospital model.

Under the idea of each teacher as a consultant, students may choose the consultant (or teacher) whom he wishes to guide him in any continuous progress area of study such as science, music, theater arts, math and other areas. This perhaps is the most unique aspect of the Wilson model.

In the hospital model, the underlying theme is individually prescribed instruction, where specialists are on extended day duty both to diagnose and prescribe. Personnel at the Wilson Campus School view this as follows:

Doctor	a master teacher
Nurse	a "regular" teacher
Nurses' aides	paraprofessionals
Candy stripers	parent and student volunteers

PENNSYLVANIA
COATSVILLE AREA SCHOOL DISTRICT,
COATSVILLE, PENNSYLVANIA

A differentiated staffing pattern designed for emphasis on a *learning system* is the major thrust for the Coatsville model.

In this model there are differentiated roles for the entire school system, nine at the professional staff level and five at the paraprofessional level as follows:

Professional teacher A
Professional teacher A
Professional teacher B
Professional teacher C
Coordinator (K–12) A or B professional teacher
Coordinator (6–12) A or B professional teacher
Department chairman (6–12) A, B, or C professional teacher
   or
Team leader (K–5) A, B, or C professional teacher
Beginning teacher
Instructional assistant A
Technician A
Technician B
Instructional assistant B
Monitors

Rather elaborate use is made of audio materials allied with learning activity packages (LAPS), film loops, and slides, and other media instructional materials, associated program elements or use of large group–small group instruction, school organization for an individualized learning system, micro teaching, and simulation games.

WISCONSIN
MENASHA PUBLIC SCHOOLS,
MENASHA, WISCONSIN

Differentiated staffing discussions in the Menasha Public Schools, Menasha, Wisconsin, centered around systems planning, research, and development which led to the following proposed staff:

Master teacher—system consultant
Department chairman
Team leader
Staff teacher
Teacher-aide

The master teacher-system consultant is viewed as both a part-time teacher and a subject area consultant for the school system. Teachers who are well versed in their field and good leaders would qualify to accomplish the role of department chairman. A team leader would work with three or more teachers and aides on some unit assignment or task force basis. The staff teacher is a full time teacher-diagnostician working directly with individual students and small groups in selecting proper instructional materials for learning needs. The staff teacher is also responsible for pupil evaluation. Teacher-aides would function on an instructional and clerical basis under direct supervision of professional staff.

8. Summary

This final chapter is meant to provide a summary and, as well, anticipate questions which might be asked concerning differentiated staffing. In this way, salient points are reemphasized and an overall framework in question-answer format is furnished which may prove useful both to educational personnel and lay citizens such as school board members.

Within the structured space dictated by the question-answer format many topics are covered. Some of these areas of interest are definitions of differentiated staffing, the differences between differentiated staffing and merit pay, the current interest in differentiated staffing, anticipated problems which might be encountered by school systems moving toward differentiated staffing, involvement of teachers in differentiated staffing, the changing principal's role, decision making in differentiated staffing, and several other general items of interest.

Many of these questions and answers will stimulate in the reader's mind still other questions and possible answers. In this regard, the authors invite both questions and answers, as well as statements from the general readership of this volume.

What is differentiated staffing?

There is no one succinct or all-inclusive definition of differentiated staffing, for there is no one universal model for differentiated staffing. As school districts incorporate the concept into their personnel organizational patterns, they tend to stylize, shape, and modify existing models in order to meet their needs, and hence develop a new and completely unique model. We believe, however, that a basic definition can be stated, which will provide for and serve as a foundation from which to deal with unique operational models.

The definition that we prefer recognizes that in order to differentiate a staff one must have the idea that there are different functions and different roles performed by the teachers, and that when these different functions and roles are clearly delineated they may be assigned to people who will conceivably perform tasks more successfully, more effectively, and perhaps less expensively. The definition that we feel is the most comprehensive is that cited in chapter one by James Olivero.[1] He states that differentiated staffing is a concept of organization that seeks to make better use of educational personnel. Teachers and other educators assume different responsibilities based on carefully prepared definitions of the many teaching functions. The differentiated staffing assignment of educational personnel goes beyond traditional staff allocations based on common subject matter distinctions and grade level assignments and seeks new ways of analyzing essential teaching tasks and greater means of implementing new educational roles.

One often associates differentiated staffing with a stairstep or hierarchical model, but this need not be so. Differentiated staffing begins when different teachers do different things. Another way to look at the answer is by looking at what the school is supposed to do. All of the thousands of tasks (jobs), little and large, are grouped into areas of commonalities. This "task grouping" then becomes the job assignment of some member of the differentiated staff.

Fenwick English has written that differentiated staffing is "a dimension and extension of the roles of the teacher through the creation of a teacher hierarchy with job responsibilities that are commensurate with a range of pay."[2]

[1]Olivero, "Meaning and Application of Differentiated Staffing," pp. 36–40.
[2]Fenwick English, *Differentiated Staffing: Giving Teaching a Chance to Improve Learning*, Tallahassee, Florida: State Department of Education, September 1968, p. 1.

Others have seen differentiated staffing as a ladder laid on its side representing horizontal differentiation with a parallel pay scale rather than a stairstep, a hierarchy, or a vertically differentiated staff. Differentiated staffing means the remaking of American education, either in its own image with slight modification or in strenuously different prototypes.

Does differentiated staffing mean the same thing as merit pay?

This question, asked more by teachers in the profession than any other, may be viewed in several ways. There are, quite frankly, some administrators who do equate differentiated staffing with merit pay. The general layman, also, makes this inaccurate extrapolation. This is unfortunate, because in all of the small (but growing) body of literature on differentiated staffing, the theoretical viewpoint is diametrically opposed to this kind of thinking.

Those administrators who desire to cloak merit pay under the guise of differentiated staffing are easily found out, for differentiated staffing in models from Temple City, California, to Sarasota, Florida, and north to the Canadian Provinces depends almost wholly on task analysis, which, among other things, provides indefatigable evidence on the importance of student learning and the centrality of the teacher's role in this moving force behind education.

Merit pay says that all teachers perform the same job, but some accomplish the job in a meritorious manner, that we know enough about the teaching-learning *gestalt* to determine who these better teachers are. In a way, given the state of art of learning theory, this is analogous to investigations in the sixteenth century to determine the leading alchemist. If this is so, it will be seen in the twenty-first century that we knew no more about learning than the seventeenth century knew about chemistry and physics!

Why is there such great interest in differentiated staffing?

Certainly the education phenomenon to which we may refer as *instant innovation* provides a partial answer to this question. Anything which is different (note the word *differentiate*) is bound to be attention-getting in the generally ultra-conservative institution of education, which resembles its seventeenth century counterpart more closely than any other comparative aspect of modern day society except perhaps youthful male hairstyles—an institution in which it is said that from theory and research to general practice takes anywhere from ten to forty years.

Other than this, differentiated staffing is an idea which has come of time. The aspirations of most persons are rising, and it is to the schools which they have turned. Societal problems have increased, have become more complex, and it is to the schools that behavioral (and traditional) societal "engineers" have turned.

Certainly in the United States the schools have never known such heated criticism. Teachers' salaries command 75 to 85 percent of a *total* multi-billion dollar outlay, and the public is expecting more and more of them for it.

Specialization, in an era of men like Chomsky, Skinner, Bruner, Piaget, and countless other learning theorists, is also a significant factor. The smothering Vesuvius fountain of knowledge forces us toward a cult of efficiency in order to survive, where, as McLuhan has said, we become not a tribe of food gatherers, but data gatherers.

Other factors, teacher militancy, aspiring educational professionalism, accountability, a systems approach view of life, also contribute. No simple and single answers exist, but the complexity of contingencies mentioned will provide the parameter for the answer to this question. H. H. McAshan in a March 25, 1968, mimeographed paper lists the current interest in differentiated staffing under an answer with multiple headings.

A. All of society has changed to include items pertaining to knowledge, teachers, students, technology, communications, transportation, and ostensibly entertainment and other roles and occupations—thus school must change to meet society's new demands.

B. Modern schools demand expertise in curriculum research and development, staff development, long- and short-range planning.

C. Teachers are different, as students and all individuals are different.

D. Really expert teachers are actually in short supply.

E. There are more and more students, teachers, innovations and less and less time to prevent a nonrecallable overload.

F. More professionalism is called for.

G. More flexibility needed.

H. Nonprofessionals need an entry into an educational career.

I. Student individualization is encouraged.

J. Competence and responsibility can be related to salary.

Finally, public schools today are in the midst of a period of crisis. Once criticism of the educational establishment was almost exclusively limited to issues related to the academic disciplines, but now the public, both in the role of concerned parents and taxpayers, have voiced deep and growing concern with the quality of public education. As parents, their concerns tend to be particularized. That is, parents as a group rarely criticize the schools as institutions. Instead they focus on particular attempts to move from the status quo to new curricula such as family life and sex education, a more permissive attitude toward discipline in the schools, new procedures such as busing for purposes of integration, or aid to private and parochial schools.

As taxpayers, their concerns with the schools are quite different. In most communities the taxpayers appear anxious by the skyrocketing increases in educational costs. Taxpayer groups have organized in the last several years and opposed, often successfully, requests for increased operating costs by boards of education. The taxpayer has indicated that he is unwilling to foot an increasing bill for a service, the quality of which he is uncertain. There are many reasons for this new uncertainty about schools. The media present a picture of total intercity schools disillusionment and disaffection by increased numbers of children. Popular books note a continued lack of stated relevant goals and objectives for public education.

For much of the public such a situation is a rather new phenomena, but such situations have long existed as deep concerns for academic critics. Men like Edgar Friedenberg and Paul Goodman have long questioned the effectiveness of schools as social institutions, but the public has most often reacted to their type of work either by rejecting their ideas as impractical or utopian or finding them completely wrongheaded.

Today the critics' call for change can no longer be lightly dismissed by the educator. Instead there is public anxiousness, because the public recognizes the need for change, yet is rather uncertain of what the change should look like.

The exact shape of the necessary changes is really not clear. Several things, though, seem obvious. The changes will need to be extensive. Some people believe that fairly extensive curriculum changes and a general upgrading of the teacher preparation colleges would be enough. Others think that the problems in the schools are so profound that nothing less than revolutionary changes are necessary. Some have suggested, for example, the implementation of a voucher system where parents could select among competing schools—some public and some private. One thing is clear: the changes advocated will have to be accomplished at little additional cost to the public. No glib explanation can convince the already overburdened taxpayer that he should pay substantially more for public education. Finally, any significant change within the structural limitations of existing school systems must have the support of teachers, once subordinate, but now stronger and more sophisticated politically, seeking better working conditions, expanded participation in decision making, better salaries, found benefits.

In the past few years the thinking, reading, and knowledgeable public has become aware that there are two yardsticks increasingly more relevant for the assessment of public school organizational patterns. Major investments and applied educational research have yielded many innovative approaches for making pupil and staff learning easier. One relevant yardstick, then, for the assessment of school organizational structures is by necessity the degree to which the public school district is readily able to assimilate innovations. A second yardstick stems from the conclusions of researchers and practitioners alike that there is no one evaluative technique which can uniformly be applied to all students and all school districts. The school district, then, must develop and be able to evaluate its own objectives, and must increase its ability in the public schools to become applied researchers.

Therefore, any new organizational pattern should be evaluated in terms of whether it is able to provide for this function within its existing structure. One promising idea which does not increase the costs so dramatically but yet does change the structure of public schools is differentiated staffing. Differentiated staffing is a relatively new and innovative idea that holds for the 70s considerable potential for resolving many conflicts that have for many decades plagued both educators and the public. The authors are convinced of the potential of this concept for America's schools and feel that it is of sufficient worth so that local districts should undertake a study of it.

In order for an idea or concept such as differentiated staffing to "come of age" there must be some rather universal problems which exist within the teaching profession. What are they?

In the last decade or so there has been a great deal written about the professionalization of teaching, so much that the idea has come to be grouped along with a number of cliches concerning education. As is the case with so many ideas, much is said but very little is done. Let us then attempt to summarize some of the problems of professionalization, at least as seen from the point of view of the teacher.

First, there are really no promotions for a teacher. Though no one would disagree that the heart of the educational enterprise is teaching, the rewards created for the institution of teaching operate in opposition to what we really believe. Teachers are rewarded financially on the basis of not teaching, that is, by being promoted to administrative positions in which they cannot teach at all. With differentiated staffing, everyone teaches at least a percentage of the time.

The lockstep concept of the single salary schedule operates on the principle that all teachers are equal and that they grow exactly in the same manner. Furthermore, there is really no provision for altering responsibilities and authority with higher salaries. The traditional salary schedule existing today in most public schools rewards teachers for longevity rather than for performance. Perhaps the most inequitable facet of public education is that we treat unequals as equal.

Still another educational problem is that all teachers are considered interchangeable parts in a rigid organizational structure. The basic organizational pattern of American education today says all of the instructional staff are in all parts equal—we have traditionally given the new teacher, the below average teacher, the superior teacher, the same number of children and the same instructional responsibilities. We do not have an organizational structure that is able to both utilize professional talents and experience in a more flexible manner. Therefore, in this type of structure many people are allowed to stagnate.

Still another problem is that we tend to treat teachers as subprofessionals. The rapidly changing nature of our society has required, especially since World War II, that public schools have as teachers better trained, better prepared specialists. But for some reason, we have maintained and certainly held to an earlier 1900s concept; the same notions of support staff for teachers that existed then is sustained today. This sustainment has resulted in much friction and maladjustment between teachers and the old support staff. The creation of even more advanced expertise in the classroom clearly reveals a need for changing the old support system.

Another problem is that teachers are largely excluded from the decision-making process and the regulation of the profession. They do not usually sit on boards which license professionals, nor do they have much to say about professional regulations at the school level. Administrative practices, perhaps logical teacher apathy, and instructional isolation have combined to limit teachers as participants in exercising these professional responsibilities.

All of these items contribute to the crux of the professionalization problem, almost universal in American public education.

In differentiated staffing schemes, can a teacher remain in the classroom and still receive increased rewards?

If this were all the new system did, then it would be adopting a type of merit pay plan, which teachers have long vehemently opposed. Those who propose differentiated staffing say that they are not suggesting a merit pay plan in order for a teacher to receive a substantially increased salary and still remain in the classroom.

First, the promoted teacher must be willing to devote more time to the job, that is more hours per week and more weeks per year. Secondly, he must be willing to take on additional responsibilities, which run the gamut from curriculum planning to abstract learning theory. Finally, as the teacher progresses up the new teacher-based career ladder, he must spend less time in the classroom. But since what he does still relates to kids, the teacher is never completely removed from the classroom. In fact, in most models, at least 40 percent of even the highest ranking master teacher's time is spent in classroom teaching.

In what ways can differentiated staffing enhance one's career opportunities?

One of the major weaknesses of current educational staff employment is the absence of a career ladder. This does not mean that there are no career opportunities in public education. However, except for the position of Department Chairman, any real advancement in public education must be to administrative ranks, counseling, or the like. This, for the most part, automatically *removes* the teacher from the classroom.

Once the teacher has had to leave the classroom and join the administrative hierarchy ostensibly for more money, numerous opportunities present themselves. But in the existing teaching career ladder, monetary and status rewards are tied to the teacher's acceptance of functions not directly related to teaching, or for that matter, the classroom. The regrettable end of this arrangement is that too often an excellent teacher who might have been a major or positive influence on the lives of youth is forced to leave the classroom in order to further his career.

It is not only the teachers already in the schools who are affected. Prospective teachers are also affected by the absence of a teaching based career ladder. Each year substantially more people complete their teacher preparation programs than are eligible to enter the teaching profession. This was true even before the shortage of teachers ceased to exist. How many of these people decided against teaching because a teaching career is severely limited? There is no way to determine the number of teachers discouraged by the realization that if they expect to make a career of teaching and remain in the classroom, they must be willing to receive restrictive incremental pay increases for their entire career. And, also, what we cannot determine is the impact on the public school systems of potentially capable teachers choosing other careers. To make teaching a more attractive profession, those who advocate differentiated staffing propose a career ladder which recognizes the importance of teaching both in its structure and its distribution of rewards.

Of the rewards which teachers can receive, having a "say" in decision making is very important. Decisions in most schools, not only about administrative matters but, also, about most other items, are made by the administration. This presents a most interesting paradox—there is hardly a school in the nation that does not include the word democracy in its philosophy. Yet, at best, most decisions are finally, often expediently, made by what through no fault of the principal seems to be a benevolent despot. Administrators, due to a lack of both time and organizational structure, are reluctant to delegate appropriate kinds of decision making to teachers. To a large degree, this administrative reluctance to share with teachers the making of decisions which affect them has led to strained relations, which contribute to what we commonly call teacher militancy.

We have seen in the past decade the image of teachers change from a docile, withdrawn group of individuals to a militant organization demanding not only higher salaries and fringe benefits, but also a voice in the decision making that affects them and their students. The nature of teacher demands not only encompasses the number of students to be assigned to each class, but the number of class periods they will teach. Furthermore, the demands include many other areas once thought to be the domain of administrators, such as choice of textbooks, selection of curricular materials, budget planning, and a voice in the recruitment of colleagues.

In order to be effective, a differentiated staffing model must allow teachers to begin to assume larger amounts of what were previously supervisory or administrative responsibilities. This change, more than anything else, should reduce the existing schism between the teachers and administrators, as well as possibly help those administrators who are overworked. Under a truly effective differentiated staffing pattern, many administrators will also be teachers. Actively involved in classroom activity, they will be more sensitive not only to teacher but to administrative issues, and at the same time will be far more vulnerable to the exercise of peer pressure by the classroom teacher. It goes without saying that this dual role will have a major positive influence in helping to reduce growing professional militancy and may help resolve many of today's problems.

Who will actually advance through the differentiated staffing hierarchy?

The advocates of differentiated staffing claim that the teacher who is willing to accept more responsibilities will be rewarded, though it seems impossible to judge who will actually be advanced if willingness to assume responsibility is the sole criteria. What is clear is that a person will probably not be directly rewarded solely for good teaching because a merit system based on rewards specifically for teaching is virtually impossible to achieve. In universities, for example, where there already exists a hierarchy similar to the one proposed by differentiated staffing, teachers seldom advance solely because of their teaching. In fact, their teaching is often ignored—only their publications and research are rewarded. There is one programmed safeguard against the employment of unqualified personnel at the higher levels of the differentiated staffing teaching structure. In the upper reaches of the career ladder, there is no tenure, but perhaps, instead, short-term contracts. If a person does not adequately fulfill his responsibilities, he will not be re-hired for the job he holds. And this is determined largely by peer evaluation.

There is one saving grace for the teacher, however. The person who is on the lower rungs of the career ladder will have tenure. Even if he moves upward in the hierarchy he retains tenure for this position and can assume this less responsible position at a later date. Given this fluid situation, one may solve the problems of poor promotional selection. A person who is a competent teacher will not necessarily be a good researcher, learning analyst or planner; therefore, there will always be a place for competent teachers.

What are the teacher preparation institutions doing about differentiated staffing?

At the present time, little or nothing is being done by teacher educational institutions to prepare teachers to undertake varying roles under differentiated staffing plans. There are two primary reasons for this vacuum. First, there is little *demand* for teachers who are prepared to fulfill the varied tasks related to a differentiated staffing model. Teacher preparation institutions generally operate on a supply and demand basis. In those instances where teacher educational institutions are attempting to work with public schools to provide the kinds of experience necessary for teachers to undertake or to function effectively within differentiated staffing, this is usually on an inservice contracted basis. Second, undergraduates are more concerned with getting their first job than they are with becoming a part of an *esoteric* professional training program.

There are many departments in schools and colleges of education which would like to move forward in an attempt to resolve glaring educational problems, yet they are unable to attract potential teachers; the beginning teacher prefers to have a *traditional program* which will allow him to be employed by *traditional school districts*. There are, after all, more traditional school districts than there are those which are pioneering.

Is there a threat to the profession through the employment of paraprofessionals?

The vast majority of schools today make very little use of part-time noncertified staff. Homemakers, for example, are often well qualified, or can be trained for meaningful educational tasks, but are seldom used part time. This potentially capable school resource is seldom employed for anything more than substitute teaching, and this at best. Too few school districts have really embarked on large scale programs of training teacher-aides. But, experiments in inner-city schools indicate that where such programs involving the use and training of paraprofessionals have been undertaken, they have met with exceptional success.

Unfortunately, the leadership of professional teachers' organizations have frequently resisted such assistance in the past. Teachers consider themselves threatened from two well founded directions. They think that in an effort to save money the school district will hire unqualified personnel, and that such a move will not only lead to a deterioration of the existing quality of education, but will also reduce the number of full time teachers employed. On the other hand, teachers fear that competent part-time people might be hired for administrative work and ultimately block any advancement they might have. Advocates of differentiated staffing, however, claim that with the establishment of career ladders these anxieties will be eliminated. The paraprofessionals will be the employed assistants of teachers and they will have specific duties assigned to them by teachers.

Furthermore, the major avenues for advancement will be open only to those who are qualified full time certified teachers.

What problems will school systems face in moving toward differentiated staffing?

School systems must look before they leap. Differentiated staffing attempts to account for all system variables in a way which no other educational innovation has done.

Teacher involvement and understanding must be sought. Systems must guard against thinking differentiated staffing is a money saver, and a replacer of professional talent by paraprofessional warm bodies.

The changing role of the principal and the personal vested interests of principals must be given great consideration. Evaluation of differentiated staffing must be considered. The group process is an important and overriding factor.

Rigid and noncreative job descriptions can lead to ennui and a shattering loss of individual psychological success.

Differentiated staffing can not be treated out of the context of the total system.

Differentiated staffing is not, as Dr. Marshal Frinks has noted, something done *to* teachers but something done through total involvement *with* teachers.

These are some few and representative areas to which much thought must be given.

How will teachers be involved in differentiated staffing projects?

The answer to this question can be seen to lie within the boundary of where the teacher works. Those instructional matters depend on the way in which the local school has defined the involvement of teachers in decisions that affect teachers. Education is a large enterprise, and the demarcation line where other institutions and agencies leave off and the school begins is difficult to discern. However, both school matters as well as professional responsibilities of teachers should be the concern of teachers. To the extent that decision making within this sphere of delimitation is manipulable by the teacher, it is to this extent that teachers will become internally committed and will strive for even higher professionalism. By the same token, the teaching profession may be held accountable.

Since decisions within the school are influenced by policies outside the school, the professional voice of the teacher must be heard and heeded at district, state, and national levels. Administration must not be peripheral to this voice but facilitating to it.

As differentiating staffing progresses, there will be more teacher involvement. All educational personnel will become more *the teacher,* more concerned with students—the clients of the educational service— and less concerned with outward and outside-oriented bureaucratic practices. The focus of education will return to the locus of the student.

How will the principal's role change?

The principal will turn more and more to administer facilitation of the professional decisions of a corps of teachers. Somewhat like a symphony conductor, teachers could be analogous to violinists as well as other orchestral players. Or, in another way, teachers could be analogous with medical doctors and principals with hospital administrators. However, here again, as always, the man himself will shape the job. It is a common game periodically to talk of administrivia and downgrade the principal, but even John Dewey, for one example, *was* the principal of his laboratory school. Just as a teacher is not a teacher is not a teacher, so a principal is not a principal is not a principal.

How "new" is differentiated staffing, really?

Differentiated staffing is not really new. The ancient Greeks had a form of it with the mother and father responsible for different aspects of the child's growth, with the state responsible for other facets of the young man's education. Finally in the Greek city state there was continual learning through service in government.

One may see differentiation in a dentist's office where one finds both a professional, a semi-professional, and a nonprofessional hierarchy. There is the oral surgeon and the dentist, the oral hygienist and the X-ray technician, but there are nurses, aides, clerk-typists, and receptionists as well. It is no great extrapolation to create a similar model for the teaching profession. But this will require rigorous attention to the science of education, which incorporates the science of learning.

Differentiated staffing is *not* an innovation which a school system may "plug in" as it may have plugged in various other innovations of the past. The life blood of staff differentiation is task analysis based on sound philosophy, goals, and objectives, which are set both by the people whom the school as an institution serves and by professional educators; more and more even the student, the client himself, is involved in this goal setting process.

All of the component parts of a school system must *fit*. There must be a systems approach with due consideration given to all of the complexities which have eventually to do with what mankind knows little enough about—human learning. A better and better science of learning must evolve.

How does the teacher involvement in decision making in a differentiated staffing model differ from teacher involvement in a traditional staffing model?

Consider that in comparisons of differentiated staffing and traditional models we are dealing with non-statistical, hypothetical terms. There are no doubt some to be sure atypical traditionally staffed schools where teacher involvement in decision making is to a great degree close to all-encompassing. As well, in some of the dozen or so differentiated staffing models there is not a truly great degree of teacher decision making, but this, too, is also atypical. We assume, after all, that a differentiated staffing model has as one of its series of objectives teacher involvement in decision making to a great extent. The point here is that teacher involvement in decision making could have occurred in the proliferation of schools of the 1900s; but, in fact, it did not (in a modal way) occur, but historically lessened as the bureaucracy of public schools burgeoned.

Let us look at a number of decisions which might be made by an assumed modal principal in a modal and traditional school as opposed to a differentiated staffing school.

In traditional schools the principal is almost forced to become a strong authoritarian figure. Teachers therefore cannot lead, and in fact are forced to follow. There are, though, remarkable exceptions to this rule.

This modal design is not seen in a light critical of the traditional school principal. He is a man caught in the middle, a transitional figure between what could almost be viewed as feudal times and the latter twentieth century of increasing "group thought." He has had a job to do, and a role to play, and he has undoubtedly done both well, as the remarkable progress of American education to this point so testifies. *But,* now times have changed. Multiple *future shock* assaults us even now. One strong authoritarian leader does not, cannot, have enough expertise to manage the complex demands placed on modern schools. Thus differentiated staffing emerges—a more sophisticated approach, recognizing complex interpersonal relationships, an organic institution to replace a simpler assembly-line approach to an earlier and (in the light of present times) simplistic approach to a *learning system.*

In differentiated staffing, the principal (or his counterpart) will continue to remain. But as his role changes, he will be the one trained to encourage and facilitate group decision making, though at times he may still be forced to make those decisions which are required immediately. However, to the extent that all teachers are emerging leaders, and are themselves facilitators of others, and to the extent that they as well encourage the system toward short- and long-range (nonexpeditious) decision making—to this extent do we presume to move to the heart of differentiated staffing.

What direction will evaluation of the teaching profession take?

The direction that evaluation of other professions has taken. Piecemeal and frequently changing rules and regulations from the oft quoted schoolmaster's duties of chopping wood for the pot-bellied stove, not to mention present day supervision of bus loading, will need to give way to a professionally responsible, publicly accountable way of service above self—something like the Hippocratic oath, or the devotion of a master artist to his canvas. As the public has a long way to go before accepting this new image of the teaching profession, so the fledgling teaching profession (ill-supported by scientific research and development) has a long way to go toward creating an image that the public may trust in a new era of teacher professionalism.

Are there some potential difficulties or inherent weaknesses in the concept of differentiated staffing?

We have attempted to show the reader what the problems are which differentiated staffing attempts to alleviate and some of the ways differentiated staffing might solve these problems. Not much has been said about potential difficulties which differentiated staffing might create of which educators should be aware. One obvious shortcoming is the degree to which overspecialization creeps in. This might take two forms—narrow specialization in subject matter or the removal of the teacher from the student. Let us examine both of these.

There has undoubtedly been a knowledge explosion in recent years which has created new demands on teachers. As more information becomes available in every field of learning, there is pressure for people to become experts in that field. There is a need for *more concentration* but committing resources to specialization are expensive.

Since we have an imprecise idea how information is transmitted and only a vague idea about how children learn, we cannot be certain of any long-term certain strategy. We should be particularly skeptical of the ultimate utility of subject specialization, particularly if it overcomes other concerns. Specialization might further an already bad practice in public schools for example, teaching children facts instead of teaching them *how to think*. Even if subject specialization is useful, it should not be equated with teacher specialization. Some subject matter might be better taught through a technological variety of learning than by a single teacher. Already, educational aids such as programmed learning, educational TV, computer assisted instruction, cassette tape teaching, etc., have been placed at the teachers' disposal. Jerome Bruner in his book, *The Process of Education*, discusses this potential: ". . . there exist devices to aid the teacher in extending the student's range of experience, in helping him to understand the underlying structure of the material he is learning, and in dramatizing the significance of what he is learning. There are also devices now being developed that can take some of the load of teaching from the teacher's shoulders. How these aids and devices should be used in concept as a system of aids is, of course, the interesting problem."[3]

A teacher might need to become a learning theory and communications specialist. If this were the case, then, rather than being viewed as a repository teacher, the teacher would be seen a kind of living conduit—a link between a body of knowledge and the learner's discovery of processes.

Now another potential problem in specialization might be the decrease in personal contact between the professional and the student. But is this all bad? If the teaching profession follows the pattern of several other professional groups, the teacher will increasingly become a diagnostician and researcher. This could be good. Over the years, for example, nurses have assumed many of the responsibilities formerly reserved for doctors, including most before and after surgery contact with the patient. Though there are numerous sound reasons for this development, it has nevertheless meant that the patient sees less and less of the doctor. Personal contact, long considered an important part of the doctor-patient relationship has decreased remarkably. But isn't this really due to a doctor shortage? Demands created by the knowledge explosion and professional career concerns have separated the professional and the client in many fields. Should professionals be, can they be, totally re-

[3] Jerome Bruner, *The Process of Education* (Cambridge, Mass.: Harvard University Press, 1960), p. 84.

moved from their clients? Such a development in public education would be most regrettable. Yet it has happened. Personal contact might be the most important ingredient in the educational process. If differentiated staffing can bring higher professionalism closer to the student it has accomplished much.

Are task analysis, mission analysis, and cost analysis really necessary for differentiated staffing? Aren't things like this merely fads?

Terminology such as *task analysis, mission analysis*, and the like may be fads, but in name only. These words speak of careful planning, of developing hypotheses before leaping into action, actions of great importance and concern to education.

So far as cost analysis goes, education has long since passed the day, if indeed it ever existed, when money is proffered simply because of an outstretched educator's hand. Education today is in a battle for funds with many other institutions, whose needs are as great and whose priorities are as high as schooling. In such an arena, cost analysis is not just a choice but an imperative.

Further, pursuing this, we find that without doubt, education in the world today is an institution inherited from the past. One keen on a sort of anthropological or historical survey of the schools could not help but find them rife with past folkways and cultural holdovers, a situation which has come about by building and adding on bits and pieces through the years. In organization, for example, it has been said that the United States inherited the grammar school from England, borrowed the high school from Austria, instituted the junior high school as an American innovation, added the Kindergarten from Germany, adapted early childhood care from Netherland dames schools, and the university system from medieval Europe. Such a remark, though somewhat superficial, does manage to state the problem.

What mission analysis, task analysis, and cost analysis set out to do is to idealize or purify as rationally as possible a new philosophy for new times, and on this base to set about systematically constructing goals and objectives. In this whole process of philosophy, goal, and objective setting, an attempt is made to involve community, students, and the total educational staff, in the belief that through this involvement may evolve a new commitment to an educational institution for our times.

Following this objective setting, studies then can lead to conceptualizing a staff to conduct this "newly formed" institution. This is how we arrive at differentiated staffing, ideally. Further role clarification, and further refinement of the system leading to continual self-seeking, ongoing, philosophy-goal-objective discussions, points toward a closed-loop system of self-renewal where there is input from within, particularly through teacher and student involvement, and from without by virtue of the citizens' groups involved in philosophy and goal setting, as well as the assessment of accountability through cost analyses. Let us hasten to add that a *full system* as herein conceived by the authors has yet to come about, but only through a rigorous examination of the institution of education is it likely to come about.

Therefore, in this volume, dwelling as it does on differentiated staffing, the authors have meant to point out step-by-step procedures, a system approach to staffing, which, though no claim has been made of its perfection, is still far in advance of the modal, the present staffing patterns in world education, and might in fact represent a state-of-the-art of personnel utilization in school systems.

Bibliography

BOOKS

ALLEN, DWIGHT W., AND ROBERT N. BUSH, *A New Design for High School Education.* New York: McGraw-Hill, 1964.

AMIDON, E. J., AND J. B. HOUGH (eds.), *Interaction Analysis: Theory, Research, and Application.* Reading, Massachusetts: Addison-Wesley, 1967.

ANDERSON, ROBERT, ELLIS A. HAGSTROM, AND WADE M. ROBINSON, "Team Teaching in an Elementary School, "in *Change and Innovation in Elementary School Organization.* New York: Holt, Rinehart and Winston, 1966.

ARGYRIS, CHRIS, *Personality and Organization.* New York: Harper & Row, 1957.

BAIR, MEDILL, AND RICHARD G. WOODWARD, *Team Teaching in Action.* Boston: Houghton Mifflin, 1964.

BANATHY, BELA H., *Instructional Systems.* Palo Alto: Fearon Publishers, 1968.

BARKER, R. G., AND H. F. WRIGHT, *Midwest and Its Children.* New York: Row, Peterson and Co., 1954.

BARZUN, JACQUES, *Teacher in America.* Boston: Little, Brown, 1945.

BENNIS, WARREN G., *Changing Organizations: Essays on the Development and Evolution of Human Organizations.* New York: McGraw-Hill, 1966.

BRUNER, JEROME, *The Process of Education.* Cambridge, Mass.: Harvard University Press, 1960.

BURKS, ROBERT H., *A Strategy for Problem Solving.* Boca Raton, Florida: Florida Atlantic University, Division of Learning Resources, 1967.

BUSH, ROBERT N. AND DWIGHT W. ALLEN, *A New Design for High School Education.* New York: McGraw-Hill, 1964.

CAMPBELL, RONALD F., AND DONALD H. LAYTON, *Policy Making for American Education*. Chicago: University of Chicago Press, 1969.

CARTER, C. F. AND B. R. WILLIAMS, *Industry and Technical Progress: Factors Governing the Speed of Application of Science*. London: Oxford University Press, 1957.

CASTETTER, WILLIAM B., *Administering the School Personnel Program*. New York: Macmillan, 1968.

CROSBY, MURIEL, *Supervision as Cooperative Action*. New York: Appleton-Century-Crofts, 1957.

DARHOF, CLARENCE, "Observations on Entrepreneurship in Agriculture," in Harvard Research Center on Entrepreneurship History (ed.), *Change and the Entrepreneur*. Cambridge, Massachusetts: Harvard University Press, 1949.

DEMPSEY, RICHARD A. AND A. JOHN FIORINO, *Differentiated Staffing: What It Is and How It Can Be Implemented*. Swarthmore, Pennsylvania: A. C. Croft, Inc., 1971.

EDELFELT, ROY A., "Differentiated Staffing and Implications for Teacher Education," in *American Association of Colleges for Teacher Education Yearbook*. Washington, D.C.: Association of Classroom Teachers of the NEA, 1968.

FESTINGER, L., et al., *Theory and Experiment in Social Communication*. Collected papers, Ann Arbor Institute for Social Research, Ann Arbor: University of Michigan, 1950.

FLANDERS, NED A., *Interaction Analysis in the Classroom*. (rev. ed.) Ann Arbor: University of Michigan Press, 1966.

FLYNN, JOHN H., CLIFTON B. CHADWICK AND A. S. FISCHLER, *An Analysis of the Role of the Teacher in an Innovative Prototype School*. Fort Lauderdale, Florida: Nova University, 1969.

GARDNER, JOHN, *Self-Renewal: The Individual and the Innovative Society*. New York: Harper and Row, 1963.

GETZELS, J. W., AND P. W. JACKSON, "The Teacher's Personality and Characteristics," in *Handbook of Research on Teaching*. American Educational Research Association, NEA. Chicago: Rand, McNally and Company, 1963.

GOULDNER, ALVIN W., *Patterns of Industrial Bureaucracy*. Glencoe, Illinois: Free Press, 1954.

HARRIS, BEN, *Supervisory Behavior in Education*. Englewood Cliffs, N.J.: Prentice-Hall, Inc., 1963.

HARRIS, BEN H. AND WAILAND BESSENT, in collaboration with KENNETH E. McINTYRE, *In-Service Education: A Guide to Better Practices*. Englewood Cliffs, N.J.: Prentice-Hall, Inc., 1968.

HONIGMAN, FRED, *Multidimensional Analysis of Classroom Interaction (MACI)*. Villanova, Pennsylvania: Villanova University Press, 1967.

JACKSON, PHILIP W., "The Teacher and Individual Differences," in *Individualizing Instruction*, Sixty-First Yearbook, Part I, National

Society for the Study of Education. Chicago: University of Chicago Press, 1962.

JACOBSON, PAUL B., WILLIAM C. REAVIS, AND JAMES D. LOGSDON, *The Effective School Principal.* Englewood Cliffs, N.J.: Prentice-Hall, 1954.

LIEBERMAN, MYRON, *The Future of Public Education.* Chicago: University of Chicago Press, 1960.

LIPPITT, RONALD, JEANNE WATSON, AND BRUCE WESTLEY, *The Dynamics of Planned Change: A Comparative Study of Principles and Techniques,* New York: Harcourt Brace Jovanovich, 1958.

MORPHET, EDGAR L., ROE L. JOHNS, AND THEODORE L. RELLER, *Educational Organization and Administration.* Englewood Cliffs, N.J.: Prentice-Hall, 1967.

National Education Association, *The Teacher and His Staff: Selected Demonstration Centers.* St. Paul, Minnesota: 3M Education Press, 1967.

National Society for the Study of Education, 65th Yearbook, *The Changing American School.* Chicago, Illinois: University of Chicago Press, 1966.

NEAGLEY, ROSS AND N. DEAN EVANS, *Handbook for Effective Supervision of Instruction.* Englewood Cliffs, N.J.: Prentice-Hall, Inc., 1967.

PARSONS, TALCOTT, *Essays in Sociological Theory.* New York: Free Press, 1963.

POPPER, SAMUEL H., *The American Middle School: An Organizational Analysis.* Waltham, Massachusetts: Blaisdell Publishing Co., 1967.

ROGERS, EVERETT, *Diffusion of Innovation.* New York: Free Press, 1962.

ROSS, DONALD H., *Administration for Adaptability: A Source Book for Drawing Together the Results of More Than 150 Individual Studies Related to the Question of Why and How Schools Improve.* New York: The Metropolitan School Study Council, Teachers College, Columbia University, 1958.

SARASON, SEYMOUR B., *Psychology in Community Settings.* New York: John Wiley, 1966.

SIMON, ANITA, AND E. GIL BOYER, eds., *Mirrors for Behavior.* Philadelphia: Research for Better Schools, Inc., 1967.

STODDARD, GEORGE G., "Generalists and Specialists in the Elementary School," *Crucial Issues in Education.* (3rd Ed.) New York: Holt, Rinehart and Winston, 1964.

WILES, KIMBALL, *Supervision for Better Schools.* Englewood Cliffs, N.J.: Prentice-Hall, 1955.

UNPUBLISHED PAPERS AND REPORTS

CHAPARRO, ALVARO, "Role Expectation and Adoption of New Farm Practices," Unpublished Doctoral Dissertation, University Park, Pennsylvania State University, 1955.

CRENSHAW, JOSEPH W., "Staff Organization and Utilization in Elementary and Secondary Schools." Mimeographed. Tallahassee, Florida: State of Florida, Department of Education, 1968.

DEMPSEY, RICHARD A. "An Analysis of Teachers' Expressed Judgments of Barriers to Curriculum Change in Relation to Factors of Individual Readiness for Change." Unpublished Doctoral Dissertation, Michigan State University, 1963.

EDELFELT, ROY A. "Interpersonal Relations and the Changing Educational Community." Mimeographed. Washington, D.C.: National Commission on Teacher Education and Professional Standards, National Education Association, December 1968.

"Goal: Maximum Educational Growth for Each Individual Learner." Temple City Unified School District, July, 1968. Single xerox copies may be obtained by writing Att. D-S Director, 274 Knott Building, Department of Education, Tallahassee, Florida 32304.

KAUFMAN, R., AND R. CORRIGAN, "Towards Educational Responsiveness to Society's Needs: A Tentative Model." Unpublished Report. Chapman College, November, 1967.

PILLOTT, GENE M., "A Conceptual Design of a System Model of Differentiated Staffing." Unpublished Dissertation. University of Florida, 1970.

QUIRK, THOMAS J., MARGARET T. STEEN, AND DEWEY LIPE, "The Development of the PLAN TOS: A Teacher Observation Scale for Individualized Instruction." Mimeographed. Project PLAN, September 1969.

"The Teacher and His Staff. Differentiated Roles for School Personnel." A Paper Distributed at the ASCD 1968 Session, March 1968.

TOSTI, D. T. "An Observation and Analysis of ASA in Plan Classrooms." Mimeographed. Westinghouse Learning Corporation, September, 1968.

PERIODICALS

ALLEN, D. W., "Differentiated Staffing: Putting Teaching Talent to Work," *Kentucky School Journal*, 47 (February, 1969), 21–23.

ALLEN, DWIGHT W. AND L. W. KLINE, Differentiated Teaching Staff," *National Business Education Quarterly*, 37 (May, 1969), 25–29.

ALLEN, DWIGHT W. AND RICHARD M. KRASNO, "New Perspectives in Teacher Preparation," *The National Elementary Principal*, Vol. 47, No. 6 (May, 1968), 36–42.

Anonymous, "Auxiliary Personnel in the Elementary School," *The National Elementary Principal*, 46 (May, 1967), 6–13.

Anonymous, "Differentiated Staffing," *Nation's Schools*, 85 (June, 1970), 43–49.

Anonymous, "Differentiated Staffing," *Education Digest*, 36 (October, 1970), 22–24.

Anonymous, "Differentiated Staffing, O.K. but More Research Wanted," *Nation's Schools*, 86 (September, 1970), 37.

Anonymous, "Differentiated Staffing: Symposium," *Today's Education*, 58 (March, 1969), 53–62.

Anonymous, "Here are Fourteen Ways to Use Non-Teachers in Your School District!" *Nation's Schools*, 76 (December, 1965), 42.

Anonymous, "Manpower Deficit: Rationale for Bold Action," *School Management*, 10 (August, 1966), 57–59.

ARNOLD, JOSEPH P., "Applying Differentiated Staffing to Vocational-Technical Education," *Journal of Industrial Teacher Education*, 7 (Fall, 1969), 13–20.

BEAUBIER, EDWARD W., "Experiences with Differentiated Staffing," *NEA Journal*, 58 (March, 1969), 56–57.

BRANNICK, J. J., "How to Train and Use Teacher Aides," *Phi Delta Kappan*, 48 (October, 1966), 61.

BRUNNER, C., "Lap to Sit on—And Much More," *Childhood Education*, 43 (September, 1966).

BUSHNELL, DONALD D., "The Role of the Computer in Future Instructional Systems," *AV Communication Review*, 11 (March–April, 1963), 1–70.

CHAFFEE, JOHN, "First Manpower Assessment: EPDA," *American Education*, Washington, D.C.: U.S. Office of Education, 5 (February, 1969), 11–12.

CLOHAN, LEWIS, "Solving Problems in Their Job," California Teachers Association, (May, 1967), 14–17.

COMBS, ARTHUR W. AND HAROLD E. MITZEL, "Can We Measure Good Teaching Objectively?" *National Educational Association Journal*, 53 (September, 1963), 34–36.

CONNORS, JOY, "Building a Career Ladder," *American Education*, 5 (February, 1969), 15–17.

CONTE, JOSEPH M., AND FENWICK ENGLISH, "The Impact of Technology on Staff Differentiation," *Audiovisual Instruction*, 14 (May, 1969), 108.

CORWIN, RONALD G., "Enhancing Teaching as a Career," *NEA Journal*, 58 (March, 1969), 55.

CORWIN, RONALD G., "Militant Professionalism, Initiative and Compliance in Public Education," *Sociology of Education*, 38 (Summer, 1965), 310–31.

COZAN, M. L., "Research on Behavior of Teachers," *Journal of Teacher Education*, 14 (September, 1963), 238–43.

CRONIN, JOSEPH H., "School Boards and Principals–Before and After Negotiations," *Phi Delta Kappan*, 49 (November, 1967), 123–27.

CUTLER, MARILYN H., "Teacher Aides Are Worth the Effort," *Nation's Schools*, 73 (April, 1964), 67–69.

CYPHERT, F. R. AND W. L. GANT, "The Delphi Technique: A Tool for Collecting Opinion in Teacher Education," *Journal of Teacher Education*, 21, No. 3, (1970), 417–25.

D'HEURLE, ADMA, et al., "New Ventures in School Organization: The Ungraded School and Use of Teacher Aides," *Elementary School Journal*, 57 (February, 1957), 268–71.

DURFLINGER, GLENN W., "Recruitment and Selection of Prospective Elementary and Secondary School Teachers," *Review of Educational Research*, 33 (October, 1963), 355–68.

EDELFELT, ROY A., "The Teacher and His Staff," *New York Education*, 5 (October, 1967), 16–19.

ENGLISH, FENWICK, "The Ailing Principalship," *Phi Delta Kappan*, 50 (November, 1968), 158–61.

ENGLISH, FENWICK, "Differentiated Staffing: Education's Techno-structure," *Educational Technology*, 10 (February, 1970), 24–27.

ENGLISH, FENWICK W., "Differentiated Staffing: Refinement, Reform or Revolution," *ISR Journal*, 1 (Fall, 1969), 220–34.

ENGLISH, FENWICK, "Questions and Answers on Differentiated Staffing," *NEA Journal*, 58 (March, 1969), 53–54.

ENGLISH, FENWICK, "Teacher May I? Take Three Giant Steps! The Differentiated Staff," *Phi Delta Kappan*, 51 (December, 1969), 211–14.

ERICKSON, DONALD A., "The School Administrator," *Review of Educational Research*, 37 (October, 1967), 417–32.

EVANS, J. S., "Improving Teacher Effectiveness," *Minnesota Journal of Education*, 44 (December, 1963), 14–15.

FLANAGAN, JOHN C., "Functional Education for the 70's," *Phi Delta Kappan*, 49 (September, 1967), 27–33.

GREGORC, ANTHONY F., "Satisfaction from Teaching," *The Educational Forum*, 35 (March, 1971), 307–13.

HAIR, D. AND E. WOLKEG, "Differentiated Staffing and Salary Pattern Underway in Kansas City," *School and Community*, 55 (August, 1969), 8–14.

HARRIS, J. W., "Salary Differentiation Is a Must," *School Management*, 13 (June, 1969), 6.

HEDGES, W. B., "Differentiated Teaching Responsibilities in the Elementary School," *National Elementary Principal*, 47 (September, 1967), 49–54.

HOWE, H., "Manpower Crisis: How 12 Districts are Beating It," *School Management*, 10 (August, 1966), 47–56.

JOYCE, BRUCE, "The Principal and His Staff," *The National Elementary Principal*, 48 (September, 1968), 24–29.

JOYCE, BRUCE R., "Staff Utilization," *Review of Educational Research*, 37 (June, 1967), 323–36.

KAPLAN, MILTON, "Teachers Belong in the Classroom," *Education Forum*, November 1968.

KRUMBEIN, GERALD, "The Determination of Personnel Costs Involved in the Creation of a Differentiated Staff," *American School Board Journal*, 157 (1970), 19–24.

KRUMBEIN, G., "How to Tell Exactly What Differentiated Staffing Will

Cost Your District," *American School Board Journal*, 157 (May, 1970), 19–24.

LEWIN, KURT, "Frontiers in Group Dynamics," *Human Relations*, 1 (1947), 34–44.

MACKAY DAVID A., "Should Schools be Bureaucratic?" *Canadian Administrator*, 4 (November, 1964), 29–31.

MARKS, MERLE B., "Assistant Teacher," *Bulletin of the National Association of Secondary School Principals*, 48 (March, 1964), 55–60.

MORROW, A. J. AND J. R. P. FRENCH, JR., "Changing a Stereotype in Industry," *Journal of Social Issues*, 13, (August, 1945), 33–37.

National Education Association: Division of Press, Radio and Television Relations, "Staff Differentiation—Answer to the Merit Pay Debate?" *California Teachers Association Journal*, (January, 1969).

NEWCOMER, KENNETH, "How Would you Like An Assistant Teacher?" *School and Community*, 50 (May, 1964), 23–24.

OLIVERO, J. L., "Meaning and Application of Differentiated Staffing in Teaching," *Phi Delta Kappan*, 7 (September, 1970), 36–40.

OLSON, CHARLES E., "The Way It Looks to a Classroom Teacher," *NEA Journal*, 58 (March, 1969), 59.

PARK, CHARLES, LUCILLE CHASE, FRANCIS CHASE, JAMES HYMES JR., DOROTHY McCUSKEY, G. E. RAST, AND P. G. RULON, "The Bay City, Michigan, Experiment: A Cooperative Study for the Better Utilization of Teacher Competencies," *Journal of Teacher Education*, 7 (June, 1956), 99–153.

"Public Schools—Bigger Teacher Shortage," *Time*, 88 (September 23, 1966), 43.

RAND, M. JOHN AND FENWICK ENGLISH, "Towards a Differentiated Teaching Staff," *Phi Delta Kappan*, 49 (January, 1968), 264–68.

ROSS, MARLENE, "Preparing School Personnel for Differentiated Staffing Patterns," *ERIC Guide to Selected Documents 1966–1968*, Washington, D.C.: ERIC, 7 (May, 1969).

SCHMUCK, RICHARD AND ARTHUR BLUMBERG, "Teacher Participation in Organizational Decisions," *NASSP Bulletin*, 53 (October, 1969), 67–69.

SILBERMAN, CHARLES E., "Technology is Knocking at the Schoolhouse Door," *Fortune*, 74 (August, 1966), 124.

SINCLAIR, ROBERT L., "Leadership Concerns," *The National Elementary Principal*, 48 (September, 1968), 16–20.

WILDMAN, WESLEY A., "What Prompts Greater Teacher Militancy?" *The American School Board Journal*, 154 (March, 1967), 27–32.

WILHELMS, FRED T., "The Principalship on the Spot," *The Bulletin of the National Association of Secondary School Principals*, 51 (November, 1967), 65–75.

PAMPHLETS, PAPERS, REPORTS

Administrative Leadership Service, *Inservice Education for Teachers*. Washington, D.C.: Educational Service Bureau, Inc., 1968.

ALLEN, DWIGHT, W., *A Differentiated Staff: Putting Teaching Talent to*

Work, Occasional Papers No. 1. Washington, D.C.: National Education Association, 1967.

ALLEN, DWIGHT W., *Needed: A New Professionalism in Education.* Washington, D.C.: American Association of Colleges for Teacher Education, May 1968.

The American Association of Colleges for Teacher Education, *Action for Americans: Proceedings of the 14th Biennial School for Executives of the American Association of Colleges for Teacher Education.* Washington, D.C.: AACTE, 1969.

Anonymous, *Guide for the Evaluation and Improvement of Professional Services,* Oakland Public Schools, Oakland, California, n.d.

Anonymous, *A Plan for Differentiated Staffing in Public Schools,* Kansas City, Missouri: Kansas City Public Schools, n.d.

Association of Classroom Teachers, *Classroom Teachers Speak on Differentiated Teaching Assignments.* Report of the Classroom Teachers National Study Conference on Differentiated Teaching Assignments for Classroom Teachers. Washington, D.C.: The Classroom Teachers Association, a department of the National Education Association, 1969.

AUGENSTEIN, MILDRED B., *Style is the Teacher: A Report of the Teacher Characteristics Project, 1967–1968.* Miami, Florida: Dade County Public Schools, 1968.

BARBEE, DON, *Differentiated Staffing: Expectations and Pitfalls.* TEPS Write-In Papers on Flexible Staffing Patterns, No. 1. Washington, D.C.: National Education Association, March 1969.

BARTLETT, D. B., "Non-Teaching Assistants: A Southend Experiment," *New York Times Educational Supplement,* No. 2615 (July 2, 1965), 29.

BHAERMAN, DR. ROBERT D., *A Study Outline on Differentiated Staffing.* AFT-QUEST Report on Differentiated Staffing, No. 2. Washington, D.C.: The American Federation of Teachers, 1969.

BROTMAN, SYLVIA, ed., *About Differentiated Staffing and Trojan Horses.* The Washington Memo. Washington, D.C.: NEA Division of Field Services, April 1970.

BUSH, ROBERT N. *The Status of the Career Teacher: Its Effect Upon the Teacher Dropout Problem.* Research and Development Memorandum No. 47. Stanford, California: Stanford Center for Research and Development in Teaching, April 1969.

CHADWICK, CLIFTON B., *A Readiness for Differentiated Staffing: Instructional Management, DS Information Report No. 3.* Tallahassee, Florida: Department of Education, Bureau of Curriculum and Instruction, November 1969.

Classroom Teachers' National Study Conference, *The Classroom Teacher Speaks on His Supportive Staff.* Washington, D.C.: National Education Association, 1966.

Classroom Teachers' National Study Conference, *The Classroom Teachers Speak on Differentiated Teaching Assignments.* Washington, D.C.: National Education Association, 1969.

Connecticut Education Association, Policy *re* Differentiated Staffing adopted by the C.E.A. Representative Assembly, May 9, 1970. Hartford, Connecticut: Connecticut Education Association, 1970.

COREY, ARTHUR P., *The Responsibility of the Organized Profession for the Improvement of Instruction.* Washington, D.C.: National Education Association Center for the Study of Instruction, 1966.

CRENSHAW, JOSEPH W., et al., *Differentiated Staffing, Technology in Education.* Tallahassee, Florida: State Department of Education, 1968.

CRENSHAW, JOSEPH W., et al., *Flexible Staff Organization Feasibility Study —Interim Report.* Tallahassee, Florida: State Department of Education, February 1969.

DANIEL, K. FRED, *Performance Assessment and Performance Based Teacher Education: The Florida Plan.* Tallahassee, Florida: State Department of Education, August 1969. A position paper.

DANIEL, K. FRED, *Whither Teacher Education.* Information Report No. 3. Tallahassee, Florida: State Department of Education, 1969.

DENEMARK, GEORGE W., *Coordinating the Team. The Supervisor: New Demands Plus New Dimensions.* Washington, D.C. Symposium of the Association for Supervision and Curriculum Development, NEA, 61–70.

Florida Department of Education, *Flexible Modular Scheduling.* Tallahassee, Florida: Bureau of Curriculum and Instruction, January 1970.

EDELFELT, ROY A., *Differentiated Staffing: Interpersonal Relationships and the Changing Educational Community,* in Florida's Twenty-Fourth Annual Supervisors' Conference, 1968. *The Proceedings.* Tallahassee, Florida: State Department of Education, 1968.

EDELFELT, ROY A., *Preservice and Professional Standards.* NEA Staff Conference, September, 1968.

EDELFELT, ROY A., *Quality and Governance,* TEPS Newsletter, March 15, 1967.

EDELFELT, ROY A., *Redesigning the Education Profession.* Washington, D.C.: National Education Association, January 1969.

EDELFELT, ROY A., *The Teacher and His Staff: Differentiated Roles for School Personnel.* Miami Beach, Florida: NCTEPS State Chairmen and Consultants Conference, June 1968.

Educational Service Bureau, Inc., *Job Descriptions: How to Write Them, How to Use Them.* 1966.

ENGLISH, FENWICK, *Differentiated Staffing: Giving Teaching a Chance to Improve Learning.* Temple City, California: Temple City Unified School District, September 1968.

ENGLISH, FENWICK, *Et Tu, Educator, Differentiated Staffing?* TEPS Write-in Paper No. 4 on Flexible Staffing Patterns. Washington, D.C.: National Education Association, August 1969.

ENGLISH, FENWICK, *Is the School Principal Obsolete?* Riverside, California: Paper written for SPEIR, Title III ESEA Pace Center, January 1968.

ENGLISH, FENWICK W., AND JAMES ZAHARIS, *How to Build a Model of*

Staff Differentiation. Claremont, California: Center for Differentiated Staffing, Claremont Graduate School, August 1970.

ESBENSEN, THORWALD, *Using Performance Objectives,* ed. by Rodney P. Smith. Tallahassee, Florida: State Department of Education, 1970.

Florida State Department of Education, *Flexible Staff Organization Feasibility Study.* Tallahassee, Florida: State Department of Education, Division of Curriculum and Instruction, Interim Report, February 1969.

Florida State Department of Education, *The Florida Educational Research and Development Program, First Annual Report.* Tallahassee, Florida: Division of Elementary and Secondary Education, February 1970.

Florida State Department of Education, *Florida Teachers Speak on Differentiated Staffing. Questions Relevant to Development and Training Activities.* Information Report No. 2. Tallahassee, Florida: Bureau of Curriculum and Instruction, October 1969.

Florida State Department of Education, *Florida Teachers Speak on Differentiated Staffing.* Tallahassee, Florida: Bureau of Curriculum and Instruction, October 1969.

FRINKS, MARSHALL L., *A Readiness for Differentiated Staffing: Questions Relevant to Development and Training Activities.* Information Report No. 2. Tallahassee, Florida: Bureau of Curriculum and Instruction, October 1969.

GALLAHER, ART, JR., "Directed Change in Formal Organizations: The School System," in *Change Processes in the Public Schools.* Eugene, Oregon: Center for the Advanced Study of Educational Administrative, University of Oregon, 1965.

GLASER, ROBERT, "The Program for Individually Prescribed Instruction," in Symposium at the American Educational Research Association meeting, Chicago, AERA, February 1966.

GOODLAD, JOHN I., *Planning and Organizing for Teaching.* National Educational Association, Project on the Instructional Program of the Public Schools. Washington, D.C.: NEA, 1963.

HABERMAN, MARTIN, *The Essence of Teaching: A Basis for Differentiating Roles.* TEPS Write-In Paper No. 5 on Flexible Staffing Patterns. Washington, D.C.: National Education Association, National Commission on Teacher Education and Professional Standards, June 1970.

HARMS, H. M., *Behavioral Analysis of Learning Objectives.* West Palm Beach, Florida: Harms and Associates, P.O. Box 15845, 1969.

JOYCE, BRUCE R., *Man, Media and Machines.* Washington, D.C.: National Commission on Teacher Education and Professional Standards, NEA, 1967.

JOYCE, BRUCE R., *The Teacher and His Staff: Man, Media, and Machines.* Washington, D.C.: National Commission on Teacher Education and Professional Standards, and Center for the Study of Instruction, National Education Association, 1967.

LIERHEIMER, ALVIN P., *An Anchor to Windward*. TEPS Write-In Paper No. 2 on Flexible Staffing Patterns. Washington, D.C.: National Education Association, National Commission on Teacher Education and Professional Standards, April 1969.

McASHAN, H. H., *Writing Behavioral Objectives*. Gainesville, Florida: Florida Educational Research and Development Council, 1969.

McKENNA, BERNARD, *The Development of School Staffs*, in *The Teacher and his Staff: Differentiating Teaching Roles*. Highlights of the Sixteenth Annual Meeting of State TEPS Chairmen and Consultants, Houston, Texas, June 25–28, 1968.

McKENNA, BERNARD, *School Staffing Patterns*. Burlingame, California: California Teachers Association, 1967.

McKENNA, BERNARD, *A Selected Annotated Bibliography on Differentiated Staffing*. Washington, D.C.: National Education Association, National Commission on Teacher Education and Professional Standards, October 1969.

MILLER, DONALD R., "The Policy Formulation and Policy Relationships of an Educational System." A speech presented to the Second Annual Conference on the Economics of Education. July 31, 1968. Tallahassee, Florida: Florida State University, 1968.

National Education Association, Szakalum, Pat, *A Checklist for Differentiation—A Recipe for Differentiation*. Washington, D.C.: National Commission on Teacher Education and Professional Standards, 1969.

National Education Association, Sharpe, Donald E., *Do We Know Enough About Teacher Classroom Behavior to Determine How Paraprofessionals Can Help in the Classroom?* Washington, D.C.: National Commission on Teacher Education and Professional Standards, 1969.

National Education Association, *Is Differentiated Staffing Worth Risking?* Washington, D.C.: National Commission on Teacher Education and Professional Standards, 1969.

National Education Association, *Is There Room for Teacher Decision Making? Who Decides What? Teacher Decisions?* Washington, D.C.: National Commission on Teacher Education and Professional Standards, 1969.

National Education Association, *A Position Paper on the Concept of Differentiated Staffing*. Washington, D.C.: National Commission on Teacher Education and Professional Standards, 1969.

National Education Association, Policy (71.4) *re* Differentiated Staffing adopted by the NEA Representative Assembly, July, 1971. Washington, D.C.: National Education Association, 1971.

National Education Association, *The Rationale for a Differentiated Teaching Staff*. Washington, D.C.: National Commission on Teacher Education and Professional Standards and English, Fenwick W., 1969.

National Education Association, *The Teacher and His Staff: Differentiation Teaching Roles*. Washington, D.C.: National Commission on Teacher Education and Professional Standards, 1969.

National Education Association, *Teacher Supply and Demand in Public Schools*. Washington, D.C.: NEA Research Report, 1967–R18.

National School Public Relations Association, "Differentiated Staffing in Schools," in *Education U.S.A.: Special Report*, Washington, D.C.: NEA, 1970.

NEWMAN, RICHARD S., *Differentiated Staffing-An Educational Alternative*. Larkspur, California: Tamalpais Uniorn High School District Research and Development Council, 1969.

NOAR, GERTRUDE, *Teacher Aids at Work*. Washington, D.C.: National Commission on Teacher Education and Professional Standards, NEA, 1967.

"Oregon Staff Differentiation, Special Issue." *Oregon Education*, 44, December 1969.

Plan for Differentiated Staffing Public Schools, Kansas City, Missouri: Kansas City Public Schools, 1966.

A Plan for Evaluating the Quality of Educational Programs in Pennsylvania. Highlights of a Report from Educational Testing Service to the State Board of Education of the Commonwealth of Pennsylvania. Princeton, New Jersey: Educational Testing Service, June 31, 1965.

Project Head Start—The Staff for a Child Development Center. Office of Economic Opportunity. Washington, D.C.: U.S. Government Printing Office, 1967.

RAND, JOHN, Superintendent and Colleagues. *The Differentiated Teaching Staff*. Presentation to the Faculty of the School of Education. Costa Mesa,, California: University of Southern California, April 1968.

RYAN, KEVIN A., *A Plan for a New Type of Professional Training for a New Type of Teaching Staff*. Occasional Papers No. 2. Washington, D.C.: NCTEPS, National Education Association, February 1968.

SHARPE, DONALD M., "Studying Teacher Classroom Behavior to Determine How Paraprofessionals Can Help in the Classroom," in *TEPS Write-In Paper No. 3 on Flexible Staffing Patterns*. Washington, D.C.: National Education Association, National Education and Professional Standards, May 1969.

SMITH, RODNEY, *Differentiated Staffing, A Guide for Understanding and Evaluating the Reorganization of Teaching Personnel*. New London, Connecticut: Croft Leadership Action Folio Number 26, 1969.

SMITH, RODNEY, "New Patterns of Differentiated Staffing." Education Summary. New London, Connecticut: Croft Educational Services, May 15, 1969.

SMITH, RODNEY, *Differentiated Staffing. A Teacher is a Teacher is a Teacher*. Tallahassee, Florida: Division of Curriculum and Instruction, State Department of Education, September 1968.

STOCKER, JOSEPH, and staff, *Education USA Special Report: Differentiated Staffing in Schools*. Washington, D.C.: National School Public Relations Association, 1970.

Teacher Supply and Demand in Public Schools, National Education Association Research Report. Washington, D.C.: NEA, 1967.

TEPS, *Auxiliary School Personnel.* National Commission on Teacher Education and Professional Standards. Washington, D.C.: National Education Association, 1969.

TEPS, *A Position Statement on the Concept of Differentiated Staffing.* National Commission on Teacher Education and Professional Standards. Washington, D.C.: National Education Association, 1969.

TEPS, *Remaking the World of the Career Teacher.* Washington, D.C.: Regional TEPS Conference Reports, June 1968.

TEPS, *The Teacher and His Staff: Differentiated Teaching Roles.* National Commission on Teacher Education and Professional Standards. Washington, D.C.: National Education Association, 1969.

TRUMP, J. LLOYD, *Images of the Future: A New Approach to the Secondary School.* Urbana, Illinois: Commission on the Experimental Study of the Utilization of the Staff in the Secondary School, 1959.

U.S. Department of Health, Education, and Welfare, Office of Education. "The Utilization of the Teacher," in *The Education Professions, 1968.* Washington, D.C.: U.S. Government Printing Office, 1969.

USOE, *Program Information: More Effective School Personnel Utilization,* United States Department of Health, Education, and Welfare. Washington, D.C.: U.S. Government Printing Office, 1969.

USOE, Staffing for Better Schools. United States Department of Health, Education, and Welfare. Washington, D.C.: U.S. Government Printing Office, 1969.

Utah Board of Education. *Proposed Utah State Plan for Differentiated Staffing.* Salt Lake City, Utah: Utah Board of Education, 1969.

WEBER, GEORGE, AND WILLIAM H. MARMION, *Merit Pay and Alternatives: Descriptions of Some Current Programs.* Occasional Papers No. 16. Washington, D.C.: Council for Basic Education, May 1969.

WEILER AND GUERIN, *School Community Relations and Educational Change.* Washington, D.C.: U.S. Office of Education, n.d.

Index

Teachers (*cont.*)
  resistance to change of, 48, 62–63
    in differentiated staffing models, 147
    see also Change—resistance to
  responsibility and, 102, 110–11, 112, 207, 209
  role of, 6–8, 9, 13–18, 19–21, 100–9, 215–16
  salaries of, 8–9, 87, 102, 109, 111–12, 203, 204
    experience and, 4, 120, 206, 208
    professionalism and, 2, 207
    responsibility and, 88, 101, 110, 206
    see also Merit pay
  specialization of, 7–8, 9, 102, 110–11, 204, 207, 214–15
  status of, 5, 7
  summer employment of, 17–18
  teacher aides, 12
  see also Academic Assistant
  tenure of, 16, 112, 210
Teaching
  exodus from, 4–5
  hierarchy, 13
Teaching as a career, 208
Teaching Curriculum Associate, 13
  functions of, 16–17
"Teaching Is a Lonely Profession," 3
Teaching Research Assistant
  allocation of work load, 17
Teaching Research Associate, 13
  functions of, 17
Team teaching, 11, 15, 109
  in differentiated staffing models, 141, 143, 150–51
Technical Assistant, 98
  functions of, 98–99
  responsibilities of, 98–99
Temple City, California, Model, 20, 42, 108, 128, 169, 170, 179, 203
  academic senate, 35–36
  Associate Teacher, 19, 21, 108
  Master Teacher, 19–21, 108
  models of schools in, 18–21, 35–36, 108, 185–91
  Paraprofessionals, 21, 108
  Senior Teacher, 19–20, 108

Temple City (*cont.*)
  Staff Teacher, 19–20, 108
Tenure, 16, 112, 210
Time
  differentiated staffing and, 107, 112
  planning for differentiated staffing and, 131
Tri-partite career ladders, 144
Trump staffing model, 108–9

U

UFT (United Federation of Teachers), 172
United Federation of Teachers (UFT), 172
United States Office of Education (USOE), 87, 96
  Bureau of Educational Personnel Development, 112–13, 133
  differentiated staffing models and, 146, 152, 155, 161, 169, 172, 179, 185
University High School (Urbana, Ill.), 195
University of Southern California, 187
Urbana, Illinois, 195
USOE, *see* United States Office of Education

V

Venice Junior High School (Sarasota Co., Fla.), 139, 178, 183, 184
Volunteers and staffing, 118

W

Watson, Jeanne, 51
Weeks, Mary Harmon Elementary School, 23, 25, 26, 139, 160–65
Weiler (author), 43
Westley, Bruce, 51
Wiles, Kimball, 92n
William E. Ferron Elementary School (Las Vegas, Nev.), 27
Williams, B. R., 54
Wilson Campus School (Mankato, Minn.), 198